Wrongs, Harms, and Compensation

OXFORD PRIVATE LAW THEORY

Oxford Private Law Theory publishes leading work in private law theory. It commissions and solicits monographs and edited collections in general private law theory as well as specific fields, including the theoretical analysis of tort law, property law, contract law, fiduciary law, trust law, remedies and restitution, and the law of equity. The series is open to diverse theoretical approaches, including those informed by philosophy, economics, history, and political theory. Oxford Private Law Theory sets the standard for rigorous and original work in private law theory.

Series Editors
Paul B. Miller, University of Notre Dame
John Oberdiek, Rutgers University

Advisory Board
Marietta Auer, Max Planck Institute for Legal History and Legal Theory
Molly Brady, Harvard University
Hanoch Dagan, University of California, Berkeley
John Goldberg, Harvard University
Matthew Harding, University of Melbourne
Irit Samet-Porat, King's College London
Seana Shiffrin, University of California, Los Angeles

ALSO PUBLISHED IN THIS SERIES
Rights, Wrongs, and Injustices
The Structure of Remedial Law
Stephen A Smith

Civil Wrongs and Justice in Private Law
Edited by Paul B Miller and John Oberdiek

Private Law and Practical Reason
Essays on John Gardner's Private Law Theory
Edited by Haris Psarras and Sandy Steel

Standing in Private Law
Powers of Enforcement in the Law of Obligations and Trusts
Edited by Timothy Liau

Wrongs, Harms, and Compensation

Paying for Our Mistakes

ADAM SLAVNY

Great Clarendon Street, Oxford, OX2 6DP,
United Kingdom

Oxford University Press is a department of the University of Oxford.
It furthers the University's objective of excellence in research, scholarship,
and education by publishing worldwide. Oxford is a registered trade mark of
Oxford University Press in the UK and in certain other countries

Public sector information reproduced under Open Government Licence v3.0
(http://www.nationalarchives.gov.uk/doc/open-government-licence/open-government-licence.htm)

Published in the United States of America by Oxford University Press
198 Madison Avenue, New York, NY 10016, United States of America

British Library Cataloguing in Publication Data

Data available

Library of Congress Control Number: 2023942152

ISBN 978–0–19–286456–7

DOI: 10.1093/oso/9780192864567.001.0001

Printed and bound in the UK by
TJ Books Limited

Acknowledgements

So many people have shaped this book over the years, it is impossible to produce an exhaustive list. I'd like to thank Christopher Bennett (the Canadian one, not the one I accidentally invited to a wine tasting, although come to think of it thanks to him too), Bill O'Brian, Matthew Clayton, Helen Frowe, Hwa Young Kim, Chris Mills, John Oberdiek, Tom Parr, Massimo Renzo, Zofia Stemplowska, Patrick Tomlin, Kartik Upadhyaya, and Andrew Williams (the Welsh one, not my head of department, although come to think of it thanks to him too). I thank the members of the Centre of Ethics, Law and Public Affairs at Warwick, the Private Law Theory Discussion Group, PEAK, and the participants of various other workshops and seminars where I have presented material that found its way into this book.

Special thanks goes to John Gardner, my thesis examiner and someone whom I wish I had the opportunity to know better. Thanks also to Chris Mills and Tom Parr for organizing a workshop on the manuscript and to Kim Ferzan, John Oberdiek, Sandy Steel, Victor Tadros, Beth Valentine, and Kate Vredenburgh for their excellent comments. Thanks also to Paul Raffield for his support, which began in week one of my undergraduate degree and has never wavered.

Parts of this book are heavily revised versions of previously published work. Chapter 3 includes content from 'Negating and Counterbalancing: A Fundamental Distinction in the Concept of a Corrective Duty' (2014) 33 Law and Philosophy 143–73. Chapters 4 and 5 include material from 'Should Tort Law Demand the Impossible?' in Paul B Miller and John Oberdiek (eds), *Civil Wrongs and Justice in Private Law* (Oxford University Press 2020). And Chapter 6 includes content from 'Nonreciprocity and the Moral Basis of Liability to Compensate' (2014) 34 Oxford Journal of Legal Studies 417–42.

There is one person to whom this book owes the greatest intellectual debt, and that is Victor Tadros. As my thesis supervisor and then colleague, he has always been a generous mentor. I have benefitted—or been indoctrinated, depending on your perspective—by his ideas, and those familiar with his work will see his influence throughout this book.

Thanks, as ever, to Alice Leonard for all her love and support over the years. And also to my daughter, Miri, the budding philosopher, who has already refuted Aristotle by being born perfect and getting better.

Summary Contents

Detailed Contents

1

Introduction

This book is concerned with corrective duties: their content, grounds, and the
legal or non-legal practices and institutions they justify. Corrective duties are a
familiar part of our daily ethical experience. If you knock someone's drink over,
you should offer to buy them another; if you break a promise to meet a friend
for lunch, you should propose a new time and place; if you hit someone with
your car, you should see they receive medical attention.

At first glance, tort law is also in the business of imposing corrective duties.
This idea is associated with theories of corrective *justice*, which treat the enforcement of corrective duties as central to the normative practice of tort law
and other parts of private law. Some corrective justice theorists insist on a juridical approach, focussing on the nature of the relationship between the doer
and sufferer of harm as embodied in the private legal action.[1]

Our approach to corrective duties will be non-juridical, however, our
starting point moral rather than legal duties. This marks a departure, not
just from the methodology favoured by corrective justice theorists, but from
that which has dominated non-instrumentalist private law theory in general: interpretivism. Interpretivism is a hybrid methodology, synthesizing
both explanatory and normative elements. Its main aim is to understand the
concepts, doctrines, and structures of the law, but to do so in rational, principled, and defensible terms.

The alternative adopted here—which I will call foundationalism—begins
with a moral conception of corrective duties and builds towards questions
of legal enforcement and institutional design. Unlike many books on private law theory, then, we will not spend much time trying to understand
the law. Not for us the wrangling over disputed judgments and doctrines,
the attempt to distil the law into its core features and structures, or the

---

[1] The leading figure here is Ernest Weinrib, to whom we will return in Chapter 2. See *The Idea of
Private Law* (first published 1995, Oxford University Press 2012) and *Corrective Justice* (Oxford
University Press 2012).

Wrongs, Harms, and Compensation. Adam Slavny, Oxford University Press. © Adam Slavny 2023.
DOI: 10.1093/oso/9780192864567.003.0001

articulation of a special type of justice inherent in it. Given this, one might wonder in what sense I propose to do legal theory at all. The answer is that legal theorists—and legal scholars, practitioners, and pretty much everyone else—should be concerned with whether legal institutions like tort law, institutions that restrict freedom, impose burdens, carry overtones of moral criticism and all at great expense, are justified. And they cannot be justified without reference to our underlying moral corrective duties, since it is these duties that determine when the expensive, coercive, and censorious apparatus of the law may be invoked against some for the purpose of winning remedies for others.

Unlike interpretivism, which tends to have an apologistic bias, foundationalism is committed neither to apologism nor reformism. Our moral duties might play an indispensable role in justifying the law's current practices, or they might recommend alternative laws or alternatives *to* the law. Failing to think about corrective duties independently of our current institutional framework risks obscuring this complex relationship. It can lead us to underestimate the malleability of the law's normative foundations, and to mistakenly think they are most naturally instantiated—or can only be instantiated—by private law mechanisms.

For a foundationalist, the question is not 'What is the best argument for tort law?' We must return to first principles and consider which are the best answers to the cluster of questions about wrongs, harms, and compensation for which tort law provides one set of answers. In formulating our methodology this way, we depart from interpretivism and from the old territory of private law theory. By entering a new territory, the realm of foundationalism, we will find a way of re-charting the old.

I. The Four-Fold Analysis

Corrective justice theorists (along with many other interpretivists) are especially interested in the form of private law. They aim to elucidate the nature of the relationship between the doer and sufferer of harm in private law interactions.[2] Our concern is the reverse. We will say something about the structure

---

[2] Weinrib is perhaps the best-known example of an interpretivist who focusses on form. There are also more substantive interpretivist approaches such as George Fletcher's non-reciprocity theory, which we examine in Chapter 6. See 'Fairness and Utility in Tort Theory' (1972) 85 Harvard Law Review 537.

of corrective duties, but our main goal is to build an account of their content and grounds. Specifically, we defend a four-fold analysis, which I summarize here.

(1) Wrongdoing: If A violates a duty not to harm B, A incurs a secondary duty to respond by giving greater regard than was previously sufficient to the values that grounded A's primary duty. This secondary duty typically requires compensating B.

(2) Conditional Permissibility: A's conduct is sometimes such that its permissibility is conditional on compensating B in the event that B is harmed. If A engages in such conduct and B is harmed, then A has a duty to compensate B.

(3) Outcome Responsibility: If A harms B, A has a duty to reduce the amount of harm caused overall, typically by compensating B.

(4) Distributive Fairness: If A harms B, the party who (i) is the primary beneficiary of A's conduct and (ii) could have avoided the harm at the lowest cost has a duty to compensate B.

This is only a sketch, and the four-fold analysis will be explained in more detail in subsequent chapters, but a few points are worth noting at the outset. First, the duties here are *pro tanto* and can be overridden by other factors. Second, as the name suggests, it is a pluralistic account of the sources of corrective duties. It does not make sense to try and assimilate them to a single grand or abstract idea. This pluralism extends to the structure of the duties as well as their content. Usually, it is the doer of harm who must compensate the sufferer—an important dictum of corrective justice theory, and an idea embodied in the law's causation requirement. But as principle (4) suggests, third parties can also owe corrective duties. When the beneficiary of the harmful conduct is someone other than the doer of harm, this beneficiary sometimes owes the duty instead.

There is another kind of pluralism implicit in the four-fold analysis: only one limb involves wrongdoing. Wrongdoing is therefore only part of the explanation of the corrective duties we owe to each other. To clarify the role wrongdoing plays in the four-fold analysis, it is worth laying out what I mean by a moral wrong here. An all-things-considered moral wrong is a violation of an all-things-considered moral duty. A moral duty is a requirement to do or refrain from doing something. Thus, wrongdoing—again, all-things-considered wrongdoing—implies impermissible action (action there is a duty not to perform) or impermissible omission (failure to perform an action there is a duty to perform).

Some interpretivists argue that tort law should be viewed as a coherent set of wrongs.[3] The four-fold analysis generates problems for this view. The first is that, as we have just seen, it is misleading to think of wrongdoing as holding a privileged place amongst the plural grounds of corrective duties. A natural response to this is to adopt a broader conception of wrongdoing that can encompass more of the law. It is not just fault-based conduct that should be regarded as wrongful, it might be argued; strict liability torts, which do not impute fault to the tortfeasor, are also properly understood as wrongs. It is often said in defence of this claim that legal wrongdoing need not imply moral blameworthiness.[4] This emphasis can be a distraction, though. True, legal wrongdoing need not imply moral blameworthiness, but if it does not imply moral *impermissibility* (whether blameworthy or not) then liability is imposed on those who were morally free to act exactly as they did.

This is either a problem or an even bigger problem. It is a problem if imposing this burden on a person is justified but not on the grounds that they are a wrongdoer. This misidentifies the justificatory reasons for liability and misappropriates the expressive function of the law. Labelling someone a tortfeasor is not quite labelling them a criminal, but if tort is—or should be—a law of wrongs, it nevertheless carries overtones of criticism and moral disapproval that are inappropriate when applied to those who act permissibly. It is an even bigger problem when imposing the burden is not justified at all. In this case, not only is a person labelled a tortfeasor, they are also coerced into repairing the harm when they have no duty to do so.

We should not conclude from this, however, that the four-fold analysis undermines the law at every turn. We will see that it also offers support for some elements of the law, such as rules regarding remedies and the distinction between strict and fault-based liability. The overlap between our moral corrective duties and the remedial side of tort law cannot be ignored when assessing the latter's justifiability. The four-fold analysis thus

---

[3] For a recent example, see John Goldberg and Benjamin Zipursky, *Recognizing Wrongs* (Harvard University Press 2022).

[4] Again, Goldberg and Zipursky's *Recognizing Wrongs* is an example (n 3) at 65.

has an ambivalent relationship with tort apologism. This ambivalence will be heightened in the latter part of the book when we examine the relationship between corrective and distributive justice and the debate between tort apologists and reformers.

We find that the practice of corrective justice it is not isolated or immune to critiques based on distributive justice. Although judges should not freely take issues of background injustice into account in tort decisions, this constraint itself presents problems for justifying the law as a whole. We also find that, despite the choice between tort law and compensation schemes usually being framed as one between irreducibly distinct paradigms of justice—corrective and distributive justice respectively—our moral duties are in fact consistent with various types of schemes. Ultimately, what emerges from a foundationalist perspective is neither a wholesale defence of nor attack on the tort system. If it can be made to work fairly and effectively, it can be justified in some form. But where it deviates significantly from our moral duties, exacerbates background injustice, and presents huge barriers to access, tort law, or at least a large portion of it, is an expensive mistake.

II. Map of the Book

Here is a map of the book. In Chapter 2 I offer some criticisms of interpretivism and develop the foundationalist methodology. Although the two methods are not inconsistent, and in some respects may be mutually supportive, I argue that the non-comparative nature of interpretivism makes it unable to evaluate the full range of views and arguments necessary to reach an all-things-considered judgement about the justification of the law. Foundationalism cannot reach an all-thing-considered evaluation either, of course, as normative theory can only do so much in the absence of empirical analysis. We need economists, social scientists, policymakers, and lawyers to consider the practicalities and consequences of any possible reforms. But foundationalism can make better *normative* progress than interpretivism. Free from considerations of fit, it can evaluate the full range of views and arguments in the relevant normative space rather than just those that best explain the law.

Chapter 2 also expands on the claim that moral corrective duties are crucial to the justification of the law. When a legal duty is imposed in the absence of an enforceable moral duty, defendants can complain that their moral freedoms are being curtailed and they are suffering an undue burden. When a legal duty is not imposed in the presence of an enforceable moral duty, would-be claimants can complain that they have no recourse for wrongs done to them and as a result their interests are de-prioritized relative to those of others. These complaints can be overridden, but they provide a powerful general case for the relevance of moral duties to the justification of the law.

In Chapter 3 I defend a distinction between negating and counterbalancing as fundamental to understanding different types of corrective action, thus disambiguating more generic terms like 'compensation', 'repair', and 'making whole'. We also distinguish between the well-known *continuity thesis* and *the responsiveness thesis*. *The continuity thesis* explains secondary duties in terms of the reasons, duties or rights that precede and survive a wrong. This thesis tends to erase or underplay the significance of wrongdoing in the derivation of secondary duties by implying that the wrong did not occur, or that it played no grounding role, or via its inability to account for the increased stringency of secondary duties. I defend *the responsiveness thesis*, which places less emphasis on trying to make it as if the wrong did not happen, and more on responding appropriately to the failures of one's moral agency. Throughout this discussion, Chapter 3 introduces the first two limbs of the four-fold analysis. *The responsiveness thesis* shows how wrongdoing grounds corrective duties, and the distinction between negating and counterbalancing helps to defend the concept of conditional permissibility.

Chapter 4 further develops the first limb of the four-fold analysis by examining the wrong of negligence. It argues the moral wrong of negligence is both capacity and cost sensitive, meaning that the level of care one owes to others depends on one's capacity to exercise that care, and the cost and difficulty to one of doing so. We consider and reject some principled arguments that some have adduced in favour of the objective standard of care (which can be restated as arguments for capacity and cost insensitivity) and conclude that, if the law is justified in departing from a capacity and cost sensitive approach, this is not for any deep reasons of principle but rather because of the difficulties of enforcing alternative standards in non-ideal conditions.

Chapters 5 and 6 develop the final two limbs of the four-fold analysis. Chapter 5 considers and rejects a range of existing justifications for some form of outcome responsibility. It defends an alternative version that connects the duty of repair to our prior duties to bear special costs to avoid harming others, grounded in the Doctrine of Doing and Allowing. On this view, we have some corrective responsibilities—though not necessarily the full burden of repair—even when we harm others through involuntary action.

Chapter 6 argues that principles of distributive fairness are relevant to individual corrective duties. In particular, we evaluate three distributive principles, *The Non-Reciprocity Principle, The Benefit Principle,* and *The Avoidance Principle.* We cast doubt on the independent significance of *The Non-Reciprocity* principle but argue that the other two interlock and play an important role in grounding corrective duties. The result is that consider-ations of fairness co-exist with the relational grounds of corrective duties such and wrongdoing and causation.

This concludes the section of the book dedicated to investigating the grounds of corrective duties, and the four-fold analysis. The remaining two chapters apply this moral account to broader institutional issues. Chapter 7 considers the relationship between corrective and distributive justice. We find that there is no straightforward generalization to be made about the priority or independence of the two spheres of justice. In some respects, corrective justice has priority, in others distributive justice has priority, and in others there is parity. This mixed picture should bring no comfort to tort apologists. Although corrective duties are not reducible to deviations from distributive justice or al-ways overridden by them, interference effects between the two spheres present systemic problems for justifying the practice of corrective justice in an un-just world.

In Chapter 8, we consider whether our moral account of corrective duties favours tort law structures over alternative institutional means of governing claims for compensation, particularly at-fault and no-fault compensation schemes. Although one might think the morality of corrective duties would favour tort, I argue this is not the case, and in fact our duties are consistent with all three institutional arrangements, in the sense that none imposes bur-dens on individuals that those individuals lack duties to bear for the sake of compensating others. This means that empirical considerations play a more decisive role in the justification (or otherwise) of tort law than many apologists would be comfortable with. Which institutional arrangement should be pre-ferred depends on issues such as deterrence, cost, and efficiency; the extent to which the effects of background injustice can be mitigated; and uptake of meri-torious claims, rather than the superiority of one arrangement over another in implementing corrective justice. This conclusion challenges the assumption that has structured the debate between reformists and apologists; that tort law and compensation schemes embody irreducibly distinct paradigms of justice. In truth, the morality of corrective duties is far more varied and flexible than this dichotomy has led us to believe.

2

Interpretivism and Foundationalism

Introduction

Non-instrumentalist tort theory, and private law theory more generally, has been dominated by a methodology I will call interpretivism.[1] There are multiple varieties of interpretivism, and those who employ the method differ on many details, but most versions tend to cohere around some central features that I will outline shortly. Interpretivism is a hybrid methodology, employing a synthesis of explanatory and normative elements, though the explanatory has a certain priority over the normative. The main aim is to understand the concepts, doctrines, structures, and practices of the law, but to understand them as embodiments of principle. This commitment to explaining the law in principled terms sets the interpretivist apart from, say, the critical legal scholar who explains the law as a camouflaged mechanism for serving dominant interests, or the legal historian who explains it as a product of its causes and origins.[2] But though interpretivism is normative in this sense, its normative ambitions are constrained by the primary aim of explanation.

The dominance of interpretivism in private law theory contrasts with methodological trends in the philosophy of criminal law. Here, there is a much greater focus on purely normative issues. Core questions such as 'What justifies punishment?' and 'What is the proper scope of criminalization?' do not ultimately depend on what the criminal justice system is doing in practice.[3]

---

[1] It is worth clarifying that interpretivism, as I understand it here, differs from Ronald Dworkin's notion of an interpretive concept, one whose correct understanding depends on the normative and evaluative facts that best justify the range of practices within that concept's scope. See Ronald Dworkin, *Justice for Hedgehogs* (Harvard University Press 2011) 6–7 and ch 8.

[2] For a categorization of various forms of legal theory—descriptive, historical, interpretive, and normative—see Stephen Smith, *Contract Theory* (Clarendon Press 2004) 3–6 (hereafter Smith, *Contract Theory*).

[3] It might be argued that a normative theory must take into account the best explanation of the criminal law, or that there is no right answer to the normative question independently of the historical, sociological, or other explanatory context within which criminal law practice must be understood. For a brief critical discussion of these ideas in relation to criminal responsibility, see Victor Tadros, *Criminal Responsibility* (Oxford University Press 2005) 3–8. Moreover, as always when pointing to general trends rather than universal laws, there are exceptions. The literature on 'public wrongs' can be seen as a closer cousin of interpretive theories of private law than much of the literature on criminalization and punishment. See Antony Duff, 'Towards a Modest Legal Moralism' (2014) 8 Criminal Law and Philosophy 217; Antony Duff, 'Towards a Theory of Criminal Law?' (2010) 84 Aristotelian Society Supp 1; Grant

Wrongs, Harms, and Compensation. Adam Slavny, Oxford University Press. © Adam Slavny 2023.
DOI: 10.1093/oso/9780192864567.003.0002

An anti-retributivist, for example, would not be moved by the conclusion that most systems of state punishment operate on retributivist grounds. If so, then so much the worse for them; they should be reformed along non-retributivist lines. Nor would an advocate of the harm principle be moved by the fact that states often criminalize non-harmful conduct or fail to prevent harm through criminalization. If so, then so much the worse for them; they should be reformed along Millian lines.

A consequence of this lack of purely normative analysis in private law theory is that a range of fundamental questions remain, if not unexplored, then underexplored. Interpretivism can make important contributions to these questions, but its inherent limitations prevent it from answering them satisfactorily—or so I will argue in this chapter. In addition, I will defend an alternative approach that I call foundationalism,[4] which will be employed in the remainder of the book. Unlike interpretivism, foundationalism is comparative, thoroughly normative, and seeks to integrate private law theory with moral and political philosophy more deeply than many thus far have been willing to accept.

I. Defining Interpretivism and Foundationalism

A. Three Features of Interpretivism

Here are three features I take to be central to interpretivist methodology. First, the ambitions of interpretivists are mainly explanatory. Interpretivists offer reconstructions of specific cases and statutes, often rationalizing apparently disparate elements of the law;[5] beyond doctrine, they seek to explain legal practices and institutions, including structural features of the law such as the bilateral form of civil actions;[6] they delineate subdivisions within private law such

---

Lamond, 'What is a Crime?' (2007) 27 Oxford Journal of Legal Studies 609; and Ambrose Lee, 'Public Wrongs and the Criminal Law' (2015) 9 Criminal Law and Philosophy 155.

[4] It is also worth clarifying that my usage of this term differs from that of Prince Saprai in his *Contract Law Without Foundations: Toward a Republican Theory of Contract Law* (Oxford University Press 2019). For Saprai, foundationalism involves the metaphysical claim that certain moral principles are constitutive or built into the fabric of the law. By contrast, foundationalism as understood in this book involves no metaphysical claims about the law, but rather treats the justification of the law as dependent on moral rights, duties, reasons, etc.

[5] There are many examples, but one discussed later in this book is George Fletcher's classic account based on non-reciprocity in George P Fletcher, 'Fairness and Utility in Tort Theory' (1972) 85 Harvard Law Review 537, which seeks to unify fault, strict, and intentional liability in tort law.

[6] The concept is central to Ernest Weinrib's well-known theory of private law. For discussion, see *The Idea of Private Law* (2nd edn, Oxford University Press 2012) (hereafter Weinrib, *The Idea of Private*

as the relationship between tort and contract, or provide general definitions of these subdivisions;[7] and they often seek to explain private law or its subdivisions on multiple levels—from doctrine to structure to practice—in terms of a cohesive idea, prominent examples being Ernest Weinrib and Jules Coleman's corrective justice theories[8] and John Goldberg and Benjamin Zipursky's civil recourse theory.[9]

Despite its explanatory focus, interpretivism is not an exercise in pure description and does not merely repeat, summarize or organize legal content. Rather, it makes the law intelligible and coherent by understanding it as an embodiment of principle. This leads us to the second feature of interpretivism: its normative dimension. Interpretive theories are normative in two distinct senses. One is that they are governed by theoretical norms such as fit with the law, coherence and transparency, among others.[10] These norms enable theories to make complex and diverse information rationally intelligible, allowing us to understand large bodies of law from a more holistic perspective. As a result of the licence afforded by these norms, interpretive theories are not beholden to legal data and may reject some aspects of positive law as wrong if they are inconsistent with a theory that is interpretively plausible more broadly.[11]

Fit, coherence, and transparency are theoretical rather than moral norms. Interpretivism is also normative in a second sense in that it has some justificatory ambitions. Although explaining the law is the primary aim, it seeks to do this in light of principles that are normatively appealing. For some, the

Law) and Corrective Justice (Oxford University Press 2016) especially ch 1 (hereafter Weinrib, Corrective Justice).

[7] For an analysis that distinguishes torts from other civil wrongs such as breach of contract, see John Gardner, Torts and Other Wrongs (Oxford University Press 2019) especially 21 (hereafter Gardner, Torts and Other Wrongs). See also Robert Stevens, Torts and Rights (Oxford University Press 2007) ch 13.

[8] Weinrib, The Idea of Private Law (n 6) and Corrective Justice (n 6); Jules Coleman, The Practice of Principle: In Defence of a Pragmatist Approach to Legal Theory (Oxford 2003) pt 1 (hereafter Coleman, The Practice of Principle) and Risks and Wrongs (Oxford University Press 1992) pt 3 (hereafter Coleman, Risks and Wrongs). For a version of corrective justice theory that responds to some recent criticisms, see Eric Encarnacion, 'Corrective Justice as Making Amends' (2014) 62 Buffalo Law Review 451.

[9] For Goldberg and Zipursky's most recent statement and defence of civil recourse theory, see Recognizing Wrongs (Harvard University Press 2020) (hereafter Goldberg and Zipursky, Recognizing Wrongs).

[10] Smith lists fit, coherence, morality, and transparency as four criteria for interpretivist theories. Smith, Contract Theory (n 2) ch 1. This is not an exhaustive list of theoretical norms, of course, and many others may be important. For a defence of determinacy as a theoretical virtue, see Jody S Kraus, 'Transparency and Determinacy in Common Law Adjudication: A Philosophical Defense of Explanatory Economic Analysis' (2007) 93 Virginia Law Review 287.

[11] Arthur Ripstein calls his methodological approach non-descriptive in recognition of the fact that his organizing principles do not fit all legal cases. Arthur Ripstein, Private Wrongs (Harvard University Press 2016) 20.

normative appeal of interpretivist principles plays a strictly causal role, helping to explain why well-motivated judges and lawmakers have made the decisions they have.[12] But for others, these principles do at least some justificatory work. For example, Coleman aims to provide 'an explanation of our practices, or important parts of them, but explanations that make sense of the practice in the light of norms ... that could withstand the test of rational reflection.'[13] Weinrib does not aim to explain the law according to external principles, but rather to articulate the normative ideas that figure in the law's own justification, or the self-understanding of law. However, he also says that rights in private law 'are not merely conclusions attached to the operations of positive law', but 'impose obligations on others that are both normatively justified as markers of reciprocal freedom and legitimately enforceable by legal institutions.'[14] Robert Stevens states that 'the first task of the academic lawyer is to explain the law so that it makes coherent sense and to account for it in the best possible light.'[15] And in reference to their civil recourse theory, Goldberg and Zipursky state that, 'our theoretical offerings are not merely descriptive, positive, or analytical, but also normative. We aim to establish not merely what tort law is, but that it is an entirely defensible feature of our liberal-democratic political and legal regime.'[16]

The third feature common to interpretive theories is that they take current law as their theoretical starting point. Coleman conceives of his methodology as 'middle level' rather than 'top down'. Top-down theory proceeds from a set of political or moral principles to a model of justified institutional structures against which actual institutions can be measured.[17] An example would be a normative economic model that begins with the claim that tort law should be a tool for the optimization of accident costs and then designs an institutional framework that best suits this purpose. Contractualism, though substantively very different from normative economic views, might also be described as top-down because implications for the law are derived from the general normative framework of reasonable agreement.[18] Middle level theory, by contrast, begins

---

[12] For discussion of this point, see Smith, *Contract Theory* (n 2) 6.

[13] Coleman, *Risks and Wrongs* (n 8) 7.

[14] Weinrib, *Corrective Justice* (n 6) 5–6

[15] Robert Stevens, 'Damages and the Right to Performance, A *Golden Victory* or Not?' in Jason W Neyers, Richard Bronaugh, and Stephen GA Pitel (eds), *Exploring Contract Law* (Hart 2009) 198.

[16] Goldberg and Zipursky, *Recognizing Wrongs* (n 9) 270.

[17] Coleman, *Risks and Wrongs* (n 8) 8–9.

[18] For an example of a fairness-based account of tort liability based on contractualism, see Gregory Keating, 'Reasonableness and Rationality in Negligence Theory' (1996) 48(2) Stanford Law Review 311 and 'The Idea of Fairness in the Law of Enterprise Liability' (1997) 95(5) Michigan Law Review 1266.

with an analysis of the law as it is, to draw out the principles that explain it or, to switch to Weinrib's terminology, to articulate the normativity immanent in the law.

This focus is sometimes driven by a belief that the law embodies a distinctive kind of justice or normative ideal, which can be understood only by attending to existing law. This is most evident in Weinrib's work, which insists on the exclusion of all 'external' factors—including ethical and policy considerations—in understanding and justifying private law. Instead, theorizing should proceed from an internal perspective.[19] According to Weinrib, the 'juridical' conception of corrective justice 'always works backward from the doctrines and institutions of private law to the most pervasive abstractions implicit in it.… The argument moves from private law as a normative practice to its presuppositions, which then serve as vehicles of criticism and intelligibility that are internal to the practice.'[20] Again, Goldberg and Zipursky strike a similar note: 'Our theorising about tort has always stayed … in close contact with doctrine and history.'[21] Though Weinrib's internalism goes further than Coleman's middle level methodology or Goldberg and Zipursky's emphasis on Anglo-American tort doctrine, they share the commitment of taking present law as their main focus.

B. An Alternative Methodology

The methodology I call foundationalism, and will pursue in the remainder of this book, differs from interpretivism in all three of these respects: it has no ambition to explain the law; it is purely normative rather than partially normative; and, rather than taking the law as its starting point, it begins with a moral conception of reasons, rights, duties, or wrongs and then builds towards questions of legal enforcement and institutional design.[22] To extend Coleman's

---

[19] Weinrib, *The Idea of Private Law* (n 6) especially ch 1.

[20] Weinrib, *Corrective Justice* (n 6) 26–27.

[21] Goldberg and Zipursky, *Recognizing Wrongs* (n 9) 7.

[22] Foundationalism shares some features with John Gardner's 'monism' about private law. He agrees that too many theorists treat private law as an 'autonomous domain, requiring a specialized apparatus of analysis and evaluation', see *From Personal Life to Private Law* (Oxford University Press 2018) 8. He also accepts that underlying moral considerations (though he avoids the term 'morality' and prefers, following Bernard Williams, to speak of 'ethics') are relevant to understanding and justifying the law. However, he does not embrace foundationalism as I have described it. One reason is that he is not enthusiastic about hypothetical examples—an important part of the moral philosopher's toolkit—preferring to discuss situations drawn from literature and drama. But, more significantly, he does not take the directional approach, beginning with morality and building to questions of legal enforcement, that I do. He prefers to think about law and personal life as raising the same set of fundamental concerns—the big

taxonomy, we might describe it as a bottom-up rather than a top-down or middle level approach. While it has affinity with top-down theory insofar as it is thoroughly normative rather than interpretive, it is not committed to any overarching moral framework such as utilitarianism or contractualism from which implications about the law are then derived. Instead, it examines more discrete units of moral assessment—individual wrongs, rights, duties, reasons etc—lending itself to the four-fold pluralistic account of corrective duties we will defend later in the book.

One of the most important differences between interpretivism and foundationalism is that the latter is entirely unconstrained by considerations of fit with the law. Its focus is purely normative. This means that, while some foundationalist theories might be apologistic, others will be critical or re-formist to varying degrees. Of course, to ask whether the law is justified we need to know something about the object of that enquiry, and thus something about what the law is. But though it is convenient to talk in general terms about the justification of the law, we will be pursuing this enquiry in a more piecemeal fashion. We will consider whether our account provides support for certain features of the law, such as the objective standard of care in negligence, rules regarding damages, the distinction between strict and fault-based liability etc, and to do this we need not commit to any *unifying* analytic view; that is, we need not produce a set of necessary and sufficient conditions for tort law as a whole, or a set of core or essential features.

Being unconstrained by considerations of fit means that the fact that a principle deviates from the law does not, in itself, count against it. To think otherwise would be to commit the conservative fallacy of assuming the law must be right because it is the law.[23] This is not to say a foundationalist cannot share the assumption that law-making procedures are likely to generate nor-matively appealing principles, or that case law, particularly appellate litiga-tion, is a treasure trove of good arguments. Indeed, this assumption is why, throughout this book, we will subject to normative analysis principles that were originally developed in an interpretivist rather than foundationalist mode. But foundationalists judge such principles on their normative rather

---

questions of law *are* the big questions of life and *vice versa*. As he puts it, 'ultimately the only consider-ations that are relevant to defending the law are considerations that are also relevant to defending what people do quite apart from the law' (Gardner, *From Personal Life to Private Law*) 8.

[23] As Charles Dickens reminds us, the crude conservative axiom that 'all that is, is right' has the troub-ling implication that 'nothing that was, was wrong'. Charles Dickens, *A Tale of Two Cities* (first pub-lished 1859, Oxford University Press 2008,) bk 2, ch 2.

than explanatory merit, and, whilst they may have a working assumption that well-established legal rules are unlikely to be completely irrational or indefensible, they are generally willing to adopt reformist rather than apologistic arguments if principles that best explain the law turn out to be normatively less plausible than those that do not.[24]

Foundationalists also begin with moral questions, temporarily bracketing issues of pragmatism and institutional enforcement. Throughout most of this book, we will be concerned with the moral duties that arise when one person wrongs or harms another, quite independently of the law, and without consideration of the problems involved in trying to institutionalize such duties. We will then apply this moral framework to some of the central questions regarding the justification of tort and related institutional arrangements. At that point we will reintroduce some of these bracketed factors into the discussion (for example, in Chapter 8 we consider how the cost, efficiency and uptake of the tort system bears on the debate about the partial replacement of tort with a compensation scheme). This is a familiar practice in what is sometimes called 'ideal theory', though this term can have multiple meanings.[25] The reason for it is not that the realities of pragmatism and institutional enforcement are irrelevant, but the opposite: because they are relevant, it is important to consider them separately from underlying questions of normative justification. Otherwise we risk confusing the two and holding the latter hostage to the former. To say a person should lack some legal right because it is too cumbersome to enforce, for example, is very different from saying they should lack that right even if it could be enforced easily. In the end, trade-offs between pragmatic or regulatory factors and ideal principles may be inevitable, but we will not even know what trade-offs we are making unless we first understand our moral duties, and for this we need a foundationalist approach.

---

[24] This is not to say that making reformist arguments does not require knowledge of the law. Tort law must be understood from the inside to provide a schematic for how to ask questions about how tort should be reformed. See John CP Goldberg and Benjamin C Zipursky, 'Unrealized Torts' (2002) 88 Virginia Law Review 1625 and John CP Goldberg, 'What are We Reforming?: Tort Theory's Place in Debates over Malpractice Reform' (2006) 59 Virginia Law Review 1075. Rather, the point is that, from a foundationalist perspective, the fact that some theory is a good explanation of the law is not in itself a reason in favour of its justifiability, except in an indirect sense, that is, via the principle that law-making processes are reliable at producing justified results.

[25] For example, John Rawls' use of the concept is slightly different to that employed here. For Rawls, ideal theory assumes compliance with duty and reasonably favourable social conditions. See John Rawls, *A Theory of Justice* (first published 1971, Harvard University Press 2005) s 39 (hereafter Rawls, *Theory of Justice*).

II. The Limits of Interpretivism

A. Non-Comparativism

We have seen that interpretivists have at least some ambition to defend tort law or private law more generally. In this part, I argue that interpretivism is incapable of providing anything close to an all-things-considered justification. The reason is that the question of justification is inherently comparative, as are all questions of permissibility and obligatoriness. Showing that one of a range of options is permissible means showing that no other option is required, and showing that one of a range of options is required means showing that no other option is permissible. The normative dimension of interpretivism, however, is non-comparative.[26] Its focus on explaining the law means that, at most, it can yield the best argument for one option (or perhaps one range of options if the interpretive theory in question is consistent with a variety of substantive laws). But this does not settle whether the law is justified until we compare it to arguments for the alternatives. Interpretivists are rather like lawyers, and their client is the law itself. They can give the best possible case for their client, but we cannot make an informed choice until we have heard the case for the other side. Given the range of principles, reforms, and institutional possibilities available in the same normative space as the current law, this is a serious limitation.[27]

Returning to our comparison with the philosophy of criminal law, note the difference in the way debates are structured. Justifying state punishment, for example, is a comparative exercise. It is not a matter of drawing out the

---

[26] Interpretivists do compare different institutional systems in enlightening ways. Weinrib uses such a comparison to describe the difference between corrective justice and systems built around the 'loss spreading' rationale (*The Idea of Private Law* (n 6) 36–37). However, this comparison is explanatory rather than normative. It helps us understand different rationales but does not provide any independent grounds on which one is to be preferred over the other. The rationale that underpins the law cannot be justified by pointing out that others are inconsistent with it.

[27] Kantians might argue that there is a necessary connection between the interpretation of law and its normative foundations. If certain legal structures are necessary to constitute persons as free and equal agents, such structures are justified by a kind of rational necessity, without the need for any comparative analysis. For a detailed development of this Kantian idea as applied to private and public rights, see Arthur Ripstein, *Force and Freedom: Kant's Legal and Political Philosophy* (Harvard University Press 2010) (hereafter Ripstein, *Force and Freedom*). I don't think any substantive moral, political, or legal principles can be justified in this way for two broad reasons. One is that I am generally sceptical that foundational normative concepts require very particular institutional structures to be properly realized (usually there are a range of such structures that can realize these concepts in different ways), and the second is that, even if some concepts do require particular structures, it remains an open question whether these normative-institutional nexuses are justified over the many others we could articulate and support. In other words, the criticism of non-comparative approaches stated above is simply re-raised at a different point. This is not an argument but a mere statement of a position, but since a full-scale evaluation of the Kantian project is not within the scope of this book, I will set this question aside.

principles embodied in current practice, but of showing that one's favoured theory can meet the objections against punishment (thus defending it against abolitionism) and is preferable to rival views, including those that defend current practices on alternative grounds and those that are reformative.[28] This is why debates about punishment usually take a thoroughly normative rather than interpretivist form. Tort theory—and perhaps private law theory more generally—must do the same if we want to make better progress towards conclusions about the justification of our private law institutions.

I am not suggesting that interpretivists are committed to a rigid acceptance of current law, with no room for criticism. In particular, those interpretivists who treat the *form* of legal requirements and arguments as crucial often acknowledge that a variety of different substantive conclusions are consistent with the same legal forms.[29] Nevertheless, these more formal varieties of interpretivism are subject to the same objection: we cannot know whether these legal forms are justified all-things-considered until we compare them with alternatives. This is notable with respect to the emphasis many interpretivists place on concepts like relationality and causality. It may be true, for example, that causation is central to the form of adjudicative reasoning in private law, but this is not by itself a justification of this form of reasoning over any others, and as I will argue in Chapter 8, this view tends to overestimate the significance of causation. Furthermore, consistency with a variety of different substantive legal conclusions can be a problem as well as an advantage for formal theories because of the possibility that they will yield substantively unjust results—an argument I will develop in pt II of this chapter.

In arguing that foundationalism can make better progress than interpretivism on these questions, I am also not saying it can settle them by itself. Normative theory can do only so much in the absence of empirical analysis. We also need economists, social scientists, policymakers, and lawyers to consider the practicalities and consequences of any possible reforms. And we must contend with path-dependency issues. When we apply theoretical ideas to the law, we do not find a philosopher's blank page but a well-established legal system with its own set of doctrines and organizing concepts. Foundationalists need not deny any of this. The claim is rather that foundationalism can make

---

[28] This is evident from any survey of the relevant literature, such as the Stanford Encyclopaedia entry on Legal Punishment, see Zachary Hoskins and Antony Duff, 'Legal Punishment', *The Stanford Encyclopedia of Philosophy* (Summer edn, 2022) <https://plato.stanford.edu/archives/sum2022/entries/legal-punishment/> accessed 8 November 2022.
[29] For example, see Benjamin C Zipursky, 'Pragmatic Conceptualism' (2000) 6 Legal Theory 457, especially 479.

better *normative* progress than interpretivism. Free from considerations of fit, it can evaluate the full range of relevant views and arguments rather than just those that best explain the law.

A final caveat. It is worth emphasizing that interpretivism and foundationalism are not inconsistent with each other. The two methodologies have largely different aims, and to an extent they are even mutually supportive. It is therefore unsurprising that at least some interpretivists have themselves recognized the limitation I am describing. As Coleman states:

> In arguing that tort law is best explained by corrective justice I do not mean to be defending tort law thereby. As it happens, the conception of corrective justice embodied in tort law expresses important moral values ... Still, even if tort law is best explained by corrective justice *and* corrective justice is an important and independent moral ideal, it does not yet follow that tort law represents a justified—let alone a morally required—institution.[30]

We can go further than Coleman, though, and identify two further problems faced by interpretivism.

B. The Relationship between Explanation and Justification

I noted that interpretivism synthesizes explanatory and normative elements. However, there is a raft of unanswered questions about the precise relationship between these elements. Is it assumed that only one principle or grand idea can fit the law? If not, how do interpretivists choose between multiple principles that meet an explanatory threshold? In particular, how do they make trade-offs between explanation and justification? Suppose there are two principles, one that is better at explaining the law but is less justifiable and another that is more justifiable but a poorer explanation. Which is to be preferred? Does explanation have lexical priority over justification, such that a principle with slightly better fit should be preferred to one that is a lot more normatively defensible, or is some degree of trade-off between explanation and justification permitted? Or is it assumed that such trade-offs cannot arise? If so, what is the reason for this assumption?

---

[30] Coleman, *The Practice of Principle* (n 8) 5. Even Weinrib says that formalism 'does not itself choose between distributive and corrective arrangements; it requires only that whatever mode of ordering a jurisdiction adopts conform to the rationality immanent in that mode of ordering'. Weinrib, *The Idea of Private Law* (n 6) 228.

There are different ways interpretivists might resist these questions. One is to turn it back on foundationalists and argue that balancing between different methodological criteria is inevitable in any approach. Within reflective equilibrium—perhaps the most common methodology in normative philosophy—one must balance intuitions about individual cases with judgements about general principles.[31] Here, though, there is at least a single overarching aim: to reach justified normative conclusions. Where there are two different aims—explanation and justification—the problem runs deeper since what remains unspecified is the purpose of the method rather than the most effective means to pursue that purpose.

Alternatively, it might be objected that the distinction between explanation and justification is drawn too sharply. John Gardner questions the distinction itself.[32] He claims that, though not all explanations are justifications, all justifications are explanations, as to justify something is to explain it rationally. However, this tells us only that explanations in terms of reasons give us *pro tanto* justifications. True, these constitute all-things-considered justifications in the absence of any countervailing considerations, but there are always countervailing considerations. Even if interpretivism picks out the single best *pro tanto* justification within that range of principles that meet an explanatory threshold, it does not follow that that principle provides an all-things-considered justification, since we still do not know how it compares with principles outside this range.

Similarly, Goldberg and Zipursky caution against too sharp a distinction between explanation and justification on the grounds that successful explanation provides the beginnings of justification. It does this by forestalling certain criticisms, such as that the law is incoherent or is ill-suited for purposes it is not intended to serve.[33] Again, this can be conceded without undermining the central point. Deeply unjust laws can be coherent and suited for their purposes; if so, incoherence and maladaptation might be positives. So defending the law from the charge of incoherence is a start, but it falls far short of the justificatory bar we ought to demand of expensive and coercive legal institutions like those of private law.

[31] The term was coined by John Rawls in his *Theory of Justice* (n 25) 111.
[32] Gardner, *Torts and Other Wrongs* (n 7) 28.
[33] Goldberg and Zipursky, *Recognizing Wrongs* (n 9) 113.

C. Normative Distinctiveness

Interpretivists often claim to reveal the distinctive normative character of the law. Weinrib holds that our understanding of the law as an embodiment of principle is lost or distorted when we attempt to think about it in terms of 'external' factors.[34] One problem for this view is that, like claims about justification, claims about distinctiveness also have a comparative dimension. Many of the principles and structures of private law have moral correlates, and it is difficult to assess the distinctiveness of the former without comparing them to the latter.

For example, corrective justice theorists point to the special relationality or correlativity of private wrongs: such wrongs are neither impersonal nor committed against the wider community; they are committed against *another private party*. Civil recourse theorists emphasize a further feature as central to understanding tort law, namely that the law does not recognize a duty arising from the commission of a wrong but a legal liability.[35] Unlike a duty, a liability does not require the performance of any corrective action by itself. It is a vulnerability corresponding to a power on behalf of the victim to force the liable party to engage in such action.[36]

Corrective justice theorists argue that the correlativity of the right/duty pairing is part of the distinctive normative character of private law, whilst civil recourse theorists argue that the imposition of liabilities rather than duties in the first instance is part of the distinctive normative character of tort law.[37] But

---

[34] Of the various proponents of corrective justice theory, Weinrib defends the most thoroughly 'juridical' version. On his view, private law does not attempt to implement the moral ideal of corrective justice, even if this is substantively similar to the principles of liability the law applies. Although Weinrib is clear on this point, it is less clear what relationship the juridical conception of corrective justice *does* have with moral duties. Does it deny the existence of underlying corrective duties? Or deny that they overlap in content with legal duties? Or does it accept their existence and overlap, but treat them as merely coincidental, of no relevance for the understanding and justification of private law?

[35] Stephen Smith, *Rights, Wrongs, and Injustices* (Oxford University Press 2019) 191–99. See also NB Oman, 'Why There is No Duty to Pay Damages: Powers, Duties, and Private Law' (2011) 39 Florida State University Law Review 137; Benjamin Zipursky, 'Civil Recourse, not Corrective Justice' (2003) 91 Georgetown Law Journal 695; and John Goldberg and Benjamin Zipursky, 'Tort Law and Responsibility' in John Oberdiek (ed), *Philosophical Foundations of the Law of Torts* (Oxford University Press 2014) 29–32; Stephen Smith, 'Duties, Liabilities, and Damages' (2011–2012) 125 Harvard Law Review 1727.

[36] Stephen Smith, 'A Duty to Make Restitution' (2013) 26 Canadian Journal of Law and Jurisprudence 157, 161. There is disagreement about whether the law really does impose liabilities rather than duties in many cases. Sandy Steel and Robert Stevens argue that the right to distrain another's property and the awarding of interest on non-pecuniary damages prior to an order both suggest a pre-existing corrective duty in positive law. Sandy Steel and Robert Stevens, 'The Secondary Legal Duty to Pay Damages' (2020) 136 Law Quarterly Review 283, 288–89.

[37] Which is not to say that civil recourse is *exclusive* to tort law—a clarification Goldberg and Zipursky make in their 'Replies to Commentators' (2022) 41 Law and Philosophy 127, pt II (hereafter Goldberg and Zipursky, *Replies to Commentators*).

these features, or at least close correlates of them, are possessed by moral duties too. Many moral wrongs are also relational. The moral wrong of negligence, like its legal counterpart, is a wrong committed against specified others, not an impersonal wrong or an offence against the community. In regard to liabilities, civil recourse theorists emphasize that they exhibit *victim empowerment*, that is, it is up to the victim whether to compel the wrongdoer to provide a remedy by bringing an action against them.[38] Again, moral corrective duties also have this feature. These duties cannot be carried out against the wishes of their beneficiaries; they are typically waivable, perhaps with some exceptions. The difference is that a duty creates a presumption in favour of performance whilst a liability implies nothing until the appropriate demand has been made. But even so, both preserve the normative core of victim empowerment, at least if this is understood in terms of control.

In any case, revealing the normatively distinctive features of the law would not make any real headway in justifying it. Distinctiveness is not the same as justification. In fact, for all that has been argued to the contrary, distinctive principles may be even worse at justifying the law than non-distinctive principles—this is also a comparative question. Consider again an analogy with the problem of punishment. Perhaps our criminal justice system embodies a 'juridical' conception of retributivism, which is distinctive in the sense that it cannot be reduced to a similar but pre-institutional conception of retributivism and is rendered incoherent when we fail to understand it on its own terms. This would be an important explanatory insight but would make almost no progress on the question of whether our current punishment practices are justified. We could simply repeat the question, asking whether this juridical conception of retributivism justifies the hard treatment of punishment, and interpretivism cannot hope to answer this question due to its non-comparative character.

III. The Relevance of Moral Duties to Tort Theory

I have said that foundationalism treats the moral underpinnings of the law as vital to the question of justification. We can now develop this claim further. The justification of the law depends on the existence of enforceable moral duties that overlap, at least in part, with our legal duties. To make this argument, we will consider two kinds of hypothetical cases: (1) those in which the law imposes a

---

[38] Goldberg and Zipursky, *Recognizing Wrongs* (n 9) 355–56.

duty in the absence of an underlying moral duty, and (2) those in which the law does not impose a duty in the presence of an underlying moral duty.

Here are some type (1) cases.[39]

> *Self-defence*: Aimee launches an unprovoked attack on Bill, which will break his arm. Bill breaks Aimee's arm before she can carry out the attack. Aimee sues Bill, and a court awards her compensation for the injury.
>
> *Well*: Charlie, along with the rest of their community, has been accessing water from a natural spring for generations. Dee appropriates the spring for profit and prohibits Charlie from using it. Charlie uses it anyway, as the alternative puts them and their community at serious risk of illness caused by unclean drinking water. Dee sues Charlie, and a court awards Dee compensation for the loss of use of her property.
>
> *Defamation*: Ecco writes an article criticizing Fin for charging extortionate fees for medical 'remedies' that are in fact placebos. Fin sues Ecco, and a court awards him compensation for the damage to his reputation.

Here are some type (2) cases, in which the law fails to impose a duty where an underlying moral duty exists.

> *Battery*: Gia breaks Harry's arm in an unprovoked attack. The law grants Harry no right to receive compensation from Gia.
>
> *Sexual Harassment*: Ian subjects Jules to a campaign of sexual harassment, including unwanted touching, phone calls, stalking, and sexist comments, resulting in serious psychological harm. The law grants Jules no right to receive compensation from Ian.
>
> *Employment*: Kit is poor and desperate and accepts dangerous employment in a local mine. Linda, Kit's employer, tells them that by accepting the job they consent to any risk of injury that comes with it. Linda negligently fails to provide a safe working environment for Kit, and as a result Kit suffers a serious injury. The law grants Kit no right to receive compensation from Linda.

---

[39] Note that the type (1) and (2) cases given here are hypothetical and are not meant to represent the current law in any particular jurisdiction, although some resonate with both contemporary and historical positions in some jurisdictions. The point of these cases is to assume a given legal position for the sake of assessing the relevance of moral duties to the justification of that position. I explain the role of the hypothetical examples to the methodology of this book in greater detail in pt V of this chapter.

In type (1) cases, the 'victim' successfully recovers compensation from the 'wrongdoer' even though no moral wrong has been committed and intuitively no moral duty to compensate is owed. If courts award damages in cases like this, the 'wrongdoer' has two objections. The first is that the law restricts their freedom to act even though they are morally free to act. We are all morally permitted to defend ourselves, to secure our survival, and to criticize charlatans, yet in these scenarios the law imposes primary duties on us to refrain from doing these things. Call this the *restricted freedom* objection.

The second, which we can call the *undue burden* objection, is that, if 'wrongdoers' are required to compensate, the law imposes a burden on them that they have no duty to bear. This burden has three elements worth distinguishing. The first is a symbolic element. In *Self-Defence*, Aimee secures a pronouncement in a court of law that Bill acted in an unjustified manner, even though he merely exercised his moral right to self-defence. This subverts one of the expressive functions of the law: to publicly communicate that one person has committed a wrong against another. It might be objected that, at least on positivist views, declaring someone a legal wrongdoer does not imply they are a moral wrongdoer, and so the symbolic effect is lessened. But the law helps itself to the language of wrongs and rights violations, with its overtones of moral criticism and disapproval, so it is somewhat artificial to suppose that this language is treated by citizens as akin to the language of fouls or infractions in sport and games, devoid of any fundamental moral implications. Moreover, many tortious acts *are* morally wrongful, which further increases the difficulty of distinguishing the symbolic significance of liability judgments in any fine-grained way. This obfuscation is itself a problem, since it can lead to inaccurate labelling.[40]

The second element of the burden faced by Bill is material, since he is lumbered with the obligation to compensate Aimee. Compensation can be expensive, especially for serious physical injury,[41] and this is imposed on Bill even though he was morally free to act exactly as he did. Even if Bill is insured, he might experience financial burden in the form of an increase in premiums, in addition to the time, cost, and stress of a legal claim against him. These burdens also serve a purpose to which he does not consent: the compensation of Aimee, and perhaps also deterrence and other forward-looking goals. This is

---

[40] For an argument that this is especially problematic in legal judgments of defamatory meaning, see Adam Slavny, 'The Normative Foundations of Defamatory Meaning' (2018) 37 Law and Philosophy 523.

[41] This complaint is mitigated by the fact that Bill will likely be insured against most common forms of liability. This does not eliminate the objection, however, since legal liability is still burdensome even when compensation is paid by a third party. If Bill is insured, he still has a legitimate complaint against undergoing the stress and cost of being sued without any justification.

distinctively objectionable, and constitutes the third element of Bill's burden, since it means that he is harmfully used for a purpose to which he does not consent, and harmful using is often regarded as more objectionable than other modes of harming.[42]

In type (2) cases, in which the law fails to impose a duty in the presence of an underlying moral duty, victims are left with no redress for the wrongs they have suffered. In *Battery*, the law fails to protect Harry's physical security from unjustified attack; in *Sexual Harassment*, the law fails to recognize the campaign of sexist abuse against Jules as wrongful; and in *Employment*, the law treats Kit, falsely, as having voluntarily assumed the risk of injury.[43] This gives rise to two distinct complaints on behalf of would-be claimants. First, that the state has failed in its obligation to provide citizens with adequate redress for wrongdoing.[44] Most believe that the state has a duty to provide such redress for at least some forms of wrongdoing, not merely that it is permissible for it to do so. Call this the *inadequate protection* complaint.

Second, if the state allows other victims to claim compensation, those who are denied it have a fairness-based complaint against the way a vital resource—opportunities to enforce corrective duties—is allocated. For example, in *Sexual Harassment*, it is perverse that Jules' interest in being free of a campaign of sexist abuse should have less protection than, say, a homeowner's interest in their neighbour's tree roots not encroaching on their land.[45] Call this the *unjust distribution* objection. These two objections, though overlapping, are distinct. To see this, consider two societies, one of which protects people against the encroachment of tree roots but not sexual harassment, and one of which protects

---

[42] The principle has been widely discussed and has Kantian roots, but for a more contemporary statement of what it is to use someone as a means, see Derek Parfit, *On What Matters: Volume 1* (Oxford University Press 2011) 213. For an analysis of different formulations of principles that prohibit using or exploiting others, see Ketan H Ramakrishnan, 'Treating People as Tools' (2016) 44 Philosophy & Public Affairs 133.

[43] Some nineteenth-century English decisions practically equate knowledge of risk with voluntary assumption, see *Woodley v Metropolitan District Railway Co* (1877) 2 Ex D 384. Together with the defences of contributory negligence and common employment, this made up the 'unholy trinity' of doctrines that made accident claims against employers near impossible.

[44] This is one of the arguments Goldberg and Zipursky appeal to in defence of their civil recourse theory, see Goldberg and Zipursky, *Recognizing Wrongs* (n 9) especially 130–35. I am less convinced that the state's prohibition on private reprisals is fundamental to this argument since some victims would not be able to exact private reprisals even if they were unconstrained by the law, and the state owes these individuals the same duty it owes to other victims of similar wrongs.

[45] For an argument that tort law fails to adequately remedy gendered harms, and sexual harassment in particular, see Joanne Conaghan, 'Gendered Harms and the Law of Tort: Remedying (Sexual) Harassment' (1996) 16 Oxford Journal of Legal Studies 407, although Conaghan's position must now be read in the light of subsequent developments such as the Protection from Harassment Act 1997 and the Equality Act 2010. See also Nikki Godden, 'Tort Claims for Rape: More Trials, Fewer Tribulations?' and Elizabeth Adjin-Tettey, 'Sexual Wrongdoing: Do the Remedies Reflect the Wrong?' in Janice Richardson and Erika Rackley (eds), *Feminist Perspectives on Tort Law* (Routledge 2012).

people against neither. Victims of sexual harassment can mount the *inadequate protection* objection in both societies, but in the first society, such victims have a distinctive objection based on their position relative to victims of less serious wrongs.

These four objections—the *restricted freedom* and *undue burden* objections in type (1) cases and the *inadequate protection* and *unjust distribution* objections in type (2) cases—create a powerful presumptive argument in favour of the relevance of underlying moral wrongs and duties to tort law. They also help us see how interpretive theories that do not address them face serious difficulties with respect to the normative side of their project. Goldberg and Zipursky's civil recourse theory is an instructive example because, by design, it avoids any reference to moral wrongs or duties.[46] Their defence of the principle of civil recourse appeals to three sub-principles which are meant to float free from moral duties: equality, fairness, and individual sovereignty.

Without rights of civil recourse, they argue, there would be *inequality* between victims of wrongdoing, similar to that which underpins the *unjust distribution* objection. The opportunities for victims of legally recognized wrongs to seek redress would depend on their ability to compel performance by other means, which in turn would depend on their resources, influence, luck, and so on. The right of action ameliorates this inequality, though it does not eliminate it entirely, by offering everyone the opportunity to bring a private suit against offenders.[47] Secondly, without civil recourse there would be *unfairness* between victims and wrongdoers. Usually, when one person wrongs another, the victim's interests are set back more severely than those of the perpetrator. Without a right of action, the victim is left powerless to redress this unfairness.[48] And finally, without conferring rights of civil recourse the state would fail to respect the *individual sovereignty* of victims of wrongdoing by monopolizing the use of force and offering citizens no recourse against wrongdoing in its place.[49]

To evaluate Goldberg and Zipursky's strategy of avoiding reliance on claims about moral wrongs and duties, we should consider the appeal of civil recourse in cases where no underlying moral wrong is committed. Failure to do this fuels the worry that the normative appeal of civil recourse in standard cases trades on an implicit recognition of underlying moral wrongdoing. Though Goldberg and Zipursky are right to emphasize that torts and moral wrongs

---

[46] Goldberg and Zipursky, *Replies to Commentators* (n 37) 130–35.
[47] Goldberg and Zipursky, *Recognizing Wrongs* (n 9) 133–34.
[48] ibid, 139.
[49] ibid, 145.

diverge, much tortious conduct involves at least some form of moral wrongness. The true test of their strategy of eliding any appeal to moral wrongness, then, is its plausibility in type (1) and (2) cases when there is no overlap whatsoever. Otherwise the costs of their view are obscured, since we are not directly presented with its harshest implications.

Consider how the principles of equality, fairness, and individual sovereignty hold up in type (1) and (2) cases.[50] In *Self-Defence*, if the law denied Aimee compensation there would be no meaningful inequality between her and other victims of wrongdoing because Aimee is not a victim of wrongdoing: she is morally liable to be harmed in self-defence by Bill. Similarly, the law would not create unfairness between Aimee and Bill for exactly the same reason. Quite the opposite. The law would generate unfairness by empowering Aimee to burden Bill and by denying Bill's moral freedom to defend himself. Finally, Aimee's individual sovereignty would not be undermined by prohibiting her from pursuing private redress, since she has no moral right to such redress. Instead, the law itself violates individual sovereignty by imposing the burden of compensation on Bill for exercising his moral right of self-defence. The problem with all three of these sub-principles is the same. The asymmetry between Aimee and Bill—or between Aimee and other victims of wrongdoing—with respect to the benefits and burdens of civil recourse tells us nothing without some criteria that determines how these benefits and burdens should be allocated, and appeal to enforceable moral duties provides us with such criteria.

Similar claims can be made about type (2) cases. In *Battery*, the law treats Harry unequally relative to other victims because it ignores his claim even though his moral rights have been seriously violated. It is unfair because it treats the wrong done to him by Gia as legally permissible. And it violates his individual sovereignty by failing to provide him with an avenue of legal recourse whilst prohibiting any private attempt to obtain redress.

What lessons can be drawn from this? One is that the law must justify itself to two constituencies of people. The first are defendants who can mount the *restricted freedom* and *undue burden* objections. This demand is more urgent in criminal law where the burdens are greater, but this is a difference of scale rather than kind. Private law still restricts people's freedom, labels them wrongdoers when they violate its norms, and burdens them for the sake of ends to which they do not consent. These practices call out for justification,

---

[50] For similar arguments, see Tom Dougherty and Johann Frick, 'Morality and Institutional Detail in the Law of Torts: Reflections on Goldberg's and Zipursky's Recognizing Wrongs' (2022) 41 Law and Philosophy 41, 1. The present argument goes further in stating that the three principles are self-defeating without some sensitivity to underlying moral wrongs.

especially to those on whom the burden is imposed. This is one reason why purely instrumentalist justifications are questionable. It is not enough to point out that holding a certain class of people liable is expected to lead to good consequences. It must also be shown that that class of people can permissibly be harmed as a means of bringing about these consequences, and instrumentalist theories struggle to meet this challenge.

The second constituency is would-be claimants who are not given any assistance in seeking redress for a wrong done to them, and who can therefore mount the *inadequate protection* and *unjust distribution* objections. This demand for justification applies both to causes of action the law refuses to recognize and to the specific procedural and substantive rules regarding the causes of action the law does recognize. For example, in *Sexual Harassment*, even if Jules can frame her grievance in terms of a valid cause of action, if this distorts her real grievance, or presents greater barriers to success relative to others, then she has a distributive complaint that the law prioritizes interests that are not as important as hers.

To these two demands for justification, we must add a third. We all pay for the law through taxes, liability insurance, and the costs of goods and services. Not only that, but the costs of civil justice have consistently been criticized,[51] and there is no sign these criticisms will be defused any time soon. Consequently, we are all owed a justification for the resources we collectively provide to keep the expensive institutions of civil justice up and running. Addressing these three justificatory demands is one of the most important tasks facing theorists of tort law. This makes it all the more surprising that they have been sidelined in favour of interpretivist questions. In the remainder of this book, I hope to show that a foundationalist approach can make some progress with them.

IV. Four Objections

Let's consider four objections to the defence of foundationalism developed above.

---

[51] For the criticism that tort is very expensive to administer compared to other compensation systems, see Patrick Atiyah's classic critique in Peter Cane and James Goudkamp, *Atiyah's Accidents, Compensation and the Law* (9th edn, 2018 Cambridge University Press) pt 1.4.5.

A. Wrongs and Duties

First, in respect of type (1) cases, it might be objected that moral wrongs are only one source of corrective duties. Such duties can also arise independently, and this limits their relevance. Consider:

> *Dangerous Animals*: Manu breeds dangerous animals. They take all reasonable precautions to ensure the animals do not escape, but, unluckily, they do escape and damage Nell's neighbouring land.
> *Joint Enterprise*: Ove and Pia own a roofing business. Ove does the books while Pia repairs the roofs, though they both benefit equally from their joint activities. While fixing a roof, Pia negligently injures Quints.[52]

In *Dangerous Animals*, Manu commits no moral wrong against Nell, yet it is plausible that they ought to compensate her for the harm. In *Joint Enterprise*, Ove commits no moral wrong against Quints, yet it is plausible that Ove and Pia ought jointly to compensate Quints. These examples point to alternative sources of corrective duties besides wrongdoing, which we will investigate further in later chapters. However, they do not undermine the objections that 'wrongdoers' have in type (1) cases, for two reasons. Most obviously, cases like *Dangerous Animals* and *Joint Enterprise* are the exception rather than the rule, and 'wrongdoers' retain valid complaints in other type (1) cases such as *Self-Defence*, *Well*, and *Defamation*.

Moreover, in *Dangerous Animals* and *Joint Enterprise*, Manu and Ove have no duty not to engage in the activity that leads to harm. Instead, they have a duty to compensate *if* that activity results in harm. This is a distinction that will also become important in later chapters. Imposing liability to compensate on them can be justified on the basis of their *conditional* duty, even if there is no prior moral wrong. If that is right, they do not have the *undue burden* complaint since they are not compelled to bear a burden they lack a duty to bear. They would have the *restricted freedom* complaint if the law imposed a duty on them not to engage in the activity in the first place. But the law can circumvent this problem by imposing a conditional duty instead.

---

[52] This case is taken from Victor Tadros, 'Orwell's Battle with Brittain: Vicarious Liability for Unjust Aggression' (2014) 42 Philosophy & Public Affairs 42, 54.

B. Indeterminacy and Disagreement

Some might think that moral duties are indeterminate, or that there is reasonable disagreement about the content and scope of these duties, and this undermines any attempt to justify legal rules or institutions by appealing to them. Let's break these ideas down into some more specific objections. One appeals to disagreement to argue that we are not epistemically justified in asserting the existence of moral duties. There are two problems with this objection, at least insofar as it is deployed as a reason to favour interpretivism over foundationalism. One is that there is also plenty of disagreement amongst interpretivists about how best to explain the law, or even what it is that needs explaining, and this is not usually taken as a sign that it is doomed from the start.[53] This is for good reason. Universal consensus is an unnecessary and unreasonable epistemic threshold to expect of any theory, normative or otherwise. The existence of disagreement does not imply that there are no right answers to the questions we are asking, or that we cannot find those answers, or that we cannot perceive what makes those answers the right ones.

Moreover, the extent of moral disagreement amongst epistemic peers is not uniform. Some judgements are more controversial than others, and we can demonstrate the relevance of moral duties by appealing to less controversial ones. How many readers doubt the assumptions made about the duties in *Self-Defence, Well, Defamation, Battery, Sexual Harassment,* and *Employment*?[54] Perhaps committed moral sceptics do, but others will admit that we are entitled to give more epistemic credence to some judgements about our moral duties than others. Even for the sceptics, there is surely value in thinking about the relationship between moral duties and legal justification conditionally. We can coherently ask what would follow regarding the justification of legal duties *if* certain moral duties existed, notwithstanding doubts as to whether these duties do indeed exist.

A second objection appeals not to indeterminacy but reasonable disagreement. Suppose we are justified in believing a given moral duty exists. Nevertheless, we might think, others may reasonably disagree, and this precludes any reliance on these duties for the purpose of justifying the law. Such justification can be founded only on premises that can be accepted from the

---

[53] Although for a criticism of interpretivist theories with universalist leanings see John Murphy, 'The Heterogeneity of Tort Law' (2019) 39 Oxford Journal of Legal Studies 455 and James Goudkamp and John Murphy, 'The Failure of Universal Theories of Tort Law' (2015) Legal Theory 21(2) 47.

[54] Those with the opposite concern that my claims about these cases are too self-evident will be reassured to know that later in the book I will defend some much less plausible views!

perspective of all reasonable views. This line of reasoning is familiar from the Rawlsian concept of liberal neutrality, or the political liberal constraint, here extended to private law.[55] One of the main replies to the political liberal view is that people should not be expected to bear high costs because of the moral mistakes of others. Consider a variation of *Self-Defence* in which Bill's life is imperilled by Aimee's attack, and suppose that, on the best conception of reasonableness, it would be reasonable to think that Bill lacks permission to defend himself, although according to the correct view, he is so permitted. When the stakes are this high, can we really disregard Bill's appeal to his moral permission to defend himself on the grounds that it is possible to reasonably disagree with it, even if it will cost him his life? I doubt it. Perhaps the argument is more plausible when applied to other areas of the law where the stakes are lower, and so has some purchase. To decide this, we need to know the rationale, or the normative motivation, for the political liberal constraint. It doesn't make sense to try and determine its scope independently of its rationale—its rationale determines its scope. Is it to achieve stability for the right reasons, stability for any reason, respect for the autonomy of citizens, reducing alienation from coercive institutions, or what? Only when we have a clear picture of this rationale will we be able to decide, in an informed way, when it applies and whether it is worth the costs that must be paid in terms of allowing mistaken but reasonable moral views to determine coercive laws.

We also need a plausible distinction between reasonable and unreasonable views. Only reasonable disagreement gains the protection of the political liberal constraint—unreasonable disagreement can be disregarded. This means that reasonable disagreement won't rule out all appeals to moral duty anyway, and so cannot be taken as a general objection to foundationalism. In the absence of significant further argument, then, I will continue with the assumption that political liberalism does not pre-empt the foundationalist approach. Of course, there is a great deal more to say about these issues. These brief comments are intended to convey the complexity of the questions that must be settled, and to carve out some space for foundationalism, rather than to deny the possibility that the justification of private law might be restricted by reasonable disagreement.

---

[55] John Rawls, *Political Liberalism* (Cambridge University Press 1993). See also Samuel Scheffler, 'Distributive Justice, the Basic Structure and the Place of Private Law' (2015) 35 Oxford Journal of Legal Studies 213 for the argument that private law forms part of the basic structure of society.

Returning now to our disambiguation of indeterminacy and disagreement as challenges to foundationalism, here is a third objection. Morality needs law to concretize moral obligations. Martin Stone states that the specification of what is owed to others in various circumstances 'is something that is both epistemically and constitutively dependent on a legal practice offering concrete judgments of that same form, you mustn't take that—it's his; you mustn't do that—he's there'.[56] Similarly, Tony Honoré argues that, 'Morality on its own is incomplete and cannot provide a viable guide to what we are required to do in particular situations',[57] and this incompleteness must be filled out by law and legal institutions. The reliance of morality on law might be taken as a reason to doubt whether moral duties can do the justificatory work foundationalists require.

In response, we can acknowledge that the law plays an important role in concretizing our moral duties, but this poses no threat to foundationalism. Morality is not indeterminate in the sense that it tells us *nothing* about our duties. Take the duty to compensate as an example. It is unreasonable to think morality could quantify compensation in any precise way, so legal processes are required to perform this task. However, it does not follow that those who wrongfully harm others without recourse to these quantifying processes owe nothing at all. Not knowing exactly what one owes independently of legal input, or there being no fact of the matter as to exactly what one owes, is not a reason to ignore the victims of one's wrongdoing entirely. What follows from this incompleteness is simply that, without the crystallizing effect of the law, the moral duty to compensate is *multiply realizable*, that is, there are different amounts and forms of compensation, any of which would fulfil the duty.[58] The law's role in crystallizing this obligation is crucial for avoiding bias, unnecessary disputes and confusion. It is not evidence that the duty does not exist, or that it is irrelevant for the justification of the law's corrective practices.

---

[56] Martin Stone, 'Legal Positivism as an Idea about Morality' (2011) 61 University of Toronto Law Journal 313, 334. Kantian theorists typically believe our moral rights, at least our moral rights to property, are indeterminate independent of specification within a legal order, see Ripstein, *Force and Freedom* (n 27) 168–76. For an argument that some property rights are determinate in a state of nature, see Victor Tadros, 'Independence Without Interests?' (2011) 31 Oxford Journal of legal Studies 193.

[57] Tony Honoré 'The Dependence of Morality on Law' (1993) 13 Oxford Journal of legal Studies 1, 3.

[58] Note also Sandy Steel's point that there may be an 'overlapping minimum' even though an authoritative legal statement is needed to fully crystalize the duty of repair, 'On the Moral Necessity of Tort Law: The Fairness Argument' (2020) 41 Oxford Journal of legal Studies 192 (hereafter Steel, 'On the Moral Necessity of Tort Law').

C. The Divergence of Torts and Moral Wrongs

Here is a third type of objection. Torts diverge in significant ways from moral wrongs, and these differences might fuel doubts about foundationalism. There are two types of divergence we should consider: moral wrongs that are not recognized as legal wrongs and legal wrongs that either have no moral correlates or differ substantially from their moral correlates.

As an example of the first type of divergence, consider the duty not to cheat on one's spouse or lie to one's friend. Can't victims of infidelity and dishonesty successfully mount the *inadequate protection* and *unjust distribution* complaints given that the law offers them no recourse? And since most will agree that the law has no business involving itself in these matters, doesn't this cast doubt on the relevance of moral duties to the law more generally? It does not, because our concerns with legal involvement in these cases flow from the fact that these moral wrongs do not meet the conditions of enforceability.[59] There can be no complaint that the law fails to enforce non-enforceable duties.

Since the concept of enforceability plays an important role in explaining why many moral wrongs should not be recognized as legal wrongs, it is worth pausing to explore it in more detail. To do so, we can borrow some terminology from Sandy Steel.[60] A duty may be either personally or institutionally enforceable. A duty is personally enforceable if the recipient of the duty has a liberty to take steps to see that the duty-bearer fulfils the duty even without their consent. This liberty is typically coupled with a power to authorize others to take similar steps on one's behalf. A duty is institutionally enforceable if the recipient has a liberty and a power to authorize a legal institution to enforce it or to authorize its enforcement. This distinction then gives us a four-fold taxonomy of duties: enforceable (in both senses), unenforceable (in both senses), only personally enforceable, and only institutionally enforceable.

We can also distinguish between questions of enforceability as applied to *types* of duties and as applied to *tokens*. Some duties seem to be unenforceable at the type level, such as duties of fidelity. We do not need to assess these duties on a case-by-case basis to determine the enforceability of each token—they are unenforceable as a class. Matters are further complicated by the fact that the

---

[59] Andrew Gold distinguishes between performance of a remedial duty by a wrongdoer (corrective justice) and enforcement by a right holder (redressive justice), and identifies several asymmetries between corrective and redressive justice, see Andrew S Gold, *The Right of Redress* (Oxford University Press 2020) ch 2. These asymmetries do not undermine the justificatory relationship described above, however, since the legal practice of both redressive and corrective justice depend, I argue, on enforceable moral duties.

[60] Steel, 'On the Moral Necessity of Tort Law' (n 58) 3.

distinction between token and type enforceability cuts across the distinction between personal and institutional enforceability. Duties of fidelity, for example, may be institutionally unenforceable as a class without being personally unenforceable as a class. Legal institutions should never meddle in romantic relationships, we might think, but it does not follow that friends and spouses cannot sometimes take steps to prevent infidelity.

It is not straightforward to find an explanation of what makes some duties, as a class, unenforceable.[61] Luckily, we do not need such an explanation for our purposes, since the duty types usually considered unenforceable—duties of fidelity and duties to keep non-contractual promises being prominent examples—will not concern us in this book, and the duties that will concern us—duties to respond to wronging and harming—are usually regarded as enforceable in both the personal and institutional senses, at least at the type level. This leaves us with the question of why some individual tokens are unenforceable, and here we can lay out a few relevant factors.

Some duties are unenforceable in the personal and institutional senses because any kind of enforcement would eliminate or reduce the value that gives rise to the duty. This is true of the duty of fidelity. The person who is forced to be loyal cannot fulfil their duty because voluntary performance is constitutive of the value of loyalty. We must tread carefully here, since I noted above that the duty not to cheat could be personally enforceable. We might say that enforcement by others impairs the moral worth of the duty-bearer's actions or their virtue, or the quality of their intentions, without making it unenforceable. Either way, in such cases enforcement impairs what I will call the *performance value* of actions. We will return to this idea when we discuss the dischargeability of corrective duties by third parties in Chapter 8. For now, we can note that, even if the prospect of undermining performance value does make a duty unenforceable, this typically will not apply to duties in relation to physical injury, which will occupy us throughout most of this book.

When duties are not unenforceable in this way, this means that the values that underpin the duties can be achieved even if the recipient, third parties, or a legal institution compels performance. Nevertheless, duties may be unenforceable for other reasons. There are many factors that determine whether a particular duty token is enforceable, but four worth mentioning are ineffectiveness, unwanted consequences, cost, and difficulty. Sometimes attempting to

[61] See Christian Barry and Emily McTernan, 'A Puzzle of Enforceability: Why do Moral Duties Differ in their Enforceability?' (2021) 19 Journal of Moral Philosophy 229 for a critical survey of different views, concluding that no single view offers a decisive explanation for the apparent unenforceability of certain types of duties.

enforce a duty is ineffective or has unintended consequences. Suppose there is a moral duty of easy rescue but enforcing a legal duty would encourage people to avoid placing themselves in situations where they might be required to perform rescues, thus reducing the number of rescues overall. If this were true, the duty of rescue would be unenforceable in the sense that it would be ineffective and counter-productive in its consequences. Other duties are too expensive to enforce relative to their importance, such as my duty to return a pen borrowed from a colleague. Yet others are too difficult to enforce because doing so would require complex fact-finding exercises or overly fine-grained legal rules.

These factors are contextual in several ways. They apply differently to the issue of personal enforcement than to institutional enforcement. My obligation to return my colleague's pen is too trivial to justify the intervention of a court, but it is not too trivial to justify my colleague simply retrieving the pen from my desk. Similarly, a duty not to break a promise to a friend may be personally but not institutionally enforceable. It may be permissible for the friend to take steps to prevent the breach, but not for institutions to do so, as this would require far-reaching powers that would conflict with privacy rights and be vulnerable to abuse. Other duties may be institutionally but not personally enforceable. As we have seen, civil recourse theorists hold that the state prohibits the private use of violence to extract remedies from wrongdoers, and this is part of what justifies its duty to provide institutions that offer civil recourse.[62]

These considerations could also be applied at the type as well as the token level. It might be that certain types of duties are unenforceable because the overall costs of doing so are too high, despite the fact that individual tokens could be enforced at a proportionate cost. This might be true if distinguishing between those tokens that are enforceable and those tokens that are unenforceable is itself too costly. It is important to note, though, that while this rationale might justify legal institutions refraining from enforcing some types of duties, it does not show that all individual tokens of that type actually are unenforceable, unless we adopt the controversial rule-consequentialist logic that what is justified as a rule itself fixes what is justified in each application of that rule.

---

[62] Some Kantians go further and argue that 'Private enforcement is not merely inconvenient: it is inconsistent with justice because it is ultimately the rule of the stronger', see Arthur Ripstein, 'Private Order and Public Justice: Kant and Rawls' (2006) 92 Virginia Law Review 1391, 1415. This view faces serious problems, however. First, that stronger individuals are more likely to be successful in their private enforcement efforts perhaps creates unfairness between parties with equally just causes, but it implies nothing about the justness of those causes. If David launches an attack on Goliath, the fact that Goliath is in a more enviable position than David is hardly relevant to the permissibility of David's attack or Goliath's defence. And second, many rights such as self-defence can plausibly be exercised privately, both inside and outside the context of a legal institutional order that protects these rights.

We can see, then, that the question of enforceability is a complex one and there is ample space for foundationalists to explain why some moral duties should not have the force of law, both at the type and token level. Let's now return to the second type of divergence: legal wrongs that either have no moral correlates or differ substantially from their moral correlates. We saw that Goldberg and Zipursky avoid appealing to moral wrongs and duties in their theory of civil recourse. In explaining this choice, they emphasize that we have reason to define legal wrongs in ways that go beyond their moral counterparts.[63] Negligence is a prominent example. There are three features of the tort of negligence that set it apart from the moral wrong of negligence. First, the tort is outcome-inclusive: one commits it only when unreasonable risks result in legally cognizable harm. By contrast, many accept that one commits a moral wrong by imposing an unreasonable risk, regardless of whether it results in harm.[64] Second, the standard of care in negligence is objective in the sense that it is fixed by what a hypothetical reasonable person would do in the relevant circumstances and is not typically affected by the limitations or impairments of a given defendant, though there are many exceptions to this. This standard has harsh consequences for those who are unable to meet it through no fault or choice of their own, and therefore does not match up to ordinary moral thinking about culpability. Finally, compensation is determined by the extent of the damage caused and is generally insensitive to the means of either the tortfeasor or the victim. An impoverished single mother who collides with a billionaire's Rolls Royce in a rare moment of oversight is liable in full for the damage, even if the cost of repair is peanuts for the billionaire and devastating for the single mother.[65] As Goldberg and Zipursky summarize, 'Given the gaps in this domain of law between law and morality, the hypothesis that its justification can be found in … a moral duty of repair seems dubious, at best'.

I agree that the moral wrong of negligence will not justify the law of negligence in its entirety. However, the moral wrong can help the law to meet the *restricted freedom* and *undue burden* objections in many, perhaps most, cases. Then any remaining divergences must either be justified in some other way, or

---

[63] Goldberg and Zipursky, *Recognizing Wrongs* (n 9) 189–98 and 205–08 and John Goldberg and Benjamin Zipursky, 'Tort Law and Moral Luck' (2007) 92 Cornell Law Review 1123.

[64] Although see John Oberdiek, 'The Wrong in Negligence' (2021) 41 Oxford Journal of Legal Studies 1174 for an argument that the wrong of negligence does not require a legally cognizable injury. If this is correct, the legal wrong of negligence—as opposed to the tort of negligence—overlaps more with the moral wrong.

[65] In reality, the claim would be covered by liability insurance. We will return to the issue of the relevance of insurance in Chapter 8.

it must be admitted that they lack justification. As I indicated previously, some divergences are justified in the light of pragmatic or regulatory considerations. For example, there is no obvious remedy for being the victim of an unjustified risk in the absence of any ensuing harm, let alone one that would merit the considerable expense of a civil lawsuit, and this is enough to explain the outcome-inclusiveness of the tort of negligence.

Equally, there are pragmatic worries about implementing a subjective standard of care, such as wasting court time interrogating the capacities of individual defendants, as well as the concern that a subjective standard would not guide action as effectively as an objective one. Perhaps these arguments justify the objective standard of care, but foundationalism shows us that this is a concession to practical realities and other forward-looking considerations rather than a deep matter of principle (see Chapter 4 for further discussion). Not only that, but foundationalism outlines the manner in which the divergence must be justified. Defendants who do not commit the moral wrong of negligence can mount the *restricted freedom* and *undue burden* objections, and it must be shown why these objections can be overridden by the need to ensure the law is more practicable or better at guiding conduct. Ignoring the divergence between law and morality on this point obscures the need to meet this challenge.

As for the impoverished single mother paying for the Rolls Royce ... there is no justification for it, or so I will argue in Chapter 7 when we address the relationship between corrective and distributive justice. Ultimately, then, foundationalists are capable of justifying some divergences between law and morality, but since their ambitions are not apologistic, they are more than willing to condemn others.

D. Legal Wrongs and Legal Authority

I have suggested that certain divergences between law and morality are either not justified or are justified only by appeal to pragmatic or regulatory considerations. This argument, it might be thought, rests on the assumption that torts must be understood as *moral* wrongs if they are to be understood as wrongs at all. Some question this. Goldberg and Zipursky say that it is the status of torts as *legal* wrongs that gives them their force. In their words:

We have all along embraced H.L.A. Hart's views that legal obligations so-called have a great deal in common with moral obligations; they are both species of a genus of obligations that has a certain phenomenological character and are appropriately viewed, under a variety of circumstances, as binding. So long as we can help ourselves to "obligations" in this sense, we do not see any problem.[66]

It is true that legal wrongs are a distinctive type of wrong in some senses. They are creatures of law rather than morality, posited by law-making bodies; they are couched in their own legal language which overlaps with, but is not identical to, everyday moral language; and they are appropriately viewed, from the internal perspective, as wrongs rather than mere prices or commands backed with threats. But this shows only that legal wrongs are distinctive, not that they are justified. Goldberg and Zipursky's description of tort duties as 'binding' and 'genuine' suggests the further claim that they are justified.

One way to defend this claim is by appealing to legal authority as a means of generating moral duties. On this view, legitimately constituted legal bodies have a normative power to create new, content-independent moral obligations. These obligations are created directly through the exercise of the power, rather than indirectly by altering the factual circumstances which themselves generate new obligations. This depends on the prior claim that there is a duty, or at least a reason, to obey the law *qua* law. This is open to doubt, although that is another debate entirely.[67] If we grant that creating a legal duty gives citizens moral reasons to obey, though, two further questions arise.

First, what is the justification for the way authority has, in fact, been exercised? Unless we concede that the specific set of torts that we have are a product of historical accident, we need an explanation why we should have *these* torts rather than some other set. The *inadequate protection* and *unjust distribution* objections might suggest that legal authority should have been exercised in some other way, and simply asserting the bindingness of legal duties does not answer this challenge. The same point applies to other normative powers. Promising generates an obligation where previously none existed, but we can have good and bad reasons to make promises. Referring to the fact that I made a promise explains the provenance of my obligation but does not demonstrate the soundness of my decision to make the promise.

---

[66] Goldberg and Zipursky, 'Replies to Commentators' (n 37) 139.

[67] For Raz's well-known service conception of authority, see Joseph Raz, *The Morality of Freedom* (Oxford University Press 1986) pt I and 'The Problem of Authority: Revisiting the Service Conception' in *Between Authority and Interpretation* (Oxford University Press 2009). For criticism of the ability of this view to justify a duty to obey orders, see Victor Tadros, *To Do, To Die, To Reason Why: Individual Ethics in War* (Oxford University Press 2022) ch 4.

Second, those who defend some form of legal authority, or obligation to obey the law *qua* law, often accept that the reasons to obey can be overridden. In *Self-Defence*, Bill has a reason not to violate the law, which tells him not to defend himself against Aimee's unjust attack. But it is a further question whether this overrides his countervailing reasons. Why is the reason to obey the law *qua* law, assuming it exists, not overridden by Bill's reason to defend his life? More generally, we need an explanation why the *restricted freedom* and *undue burden* objections don't override the moral reason to obey the law. Moral freedoms, especially important ones like the right to self-defence, cannot be overridden by legal fiat so easily. Appealing to legal authority or the duty to obey the law does not free us from the need to provide a normative justification.

V. Hypothetical Case Analysis

Before moving on from our discussion of methodology, it will be helpful to say something about the use of hypothetical cases throughout this book. The bread and butter of interpretivism is the analysis of legal content and structure. The bread and butter of top-down theory is the derivation of implications for the law from an overarching normative framework. Our bottom-up alternative—foundationalism—lends itself to a different method, one familiar to moral and political philosophers, in which we assess the intuitiveness of different ideas and principles in a range of hypothetical cases.

Hypothetical case analysis is a versatile tool that has helped many areas of philosophy, including normative legal theory, to achieve new levels of depth and sophistication. It also has its critics. Among the complaints I have encountered are that hypothetical cases are too pared down (that's the point—they give us control over contextual detail and often it is better to consider one or two salient normative factors at a time rather than five or six); that judgements about them are potentially biased or subject to debunking (as are all judgements, so this must be determined on a case-by-case basis rather than a generalization); that arguments cannot be settled by 'intuitions' (this is why moral intuitions are the beginning rather than the end of normative inquiry: the question is whether we can articulate a rationale for the intuition that shows it is worth keeping rather than abandoning in the broader search for reflective equilibrium); or that they misrepresent the messiness and complexity of our ethical lives (only in the way an engineer 'misrepresents' the complexity of a machine by taking it apart and examining its components individually before putting it back together). There is no space to rehearse these broader arguments here (though I couldn't resist those parenthetical pot-shots)[68] but we can set out some advantages of case-based analysis in comparison to interpretivism.

As we noted previously, some interpretivists seek to explain large swathes of law and practice in terms of a single principle or overarching idea. The case-based method is a corrective for such 'one principle to rule them all' approaches. As we will see in Chapters 3–6, case analysis pushes us towards a more plural-istic and dynamic account of the grounds of corrective duties, throwing doubt on the idea that any single principle is sufficient. It is also useful to draw con-clusions about the *content* of the moral duties relevant to tort law, rather than just their form. Views about the structure of corrective justice, for example, are consistent with a wide range of substantive accounts of their content. One of the main aims of this book is to offer a four-fold account of the grounds of corrective duties, which cannot be achieved by attending to their form alone. Hypothetical cases will be indispensable in realizing this aim.

The inherent pluralism of the normative considerations that ground cor-rective duties can create problems for methodologies that are not fine-grained enough to identify and separate them. In some cases, especially paradigmatic examples of tort liability, multiples principles have similar implications. The case-based methodology is an analytic tool we can use to separate and examine distinct considerations that are otherwise likely to be conflated. For example, theories that attach liability to causation[69] and those that attach it to fault will converge on cases where fault and causation are both present, and a large pro-portion of tort cases fall within this overlap. But without assessing cases of causing harm without fault and cases of being at fault without causing harm, we will not know which principle provides the most robust support for the core cases.

We will also fail to develop a sophisticated understanding of the relationship between the various grounds of corrective duties. Two principles that yield the same implication in a given case may be separately sufficient to support the conclusion (in which case the conclusion is overdetermined), or they may be jointly necessary. The relative strength of the principles may also vary, or admit of exceptions, in ways that are discoverable only once they have been assessed

---

[68] A 'directed' version of reflective equilibrium, which distinguishes between various types and uses of hypothetical cases, is defended in Adam Slavny and others, 'Directed Reflected Equilibrium: Thought Experiments and How to Use Them' (2020) 18 Journal of Moral Philosophy 1. For further discussion, see Francis Kamm, *Intricate Ethics: Rights, Responsibilities, and Permissible Harms* (Oxford University Press 2007); Allen Wood, 'Humanity as an End in Itself' in Derek Parfit (ed), *On What Matters: Volume 2* (Oxford University Press 2011) 58–82, 66; and Jeff McMahan, 'Moral Intuition' in Hugh LaFollette (ed), *The Blackwell Guide to Ethical Theory* (Blackwell 2000) 103–20.
[69] For a well-known example of such a theory, see Richard A Epstein, 'A Theory of Strict Liability' (1973) 2 Journal of Legal Studies 151.

against a range of cases, including situations that are not represented in the law books. The methodology of hypothetical case analysis helps us solve such problems. We can separate distinct and often conflated considerations in order to examine them independently. We can show how these factors are either more opposed or complimentary than typical cases lead us to believe. We can construct cases that compare these factors more cleanly than most real scenarios. And we can test principles more systematically against our considered judgements in a wider range of cases than would be possible were we to focus only on the case law.

Conclusion

In this chapter, I have argued that the internal constraints of interpretivism make it unable to evaluate the full range of views and arguments necessary to reach an all-things-considered judgement about the justification of the law. I defended an alternative—foundationalism—that begins with a moral conception of rights, wrongs, duties, or reasons and builds towards questions of enforcement and institutional design. Foundationalism appeals to the moral underpinnings of the law that bear upon, but do not by themselves determine, the justifiability of the law. I argued that, although questions about the justification of our law and institutional practices are not purely normative, they are necessarily normative since they depend on the enforceable moral duties that we owe one another. In the remainder of this book, we will pursue this foundationalist method to develop a moral account of our corrective duties, before applying this to some of these central questions. If our method is fruitful in this endeavour, this will be the most powerful argument of all in its favour.

3

Unpacking Corrective Duties

Introduction

Having set out our methodology, our next aim is to build the four-fold ac-count of moral corrective duties. To do this, we need to know what a corrective duty aims to do. An initial answer is that it aims to compensate for harm. Compensation is central to the ethics and legal practice of corrective justice. Although not all tort remedies have a corrective function, compensatory prin-ciples feature heavily in the remedial side of tort law.[1] And from a moral per-spective, it is intuitive that those who inflict wrongful harm ought to undo or repair what they have done, and that compensation seeks to do this as far as is practical. Nevertheless, metaphorical talk of 'making whole' or even terms like 'compensation' can cloud distinctions between different types of corrective ac-tion, so we must examine corrective duties in more detail.

This chapter has two primary aims. The first is to defend a distinction be-tween negating and counterbalancing as two fundamentally different forms of corrective action. The distinction can be defined in the following way. Negating the effects of some event renders a person's future wellbeing *identical* to what it would have been if not for that event, and counterbalancing renders it *equal* to what it would have been if not for that event. Exploring this distinction is useful, not just because it clarifies concepts that might otherwise be obscured under a more generic rubric, but because it makes a difference to the moral per-missions and duties we have by helping us spell out the conditions under which *ex post* corrective action makes otherwise wrongful conduct permissible. This will yield one ground of corrective duties—conditional permissibility—in the four-fold analysis that we will develop over the next three chapters.

---

[1] John CP Goldberg and Benjamin C Zipursky, *Recognizing Wrongs* (Harvard University Press 2020) 157 (hereafter Goldberg and Zipursky, *Recognizing Wrongs*) argue that making whole is not the func-tion of damages in tort. The range of civil law remedies apart from compensatory damages shows that the central purpose of tort is rather to provide adequate recourse to the victims of wrongdoing. Goldberg and Zipursky do not deny that remedies play a compensatory role, but others argue that their theory underplays the centrality of compensation. John Gardner, for example, argues that compensa-tion is the only remedy as of right, or the default option. See *Torts and Other Wrongs* (Oxford University Press 2019) 62 (hereafter Gardner, *Torts and Other Wrongs*).

Wrongs, Harms, and Compensation. Adam Slavny, Oxford University Press. © Adam Slavny 2023.
DOI: 10.1093/oso/9780192864567.003.0003

The distinction also reveals the similarities and differences between primary and secondary duties, elucidating the relationship between them. This might lead us to adopt the well-known *continuity thesis*, the idea that secondary duties are generated by the reasons, duties, or rights that precede and survive a wrong. The second aim of the chapter is to argue that we should adopt an alternative—*the responsiveness thesis*—which understands secondary duties as appropriate responses to the breach of primary duties, rather than the continuation of any normative factor that preceded the wrong. This captures the role of wrongdoing in grounding secondary duties and represents another limb of the four-fold analysis.

I. Negating and Counterbalancing

A. Understanding the Distinction

To illuminate the distinction between negating and counterbalancing, consider:

(1) Rich wrongfully injures Sneh by breaking her leg but because Sneh is unconscious, she suffers no pain. An operation can fully repair her leg before she regains consciousness and prevent her suffering future pain.

(2) Rich wrongfully injures Sneh by breaking her leg, causing her pain. An operation will fully repair her leg and prevent her suffering future pain.

(3) Rich wrongfully injures Sneh by breaking her leg, causing her pain. The most effective treatment on Sneh's leg will render the limb usable but will not remove the pain.

(4) Rich wrongfully injures Sneh by breaking her leg. No treatment can restore the use of her leg or remove the pain.

In (1), the operation *negates* the threat to Sneh's wellbeing posed by the damage to her leg by restoring functionality and averting future pain. In (2), the situation is more complex. The operation negates a portion of the harm, but the pain Sneh suffered before she was placed under anaesthetic cannot now be undone. Instead, Rich ought to provide some benefit to *counterbalance* the harm, such as a sum of money that reflects the intensity and duration of Sneh's pain.[2]

---

[2] Stephen Smith argues that damages for pain and suffering cannot be compensatory; rather such damages express the wrongfulness of the defendant's conduct. See Stephen Smith, *Rights, Wrongs, and Injustices: The Structure of Remedial Law* (Oxford University Press 2020) 233. However, though past

(3) is similar in the sense that treatment negates the harm only partially. In this case, Rich must counterbalance the pain that Sneh suffered before the operation and the future pain that medical treatment cannot now prevent. Finally, in (4), none of Sneh's harm can be negated; Rich can seek only to counterbalance it.[3]

These cases illustrate the distinction between negating and counterbalancing on an intuitive level, but we can render it more precise. I said negating the effects of an event makes a person's future wellbeing identical to what it would have been. This means more than ensuring a person has the same *amount* of wellbeing that they would have had if not for the event. It also means ensuring that their wellbeing is of the same *shape* and *quality*. Conversely, counterbalancing makes a person's future wellbeing equal in amount to what it would have been, though it may differ in shape and quality.

Let's begin with the distinction between the shape and amount of wellbeing. Suppose Sneh suffers a broken leg and her wellbeing decreases, after which she receives a benefit that increases her wellbeing, and assume that her gain in wellbeing is equal to her loss, making her overall wellbeing in the world in which she is harmed and benefitted equal to her overall wellbeing in the world in which she is not harmed.[4] In this case, the benefit counterbalances Sneh's harm because she ends up with the same amount of wellbeing that she would have had if not for the injury. But although the amount is the same, its shape through time is not. It has undergone a trough followed by a peak rather than

---

pain cannot be negated, it can be counterbalanced with benefits that render the victim equally well off. Once we recognize the distinction between negating and counterbalancing, damages for pain and suffering are readily explicable in compensatory rather than expressive terms. See also Sandy Steel, 'Remedies, Analysed' (2021) 41 Oxford Journal of Legal Studies 539, 21.

[3] For two similar distinctions, see Robert Goodin, 'Theories of Compensation' (1989) 9 Oxford Journal of Legal Studies 56 (hereafter Goodin, *Theories of Compensation*) (on the distinction between means-replacing and ends-displacing compensation) and Shelly Kagan, 'Causation and Responsibility' (1988) 25 American Philosophical Quarterly 293 (on the distinction between compensation and correction) (hereafter Kagan, 'Causation and Responsibility').

[4] This is similar to Robert Nozick's indifference view of compensation, except that it appeals to an objective account of wellbeing rather than a preference-based account. For Nozick's view, see *Anarchy, State, and Utopia* (Blackwell 1974) 57. For the reasons why a preference-based account is untenable, see Victor Tadros, 'What Might Have Been' in John Oberdiek (ed), *Philosophical Foundations of the Law of Torts* (Oxford University Press 2014) 170, 173–75. To simplify, I assume throughout this chapter that the victim's wellbeing would remain constant if not for the harmful event. This will not be true in some cases, such as those involving pre-emptive harms, where the harm inflicted on a victim by one agent prevents an equivalent or greater harm being inflicted on the same victim by another. In these cases, the victim's wellbeing would not have remained constant had the first agent not inflicted harm. It is important that we have the theoretical resources to deal with these cases, as they pose difficulties for the measurement of harm. But all attempts to measure the impact of events on a person's wellbeing face these problems, so I leave them to one side here. For an in-depth discussion of pre-emption and overdetermination problems, see LA Paul and Ned Hall, *Causation: A User's Guide* (Oxford University Press 2013).

remaining constant. By contrast, negating ensures that the shape of a person's wellbeing is identical to what it would have been if not for the harm. In (1), where Rich breaks Sneh's leg but repairs it before she regains consciousness, the shape of her wellbeing is identical to what it would have been if not for the injury.

Negating also differs from counterbalancing because it renders a person's wellbeing identical in qualitative terms. When Sneh suffers a broken leg in cases (2)–(4), several factors have an impact on her, including physical pain, reduced ability to pursue her projects, the effect of the injury on her emotional life, and so on. In (4), even if Rich gives Sneh a benefit that makes her equally well off, her wellbeing still differs in quality. For example, if Rich builds her a dream house, this might counterbalance the harm, but the ingredients of her wellbeing are different. In (1), however, where Rich negates the damage to Sneh's leg while she is still unconscious, her future wellbeing is not only equal in amount but also identical in quality with what it would have been if not for the injury.

B. Overriding the Presumption

Cases (1)–(4) suggest that our duty to repair harm usually entails negating it where possible and counterbalancing the remainder. This is why, in (1), it would be wrong for Rich merely to counterbalance Sneh's harm when it could just as easily be negated. This illustrates the presumptive priority of negating over counterbalancing. It is usually better to put a person in exactly the position they would have been in if not for the harm than some equivalent position in terms of wellbeing. Shortly, we will justify this presumption by explaining why we have an interest in harm being negated rather than counterbalanced. For now, note that this presumption can be overturned. Consider:

(5) Rich wrongfully injures Sneh by breaking her leg. Rich could either negate the remaining harm by fixing Sneh's leg or give her a sum of money that would make her equally well off. Sneh would prefer the sum of money.

(6) Rich wrongfully injures Sneh by breaking her leg. Rich could either negate the remaining harm by fixing Sneh's leg or give her a sum of money that would make her equally well off. Fixing Sneh's leg would require medical resources that could save the lives of five other people who would otherwise die.

(7) Rich wrongfully injures Sneh by breaking her leg. Rich could either negate the remaining harm by fixing Sneh leg or give her a sum of money that would make her equally well off. Sneh would prefer her leg to be fixed but this would be hugely more costly for Rich, making him destitute.

In (1), the presumption is overridden because of Sneh's own preferences. Counterbalancing the harm serves her autonomous choice despite her interest in its being negated. What if victims are mistaken in their preferences? This possibility raises complex questions that I cannot address here,[5] except to say that, on plausible assumptions about value pluralism, it is at least possible for Sneh to prefer counterbalancing over negating without being mistaken about her own wellbeing. Even if the projects that required the use of her leg were valuable, this does not preclude the possibility that other projects, made possible by the sum of money, are equally or more valuable. And even if Sneh's new projects are less valuable in some objective sense, she surely has some prerogative to choose them despite being owed something objectively better, that is, negation.

In (7), the presumption in favour of negating is overridden by the benefit to third parties. Sneh's interest in the harm being negated is not strong enough to justify the loss of five people's lives. This is a stark comparison, but other public benefits that do not involve the loss of life or limb might also override the presumption, which include the considerations courts use to justify imposing damages over injunctions. In *Lawrence v Fen Tigers*, for example, Lord Neuberger accepted that claimants who have demonstrated the existence of a nuisance are *prima facie* entitled to an injunction but held that the public interest can be relevant in deciding whether the court should exercise its discretion to award damages instead.[6]

(7) is perhaps more controversial since it is the wrongdoer's interests, not those of the victim, that override the presumption to negate. It is controversial because some may balk at the idea that victims should have to take into account the interests of their wrongdoers when demanding corrective responses. Yet Sneh's victimhood does not give her the right to disregard Rich's interests entirely. If negating is *hugely* more costly for Rich, and not much better for Sneh, the presumption in favour of negating can be overridden, especially if Rich's wrongdoing is not highly culpable. On a strong version of this claim, Rich is

---

[5] For more detailed discussion, see Adam Slavny, 'On Being Wronged and Being Wrong' (2017) 16 Politics, Philosophy & Economics 3.

[6] For a recent discussion of the circumstances in which courts may award damages *in lieu* of an injunction in cases of private nuisance, see *Lawrence v Fen Tigers Ltd* [2014] AC 822, [124]–[127].

permitted to counterbalance rather than negate if in doing so he can prevent great cost to himself at small cost to Sneh. On a weaker version, Rich can do this only if his basic interests are at stake, or if negating rather than counterbalancing leaves him very badly off in absolute terms, as in case (6). We need not decide which version to adopt here. What matters is the claim, common to both interpretations, that the priority of negating over counterbalancing does not hold regardless of the costs for the wrongdoer.

This claim relies on an idea that recurs throughout this book and is worth making explicit. Our duties have a *stringency threshold*, which specifies the maximum cost that an agent can be expected to bear for the sake of fulfilling that duty.[7] The notion of cost employed here—and throughout this book—encompasses any negative consequence for the duty-bearer that is relevant in determining whether they can be required to fulfil that duty. These may be financial costs, as when one has a duty to pay for a fence to be erected around one's land to protect others from danger, or when one has a duty to ensure one's car is road safe. They may be costs in terms of time and effort, as when one builds the fence oneself instead of contracting a third party. Other costs such as pain, stress, and discomfort should also play a role, though these are of course harder to measure. This is not an exhaustive list. 'Cost', in this context, is an umbrella term designed to capture any consideration relevant to the question of whether the performance of some act is so burdensome as to relieve a person from having to perform it.

One of the key principles motivating stringency thresholds is that of narrow proportionality.[8] The burden of fulfilling one's duty should not be completely out of proportion to the seriousness of the wrong. If Rich's wrong is not very culpable, and the costs to him of compensating are extreme, imposing this duty on him is disproportionate. This form of proportionality is widely accepted in other areas of legal philosophy but is more alien to tort liability, which is famously insensitive to the means of the tortfeasor, regardless of the impact this has on those with limited resources.

In practice, this harshness is tempered by the availability of insurance, bankruptcy protection, and the pointlessness of pursuing a claim against those unable to pay. This must be acknowledged, though with two important caveats. First, this point mitigates rather than eliminates the problem. Being sued is still burdensome, either because one incurs financial penalties such as increased

---

[7] The concept of a stringency threshold employed here is what Victor Tadros call 'self-focussed stringency', see *Wrongs and Crimes* (Oxford University Press 2016) 55.

[8] For the distinction between narrow and wide proportionality, see Jeff McMahan, *Killing in War* (Oxford University Press 2009) 20–21.

insurance premiums and legal costs, or because of the time, energy, and emotional toll of suing or being sued. These costs also need justification and are subject to considerations of narrow proportionality. Second, many theorists view the insensitivity of liability to a tortfeasor's means as a justified or principled feature of the law rather than an iniquity we tolerate in principle only because it rarely comes up in practice.[9] Given this, it is important to respond directly to such arguments rather than ignoring the question on pragmatic grounds.

The concept of stringency thresholds suggests that—in this respect at least—there is no fundamental divide between corrective duties and, say, criminal or defensive liability. Wrongdoers are required to correct the harm they cause only up to a point. Their interests are not disregarded in the determination of their corrective duties. If it were otherwise, we would expect the presence of insurance to be largely irrelevant to the justification of enforcing corrective duties. Imagine a society in which insurance and bankruptcy protection were unavailable and legal institutions routinely made people destitute by forcing them to compensate for barely culpable wrongdoing. I take it most will agree that such practices would be unconscionable. One interpretation of this judgement is that insurance allows the costs of fulfilling our corrective duties to drop below the stringency threshold, thus making them enforceable. As a consequence, the fact that legal liability is insensitive to the means of tortfeasors in the context of a system underpinned by widespread liability insurance should not lead us to conclude that our corrective duties are not subject to stringency thresholds.

C. Two Objections

It is worth addressing two initial objections to the distinction between negating and counterbalancing. The first is that it wrongly presupposes that wellbeing is a quantifiable value. It is sometimes argued that conceptualizing human flourishing as a 'market good' distorts its value,[10] treating it as measurable and mathematically precise when in fact it is complex, messy, and contextual.

---

[9] For a recent example, see John CP Goldberg and Benjamin C Zipursky, 'Replies to Commentators' (2022) 41 Law and Philosophy 127, 134. Goldberg and Zipursky do not claim to offer a full-blooded justification of this feature, often emphasizing that it is an interpretive claim. Nevertheless, given their methodological approach as a whole, they presumably see this feature as based in an overarching framework of legal wrongs that is defensible and principled.

[10] For this type of objection against weighing human lives to resolve moral dilemmas, see Alon Harel, *Why Law Matters* (Oxford University Press 2014) ch 4.

This objection conflates commensurability with comparability. Two bearers of value are commensurable if they are measurable along a common scale, such as monetary value. Two items are commensurable in monetary terms if they can be given a price, which permits both precise quantification and fine-grained value comparisons. I agree that wellbeing outcomes are not commensurable in this way, and therefore do not admit of precise quantification or fine-grained value comparisons. It may be worth using such measures as heuristics—such as the health economist's quality adjusted life year or QUALY—providing we recognize such scales serve a practical purpose and do not represent deep truths about human wellbeing. But the distinction between negating and counterbalancing does not assume that different elements of wellbeing are commensurable. It assumes only that, in some cases, outcomes involving losses and gains in wellbeing are comparable. Here I follow the conception of comparability developed by Ruth Chang, according to which two bearers of value are comparable if a positive comparative judgement of their value is true.[11] There are three familiar comparative relations: 'better than', 'worse than', and 'equally as good as'. A comparative judgement is complete when one of these relations is specified between two items in terms of what Chang calls a 'covering value', which expresses the criteria by which the comparative evaluation is to be made (in our case the covering value is wellbeing). Although many take exception to mathematical quantifications of wellbeing, the claim that events can make us better or worse off is uncontroversial, and this already commits us to some degree of comparability. In addition, although I will continue to talk of benefits making a person equally well off, we could interpret this as rough equality, using Chang's notion of parity, rather than a mathematically precise type of equality.[12] So the distinction between negating and counterbalancing does not presuppose the quantifiability or commensurability of wellbeing; a small stock of comparative judgements—that one outcome is better or worse or roughly equal for a person in terms of wellbeing than another—is sufficient. Far from being artificial or fanciful, such judgements are a staple feature of our everyday assessment of wellbeing.

[11]   Ruth Chang, 'The Possibility of Parity' (2002) 112 Ethics 659.

[12]   We could also adopt Parfit's conception of imprecise equality, or imprecise comparison, which does not require that an item's value can be determined along a linear scale. See Derek Parfit, 'Can We Avoid the Repugnant Conclusion?' (2016) 82 Theoria 110, 114. Even if imprecise judgements of equality of value, or of parity of value, are impossible, we could also interpret the duty to counterbalance as a duty to make a reasonable attempt at equalizing wellbeing. Ultimately, whatever the limits of evaluative precision turn out to be, it is doubtful that they will undermine the distinction between negating and counterbalancing.

A second objection is that I claim that a person can be made equally well off even though the shape and quality of their wellbeing is altered. Some might argue that altering the shape and quality of someone's wellbeing itself reduces their wellbeing. When a person's projects and pleasures are usurped by injury, can they really be made equally well off by replacing them with different, albeit equally valuable, projects and pleasures? Although it is plausible to see interference of this kind as a reduction in wellbeing, in pt II.B I hope to show that this type of interference is importantly distinctive. I also think it is intuitive to talk of compensation making a person equally well off even though their ends have been interfered with. These preliminary remarks suggest that we should distinguish between wellbeing and interference,[13] although the arguments of this chapter do not rely on this, and I will not commit to any conceptual or metaphysical view about wellbeing. We could adopt a more capacious concept of wellbeing and reformulate the distinction to say that counterbalancing redresses one *type* of wellbeing-impairment whilst negating redresses another. That formulation would allow us to accept the relevance of the distinction without taking a stand on the exact boundaries of concepts such as harm and wellbeing.[14]

II. The Normative Significance of Negating and Counterbalancing

A. Implications for Permissibility

The distinction between negating and counterbalancing is normatively significant in the sense that it makes a difference to the moral permissions and duties we have. We can see this by comparing two types of cases: those in which an agent makes someone identically well off (negation) and has done nothing wrong, and those in which an agent makes someone equally well off (counterbalancing) but acts wrongly. Consider:

---

[13] Another reason is to recognize the category of harmless wrongdoing. For an argument that wrongful discrimination need not result in harm, see Tom Parr and Adam Slavny, 'Harmless Discrimination' (2015) 21 Legal Theory 100 (hereafter Parr and Slavny, 'Harmless Discrimination').

[14] Some argue that compensation is inappropriate if it improves a dimension of wellbeing unrelated to that set back by the wrong. See Bruce Chapman 'Wrongdoing, Welfare, and Damages: Recovery for Non-Pecuniary Loss in Corrective Justice' in David G Owen (ed), *The Philosophical Foundations of Tort Law* (Oxford University Press 1995) 409, 425. The view I present here shows, I think, that this goes too far. Rendering a person equally well off is an important way to address the wrong, since it ensures they are not harmed overall. This can be achieved purely through counterbalancing, even if the components of the victim's wellbeing are different.

Fence 1: Tully's fence is in Una's way. Una takes it down and puts it back exactly as it was before Tully suffers any harm or loss.

Fence 2: Tully's fence is in Una's way. Una knocks it down but cannot put it back up before Tully's chickens escape. Instead, Una gives Tully a bread oven that counterbalances the decrease in their wellbeing caused by the escape of their chickens, making them equally well off overall.

Let's assume that, in both cases, Una's reason to knock down the fence is not strong enough to give her a necessity justification, for example it is not required to save life or limb.[15] On the other hand, assume that she does not do it capriciously or on a whim. My suggestion is that the threshold of justification that Una must reach for knocking down Tully's fence is lower in *Fence 1* where she negates the harm than in *Fence 2* where she counterbalances it. If Una has a good enough reason to knock down the fence, and she can make Tully identically well off, it is difficult to see why Tully should have a moral permission to exclude Una from their property. In the second case, the threshold of justification is higher. Reasons that justify tampering with the fence may well not justify causing the loss of Tully's chickens, even if Tully will not be left worse off as a result.

The distinction is also relevant when more serious bodily harms are at stake. Consider:

Finger 1: Una's finger is trapped under some wreckage. If she moves the wreckage, she will emerge unscathed, but if not, she will lose the finger. The only way she can remove the wreckage is by moving Tully's unconscious body, which is lying in the way. If Una does this, Tully will suffer a broken leg, which will cause permanent damage unless treated quickly. Una can fully repair Tully's leg before they wake up, making it as good as new and averting any future pain.

Finger 2: Identical to 1, except Una cannot repair Tully's leg before they wake up. If Una moves Tully's body to save her finger, Tully's leg will be permanently damaged. However, Una can build Tully their dream house, which will make them equally well off overall.

---

[15] For a discussion of liability to compensate in cases where an infringement of a right is necessary to avert a significant loss, see Joel Feinberg, *Rights Justice, and the Bounds of Liberty* (Princeton University Press 1980) 230 and Judith Jarvis Thomson, *Rights, Restitution, and Risk* (Harvard University Press 1986) 71.

In *Finger 1*, it is plausible that Una is permitted to move Tully. She must damage their body to do this, but Una can negate the effects of this damage, and the need to save her finger justifies this. In *Finger 2*, however, it is doubtful that Una is permitted to injure Tully even if she counterbalances the harm. The use of Tully's leg is vital to their projects, and Una is not entitled to deprive them of this use even if she makes them equally well off, and even if doing this is necessary to save Una's finger.

B. Five Features of Interference

What motivates the different judgements in these cases and thus the presumption of negating over counterbalancing? We can identify at least five types of morally significant interference that take place when one's harm is counterbalanced but not negated. One is that counterbalancing, unlike negating, sometimes reduces a person's ability to set their ends. In *Finger 2*, although the house is a source of happiness for Tully, it may not facilitate their ability to set their ends as much as the use of their leg. A permanently damaged leg rules out a broader range of ends than not having a dream house, and so the injury restricts Tully's end-setting capacity.

A second feature of interference is that counterbalancing sometimes forces a person to pursue ends that they do not value as highly as those they originally set.[16] Consider:

> *Donation*: Una wrongfully injures Tully, causing them to lose a kidney. Tully was planning to donate the kidney to a stranger. Una then gives Tully a sum of money that makes them equally well off.

Making Tully equally well off by counterbalancing the harm does not rectify the interference because Tully is no longer able to pursue an end that they value above their own wellbeing: saving someone's life. Counterbalancing is a shadow of negating when the end that is frustrated is one that either does not increase, or undermines, a person's wellbeing. Of course, saving a life *does* improve Tully's wellbeing by giving them a sense of altruistic satisfaction, but this is not sufficient to counterbalance the suffering associated with the loss of a kidney. We should not infer that it is from the fact that Tully chooses to donate

---

[16] For a discussion of how compensation can displace a victim's ends, see Goodin, 'Theories of Compensation' (n 3).

as this would distort their motivating reason. Tully chooses to donate because they value saving a life for its own sake and are willing to sacrifice personal wellbeing to achieve this.[17] *Donation* also demonstrates how the importance of this form of interference is distinct from the first. The sum of money Una gives Tully arguably *increases* their end-setting capacity, but also prevents them pursuing a specific end they value more than any of those that are now open to them.

A third and closely related form of interference is that counterbalancing, unlike negating, can prevent one pursuing the specific ends one has set. In *Donation*, suppose that Tully's compensation allows them to pursue an end that they value as highly as saving a life. Tully's end-setting capacity is thus not diminished, and they are not forced to pursue an end they value less than their previous ones. Nevertheless, it matters that they are prevented from pursuing the specific ends they set for themselves. Consider a comparison with the way we value relationships. Suppose Una sabotages one of Tully's friendships and proposes to fix the damage by introducing them to a new friend. Even if the new friendship will be just as valuable to Tully as their old friendship, this cannot replace the loss. We attach value to the specific and unique qualities of our relationships, and although an alternative relationship with its own distinct qualities can serve a similar social and emotional function, it cannot negate the loss of a prior relationship. The same holds true, I suggest, for our relationships to the projects and goals we set ourselves. These projects give shape and meaning to our lives, partly because they are valuable and partly because they are *ours*. Replacing one project with another cannot replace the specific qualities we value about our thwarted projects, no matter how much we come to value the special qualities of our new projects.

Fourth, our most important ends shape large sections of our lives. Intellectual pursuits, sporting excellence, building a family, being a socialite, or travelling the world—all of these are important to us partly because they define our values, goals, and preferences over long periods. It is not just that these projects have temporal longevity. They are also associated with meaningful narratives. Writing a book or having a child or being an athlete can give narrative structure to a person's life. This diachronic relationship between different segments of a life has been called 'narrative unity'.[18] Part of the insight here is that later events can alter the significance of what has gone before. If a writer

---

[17] For an argument that acts of self-sacrifice are possible, see Victor Tadros, 'Harm, Sovereignty and Prohibition' (2011) 17 Legal Theory 35.

[18] See Jeff McMahan, *The Ethics of Killing: Problems at the Margins of Life* (Oxford University Press 2002) 174–85 (hereafter McMahan, *The Ethics of Killing*).

suffers a stroke and dies before completing their magnum opus, the event has a calamitous significance in their life. They are a promising writer tragically cut short before realizing their greatest achievement. Alternatively, if they complete their novel before they die, this fact changes the significance of the stroke. It mitigates its effects because it does not disrupt the narrative unity of completing their life's work. In some respects, it might even add value to the work, in the same way that Beethoven's *Pastorale* is regarded as a greater achievement because it was composed in the advanced stages of hearing loss. This suggests we have special reasons to continue to pursue the projects we have set to give them narrative unity. We recognize that a person who starts projects and never finishes them due to poor concentration or flightiness is missing an important facet of the good life, and this cannot be made up by replacing each unfinished project with another one of equal value.

Finally, counterbalancing may affect the time at which a person can pursue the ends they set for themselves. Suppose that, in *Finger 2*, Tully's injuries will prevent them from pursuing a set of ends, S, between $t1$ and $t2$. After this period, the damage to their leg will be repaired. However, at $t2$, Tully's ability to pursue S will be removed anyway by a genetic medical condition until $t3$, and the duration between $t1$ and $t2$ is equal to the duration between $t2$ and $t3$. Una can treat Tully's genetic condition, enabling them to pursue S between $t2$ and $t3$. In this variation, if Tully's condition is treated, they suffer no disruption in terms of their capacity to set ends, their ability to pursue the ends they have set, or the narrative unity of those ends, but Una still interferes with the time at which Tully can pursue them. The value of control over our ends has a temporal dimension: some projects we wish to pursue when we're young, others when we're older, and the change in our priorities and pursuits through time reflects the exercise of our rational agency and our evolving personalities. Disrupting the time at which Tully can pursue their ends is another type of morally significant interference.

C. The Anti-Holmesian Argument

As the cases of *Fence 1* and *Finger 1* suggest, there are circumstances in which *ex post* corrective action renders otherwise wrongful conduct permissible. One objection to this claim is that it courts the view, attributed to Oliver Wendel Holmes,[19] that actions we ordinarily consider wrong are in fact permissible as

---

[19] See Gardner, *Torts and Other Wrongs* (n 1) 5, noting also that this attribution has been contested.

long as one pays the relevant price. This seems to imply that we can alchemize wrongs into rights by repairing harm after the fact,[20] and this is implausible in most ordinary cases. For example, placing enough cash in your pocket to compensate for a broken nose does not give me permission to wind up a right hook.

I don't deny the plausibility of this anti-Holmsian thought but it should not be overgeneralized. Conditional permissibility is one part of the four-fold analysis and therefore exists alongside wrongdoing and other sources of corrective duties. All we need to resist the anti-Holmsian argument, then, is the claim that at least some actions are conditionally permissible. Here is a schematic argument for this idea. There are some acts that are impermissible because they are too harmful, where if they were less harmful, they would be permissible. Call the threshold of harm at which such an act is impermissible, n. Compensation reduces the overall harmfulness of acts. This means there will be some acts that cause >n harm without compensation, but <n harm with compensation. For these acts, compensation makes otherwise wrongful acts permissible.

The best candidates here are acts that cause >n harm, though not by much, such as harms that are slightly but not greatly disproportionate.[21] For example, suppose an unjust attacker threatens to break my leg. I can defend myself against the attack, but if I do, I will break the leg of a bystander. Stipulate that protecting myself at the expense of the bystander's leg is disproportionate, but only just (the level of harm can be adjusted to suit any view of proportionality). Then it follows that, if I compensate the bystander, this makes it proportionate—and therefore permissible—for me to defend myself. One way to see this is to imagine that the benefit can be provided before the harm, as in cases of negating. Suppose the bystander is unconscious and I can fix any physical damage I cause in defending myself before they wake up. Here, it is implausible that defending myself is disproportionate when I not only make the bystander equally well off, but identically well off.

This concept of conditional permissibility represents one limb of the four-fold analysis summarized in Chapter 1. It is sometimes called licensing-based liability, as paying compensation after the fact effectively buys a licence to engage in the harmful activity. This is the best interpretation of *Dangerous Animals*, where although Manu takes reasonable precautions against the escape of his animals, they do escape and harm Nell. The famous rule in *Rylands v*

---

[20] For an argument that licensing-based liability, as opposed to wrongs-based liability, is relatively rare in tort law, see Goldberg and Zipursky, *Recognizing Wrongs* (n 1) 189–98.

[21] For an argument that compensation can affect proportionality calculations in war, see Saba Bazargan-Forward, 'Compensation Proportionality and in War' in Jens David Ohlin, Larry May, and Claire Finkelstein (eds), *Weighing Lives in War* (Oxford University Press 2017).

Fletcher[22] can also be understood in terms of conditional permissibility. Those who view torts as a coherent set of wrongs sometimes accept the possibility of conditional permissibility justifications for liability but downplay their significance across tort law as a whole.[23] However, conditional permissibility has the potential to apply well beyond the rule in *Rylands*. In principle, it could justify liability for harm caused by all forms of unusually risky activity, and we have already seen its relevance for self-defence.

Once we have established that corrective responses can sometimes justify otherwise wrongful acts, the distinction between negating and counterbalancing helps us explore this idea by revealing both its plausibility and its limitations. It shows that negating can justify some otherwise wrongful acts because it prevents interference, but also why counterbalancing often does not have the same effect, since it causes interference.

It might be objected that some wrongful acts cannot be made permissible regardless of whether negating or counterbalancing takes place. This is true. To take one example I have given elsewhere, a person who votes against the appointment of a person of colour for racist reasons commits an act of wrongful discrimination, even if they are outvoted by their peers and the candidate is appointed. In fact, they would commit this wrong if they personally ensured it did not result in harm, say by securing the candidate a better job elsewhere.[24] Similarly, serious wrongs such as sexual assault committed against unconscious victims cannot be justified by negating the effects of the wrong, say by ensuring the act forever remains undiscovered, including by the victim.[25] But the claim here is not that negating always makes otherwise wrongful action permissible—this would be to collapse it into the Holmesian view. Rather the claim is that negating (and to a lesser extent counterbalancing) can make otherwise wrongful acts permissible in that subset of cases when what would make the act wrong is either harm or interference. When harm or interference are not what grounds the wrongness of the act, negating and counterbalancing generally do not have this effect.

---

[22] (1868) LR 3 HL 330.

[23] Goldberg and Zipursky deal with conditional permissibility this way. See *Recognizing Wrongs* (n 1) 191.

[24] Parr and Slavny, 'Harmless Discrimination' (n 13) 107.

[25] Many rapes perpetrated against unconscious victims do not remain undiscovered, however. Quite the opposite, as Kelly Oliver notes in her analysis, see *Hunting Girls: Sexual Violence from The Hunger Games to Campus Rape* (Columbia University Press 2016) 59–60. We must also distinguish cases where the victim themselves do not discover the wrong from cases where they do. In the latter cases, there are distinctive harms attached to the knowledge of the violation even if the person was unconscious when it took place. For an account of such harms, see Cressida Heyes, 'Dead to the World: Rape, Unconsciousness, and Social Media' (2016) 41 Signs 361, 365.

Here are three other factors that can ground wrongness besides harm and interference: the intentions with which one acts, the expressive content of action, and the violation of non-material values such as autonomy. From these factors we can see that cases of harmless discrimination and undiscovered sexual assault are disanalogous to *Fence 1* and *Finger 1* in several ways: they are committed for immoral rather than valid reasons; their expressive content is humiliating, demeaning, or prejudicial;[26] and other important values are at stake, such as control over sexual autonomy, which is more important than control over one's property or other non-sexual interferences with one's body. In *Fence 1* and *Finger 1*, by contrast, none of this applies. Una acts to save herself from injury, not from objectionable motivations such as racism or misogyny. Her act, though it interferes with Tully's property in *Fence 1* and body in *Finger 1*, does not communicate any demeaning or humiliating message of the kind comparable to racial discrimination. And although Una interferes with Tully's interest in excluding others from using their property, or from harmlessly damaging their body, this interest is far less strong than a person's interest in sexual autonomy. Of course, if we attend only to acts that there is no good reason to perform, and which are typically performed for objectionable reasons, we will naturally be led to a thoroughly anti-Holmesian view. This would be a mistake, however. Sometimes we have good (albeit outweighed) reasons to perform *pro tanto* wrongful acts, as the case of disproportionate self-defence, *Fence 1* and *Finger 1* show. If an agent has such reasons, and in addition any harm-based or interference-based reasons against performing the act can be eliminated *ex post*, this will often be sufficient to make it permissible.

Now, one might insist that in *Fence 1* and *Finger 1*, something very important *is* at stake, namely Tully's control over their property and bodily integrity, and the reasons against interference—as I have described that concept here—do not capture the degree of control we ought to have over our property and person. One of the most forceful proponents of the right to such robust control is Arthur Ripstein, who argues that no other person may determine the purposes one's own means are used to pursue. As Ripstein puts it: 'Another person is not entitled to so much as touch your body, or enter your land, or use your chattels without your authorization.'[27] Others hold the right to exclude to be central to the practice and justification of property rights. James Penner

---

[26] Michelle Anderson emphasizes 'dehumanization, objectification, and domination' as featuring in the testimony of both victims and perpetrators of rape, see 'All-American Rape' (2005) 79 St. John's Law Review 625, 641.

[27] Arthur Ripstein, *Private Wrongs* (Harvard University Press 2016) 30 (hereafter Ripstein, *Private Wrongs*).

argues that ownership is 'the right to determine the use … of a thing in so far as that can be achieved by others excluding themselves from it',[28] and we could apply a similar argument to self-ownership; that is, ownership of one's own body and bodily resources as opposed to external property.[29]

The distinction between negating and counterbalancing suggests that the five points discussed above, relating to the value of a person's means, do not always justify absolute control. In *Fence 1*, Una acts without authorization but she does not reduce Tully's end-setting capacity, force Tully to pursue ends they do not value as much, prevent pursuit of ends they have already set, frustrate the narrative unity of their ends, or affect the time at which they can pursue them. When all these forms of interference are absent, it is hard to see the normative motivation for insisting on further control.

We can see this by comparing Ripstein's famous case of harmless trespass with *Fence 1* and *Finger 1*. Ripstein imagines a man who creeps into your house to take a nap in your bed while you are out, leaving no trace of his activity.[30] Most people intuitively think such harmless trespasses are wrong. However, there are two differences between Ripstein's case and *Fence 1* and *Finger 1*. First, the motivations in the harmless trespass case are unspecified, and we are tempted to fill in the blanks by imputing deviousness to the trespasser. Suppose we clarify that the trespasser's motives are good. Say he enters your property to drink from an outdoor tap, not to save his life but to stave off some lesser but still significant harm, once again making sure to leave no trace of his activity. I find this trespass intuitively less objectionable than the one described by Ripstein. Second, there is something uncomfortably intimate about the man's activity in Ripstein's case, and this suggests that certain privacy interests are at stake. But whilst property rights often allow us to safeguard our privacy, this is not true of all forms of property all the time. When Una takes down Tully's fence, it is less plausible that Tully's privacy is at stake, especially if we stipulate that the land beyond the fence does not grant access to any intimate spaces such as the interior of Tully's house.[31]

---

[28] James E Penner, *The Idea of Property in Law* (Oxford University Press 1997) 103.

[29] This view is associated with Robert Nozick, see *Anarchy, State, and Utopia* (Blackwell 1974). For criticisms, see D Sobel, 'Backing Away from Libertarian Self-Ownership' (2012) 123 Ethics 32 and Kasper Lippert-Rasmussen, 'Against Self-Ownership: There are No Fact-Insensitive Ownership Rights over One's Body' (2008) 36 Philosophy and Public Affairs 86.

[30] Arthur Ripstein, 'Beyond the Harm Principle' (2006) 34 Philosophy and Public Affairs 215, 219.

[31] Admittedly, Ripstein is not absolutist about the prohibition on interfering with another person's means. He allows that there is a privilege to use someone else's land, for example, to recover or preserve a chattel, see Ripstein, *Private Wrongs* (n 27) 155. This does not account for the difference between *Fence 1* and *Fence 2*, though, since it does not concede that a weighty interest can justify even a negated intrusion. This stark asymmetry between rights and interests is difficult to support. It means, for example,

We should distinguish, then, between an interest in the use of one's means, and an interest in mere exclusion of others from one's means. It is the use of our means to pursue our ends rather than mere control over them that is of central importance, and though these two interests usually go hand in hand, cases of negation show that they can come apart. This chimes with some views of property rights which seek to decentre the role of exclusion. Larissa Katz, for example, argues that the essence of property is an authority to set the agenda for the owned thing rather than the right to exclude others from it. On her view, what matters is whether exclusion preserves or encroaches upon the owner's actual or imputed agenda, and when the owner retains this authority, the argument for exclusion is considerably weaker.[32] Negating, and counterbalancing to a lesser extent, is one way those who encroach on others' property can preserve the authority of the owner to use their property in the service of their chosen ends.

It must be remembered that, so far, I have been arguing that Una has a moral permission to act as she does in *Fence 1* and *Finger 1*, not that she should have a legal permission. Our discussion in the previous chapter cautions us against drawing any straightforward conclusions about the justification of legal rights on the basis of moral rights. Herein lies another objection. It's all very well making claims about moral rights, we might think, but what does this imply about what regimes of legal rights should be adopted?

When individuals act morally permissibly but unlawfully, they can mount the *restricted freedom* and *undue burden* objections. Their freedom is restricted because they are acting within their moral permissions, but in ways that are unlawful, and they are burdened with duties to provide appropriate remedies merely for exercising these freedoms. However, these objections may be met, at least in some cases. Legal rights must possess certain properties that moral rights need not. They must be stable over time in circumstances where the relevant facts that would justify their infringement are not always available or are costly to determine. In these epistemically limited conditions, it is undesirable to grant a legal permission to infringe rights, as this may lead to a situation in which people frequently claim moral permissions they do not in fact possess, as well as causing other unwanted side effects such as a general lack of confidence in the regime of legal rights.

---

that I may climb your fence to retrieve my medicinal herbs but not to gain access to medicinal herbs that are unowned, even if my interest in obtaining them is equally weighty.

[32] Larissa Katz, 'Exclusion and Exclusivity' (2008) 58 University of Toronto Law Journal, 275, especially pt A1.

This argument is more plausible in *Fence 1* than *Finger 1*, though. Denying a general permission to override others' property rights when it is morally permissible to do so may well be worth it if it is necessary to ensure the stability of a regime of property rights. In cases like *Finger 1*, on the other hand, when more serious interests are at stake such as Una's freedom from severe injury, it is less plausible to legally prohibit her from exercising her moral permission for the sake of these forward-looking concerns. After all, the same is true of self-defence—it is easy to abuse the right or be mistaken as to whether it applies—yet the protection of oneself from serious injury is considered significant enough to tolerate this.[33]

In any case, the important point is not that the law should allow more widespread rights violations on the condition that compensation is given, but rather that Una does not commit a moral wrong in *Fence 1* or *Finger 1*, and thus the justification of the legal rule depends, not on any underlying moral right, but on the non-ideal conditions in which the rule applies.[34] The claim that Una does not commit a moral wrong in *Fence 1* and *Finger 1* does not commit us to the view that her actions should be legally permissible, but it does mean that any legal prohibition will have to overcome the *restricted freedom* and *undue burden* objections.

III. Primary and Secondary Duties

A. The Forward-looking Character of Secondary Duties

Understanding the relationship between primary and secondary duties is an abiding theme of tort theory. It is often pointed out that imposing a secondary duty is the next best way to uphold the right that was violated. For example, Robert Stevens argues that 'the secondary obligation to pay money imposed upon the wrongdoer can be seen as the law's attempt to reach the "next best" position to the wrong not having been committed by him in the first place'.[35]

---

[33] For a similar argument in relation to assisted dying, see McMahan, *The Ethics of Killing* (n 18) 486.

[34] Those sympathetic to rule-consequentialism may argue that the best rule, applied in non-ideal circumstances, fixes what is morally permissible in the individual case. I lack the space to elaborate, but others have questioned this move on the grounds that it makes basic normative truths contingent on empirical facts. For example, see David McNaughton and Piers Rawling, 'On Defending Deontology' (1998) 11 Ratio 37 and Jussi Suikkanen, 'A Dilemma for Rule-Consequentialism' (2008) 36 Philosophia 141.

[35] Robert Stevens, *Torts and Rights* (Oxford University Press 2007) 59. See also Arthur Ripstein, 'As If It Had Never Happened' (2007) 48 William & Mary Law Review 1957, 1968.

Similarly, Weinrib claims that 'with the materialization of wrongful injury, the only way the defendant can discharge his or her obligation respecting the plaintiff's right is to undo the effects of the breach of duty'.[36] Although intuitive, this relationship between primary and secondary duties requires further explanation. One familiar problem is that, if primary duties are forward-looking while secondary duties are backward-looking, how do the former ground the latter?

The distinction between negating and counterbalancing helps us answer this question by showing that the characterization of secondary duties as backward-looking is misleading. Negating and counterbalancing duties are both, in a sense, forward-looking. Negating duties require agents to avert future harms that would otherwise obtain. Counterbalancing duties require agents to avert the future impact an event would otherwise have on a person's overall wellbeing. Both are therefore preventive, albeit in different ways. Although both types of duties respond to past wrongs, they have importantly forward-looking functions.[37]

.Applying these observations to the primary/secondary duty distinction, note the close connection between primary duties and duties to negate. Suppose Una wrongfully causes Tully to be in a harmed state, H, at *t1*. Una cannot now discharge her primary duty not to cause Tully to be in H because Tully is already in H and 'ought implies can'. But Una can discharge her duty not to cause Tully to be in H at *t2*, where *t2* is the earliest point at which Una is able to negate the effects of her wrong. If she fails to do this, she will have caused Tully to be in H at *t2*. The main difference between the descriptions of these duties is temporal. Both are preventive because they require Una to avoid causing Tully to be in H, albeit at different times. If the continuation of H cannot be prevented but its impact on Tully's wellbeing can be counterbalanced, Una's reasons to do this are also similar to the reasons that support her primary duty. The primary duty is grounded not just on the importance of Una not harming Tully initially, but on the importance of her not harming Tully overall.

---

[36] Ernest Weinrib, *The Idea of Private Law* (first published 1995, Oxford University Press 2012) 135 (hereafter Weinrib, *The Idea of Private Law*).

[37] See also Sandy Steel, 'Compensation and Continuity' (2020) 26 Legal Theory 250, 257 (hereafter Steel, 'Compensation and Continuity') arguing that placing rock on a person's toe means you are continuing cause of my harm.

B. Two Objections

Let's consider two objections to this explanation of the relationship between primary and secondary duties. First, Shelly Kagan argues that explanations like this fail to distinguish between doing and allowing harm.[38] For example, in case (4) of our original sequence, in which Rich breaks Sneh's leg but cannot restore its functionality or prevent her pain, the harm Rich inflicts on Sneh is complete in the sense that there is no way of negating it. Rich is no longer doing harm to Sneh—that is in the past. He is now merely allowing Sneh's harm to go uncompensated. Since it is worse to do harm than to allow it, the duty to counterbalance, at least, cannot be understood as preventive in the same way as the primary duty.

The plausibility of this argument depends on exactly how we understand Kagan's claim that the harm to Sneh is complete. Kagan applies his view to cases where the harm is either 'in the past, or it is at least fixed in its size and nature'.[39] But though we cannot negate a past or fixed harm, we might be able to prevent a *related* state of affairs by counterbalancing: that of the harm reducing the victim's overall wellbeing. By letting the harm go uncompensated, the injurer brings about a state of affairs in which the victim is worse off than they would have been if not for the injurer's actions. The fact that harm is 'fixed in its size and nature' might mean it cannot be negated, but it does not mean its overall impact is fixed. When an injurer fails to counterbalance the harm they wrongfully cause, they do not merely fail to prevent this state of affairs, they cause it.

It could be replied that the distinction between doing and allowing applies only to harming rather than causing a state of affairs in which overall wellbeing is reduced. Leaving aside the objection that this is an arbitrary and convoluted way to carve up the concept of 'harm', this reply still misses the mark. This is because the moral relevance of the distinction between doing and allowing is independent of the metaphysics of harm. To see this, assume the truth of a particular view of the metaphysics of harm. Joel Feinberg's interest theory will serve. According to Feinberg, mere pain is not harm because it does not set back a relevant interest.[40] Granting this view *arguendo*, it is still intuitive that

---

[38] Kagan, 'Causation and Responsibility' (n 3).

[39] ibid, 300.

[40] Joel Feinberg, *The Moral Limits of the Criminal Law Volume 1: Harm to Others* (Oxford University Press 1987).

causing pain is harder to justify than failing to prevent pain. In other words, if Feinberg's view were correct, it would not change our intuitions about doing and allowing. We would simply say the distinction ranges over more outcomes than those that are, strictly speaking, harms.

Here is the second objection. Suppose we concede that secondary duties have a forward-looking function, as I have suggested. We might still insist they have other features that distinguish them from primary duties. It is often more burdensome to fulfil secondary duties than primary duties. Most wrongs are avoidable without a significant degree of effort, while compensating serious injuries can cost substantially more than it would have cost to avoid causing them in the first place. Moreover, many primary obligations are negative and do not impose ends on the duty-bearer. They require them to refrain from doing something, leaving them free to do anything but the prohibited thing. Corrective duties are positive in the sense that they require the duty-bearer to set compensation as their end and are therefore more burdensome in terms of restricting liberty.

Both points are subject to the same response. Whether secondary duties are more costly than primary duties is a contingent matter. We can imagine a careless billionaire, for example, for whom counterbalancing harm *ex post* is less costly than adhering to duty *ex ante*. Similarly, not all primary duties are negative and therefore less liberty-restricting than secondary duties. The moral duty of rescue, for example, which is widely accepted by non-libertarian philosophers, is positive. As a result, these points do not undermine the relationship between primary and secondary duties I have described. Rather, they suggest that secondary duties are more likely to exceed the stringency threshold of primary duties. As we will see, this is a problem for views that treat primary and secondary duties as having the same stringency. But it is not a problem for the view I will defend, which treats secondary duties as more stringent than primary duties—in fact it is a reason in favour of it.

IV. Continuity or Responsiveness?

A. The Two Theses

We have identified some similarities between primary and secondary duties. Some theorists go further and accept *the continuity thesis*, which can be stated as follows:

> *The Continuity Thesis*: When someone violates a primary right/duty, that right/duty or the reason(s) that underpin it survive the violation and justify a secondary right/duty of repair.

One of the most widely discussed versions of *the continuity thesis* is offered by John Gardner, who frames it in terms of reasons. Gardner argues that when one breaches a duty, the reasons that supported the duty continue to exist and call for 'next best' conformity.[41] If I break a promise to meet a friend for lunch, the reasons that supported my duty (keeping my word, spending time with the friend) can be partially complied with by performing a related action such as meeting for lunch the following day. Compensation, on this view, can be understood as 'next best' conformity with reasons not to harm others.

Ripstein and Weinrib also advocate *the continuity thesis*, though they frame it in terms of the continuity of rights and obligations respectively, rather than reasons.[42] On these variations, the primary obligation, or the right that correlates with this obligation, survives the breach and subsequently requires compensation. 'Secondary' rights and obligations are justified because they are, in fact, identical to the original right/obligation pairing.

It might be thought that our discussion above supports *the continuity thesis*. I have argued that secondary duties share with primary duties two important features: they are negative (at least when their corresponding primary duties are negative) and preventive. They are preventive because by negating or counterbalancing they avert specific harms or overall reductions in wellbeing that would otherwise occur; and they are negative (when their corresponding primary duties are negative) because failing to mitigate the harm one causes is equivalent to causing it. These similarities help to justify the imposition of secondary duties and to explain their content. However, I argue below that we should not accept *the continuity thesis*, but rather an alternative that we can call *the responsiveness thesis*:

> *The Responsiveness Thesis*: When someone violates a primary right/duty, they pay insufficient regard to the values that underpin it, and thus incur a duty to respond by paying proportionally greater regard than was previously sufficient to those values.[43]

---

[41] Gardner, *Torts and Other Wrongs* (n 1) 65.

[42] Ripstein, *Private Wrongs* (n 27) 241–51, 263 and Ernest Weinrib, *Corrective Justice* (Oxford University Press 2012) 81–91 (hereafter Weinrib, *Corrective Justice*).

[43] A view like this is implicit in Victor Tadros' argument that the duties of moral wrongdoers sometimes go beyond rectification. See Victor Tadros, *The Ends of Harm: The Moral Foundations of Criminal Law* (Oxford University Press 2011) 283–91 (hereafter Tadros, *Ends*).

The responsiveness thesis explains the duty of repair in a different way. When we violate a primary duty, we acquire a *separate* duty to promote or further the values that underpinned the duty we violated. This is an intuitive way to respond to our wrongdoing. We should correct for disregarding these values in the exercise or our moral agency by giving them more regard than we would otherwise be required to give them in future. This involves, at a minimum, securing the same aims as the primary duty (subject to the stringency threshold), that is, negating and counterbalancing. However, it often involves more than this, and this is one reason why *the responsiveness thesis* is more plausible than *the continuity thesis.*

B. The Central Objection to *The Continuity Thesis*

The central problem for *the continuity thesis* is that it appears to eliminate the role of wrongdoing in explaining secondary duties. If such duties are justified by the continuation of some normative feature that preceded the breach, the wrong itself becomes explanatorily redundant.[44] Intuitively, though, the wrong plays a crucial role in generating secondary duties.

This worry can be disambiguated into two distinct objections, which we will address in turn. This first is that some versions of *the continuity thesis* treat secondary duties as identical to primary duties, and this suggests not only that the wrong plays no role in grounding secondary duties, but that there *is* no wrong. This version of the objection prompts Gardner to frame *the continuity thesis* in terms of reasons. A secondary duty cannot literally be the same duty as the primary duty that was breached, but the reasons that supported the primary duty can be partially complied with. Here Gardner assumes that, while duties are individuated according to the actions they direct us to perform, reasons are not.[45]

---

[44] For example, see Benjamin Zipursky, 'Rights, Wrongs, and Recourse in the Law of Torts' (1998) 51 Vanderbilt Law Review 1, 74 and Charlie Webb, 'Duties and Damages' in Paul B Miller and John Oberdiek (eds), *Oxford Studies in Private Law Theory: Volume I* (Oxford University Press 2020) 23–24 and Goldberg and Zipursky, *Recognizing Wrongs* (n 1) 159. Similarly, Stephen Smith objects to the continuity thesis on the basis that it implies that conformity with a secondary duty is just as good as conformity with a primary duty, see 'Duties, Liabilities, and Damages' (2011) 125 Harvard Law Review 1727, 1753. Interestingly, Gardner himself has observed that breach of a primary duty is not a mere condition of a secondary duty as this fails to capture the justificatory relationship between the two duties—a secondary duty is imposed if and *because* a primary duty has been violated. See Gardner, *Torts and Other Wrongs* (n 1) 127.

[45] John Gardner 'The Negligence Standard: Political Not Metaphysical' (2017) 80 Modern Law Review 1, 6.

An initial problem with this claim is that it is not clear why we should distinguish between reasons and duties in this way given that they are both action-directed. The objection can be repeated with respect to reasons. The reasons that support a secondary duty cannot be the same as those that supported the primary duty because it is impossible to fulfil these reasons after the primary duty has been breached. Reasons are time-indexed just as duties are. If I have a reason to catch the 12:00 o'clock train, my failure to arrive at the station in time might give rise to a reason to catch the 12:10, but this is a quantitatively different reason to my reason to catch the earlier train.[46] Gardner's view holds, to the contrary, that reasons sometimes do not disappear when it is no longer possible to adhere to them. Since we will engage with this claim in more detail in Chapter 5, I will put it to one side here and focus on the objection to *the continuity thesis* as it applies to Weinrib and Ripstein's claims that the secondary obligation/right is the same as the primary obligation/right.

One argument Weinrib offers is that, if breach brings an obligation to an end, then the obligation is absurdly discharged by its breach.[47] This argument rests on a confusion of concepts, though. The obligation is not discharged by its breach, it is violated. It is true that violating an obligation makes it cease to exist,[48] but there is nothing unusual or absurd about this phenomenon. When a necessary condition of an obligation's existence is removed, the obligation disappears. For example, the obligation not to kill a person is ended by killing them—it *would* be absurd to think there is an obligation not to kill a dead person—yet clearly murderers violate rather than discharge this obligation. Perhaps Weinrib's argument is really motivated by the idea that, if an obligation disappears because it has been breached, the wrongdoer will have gotten away with something. They will have 'hacked' morality, escaping from their moral constraints by disregarding them. Except this is also false since a wrongdoer may be liable to compensate or be punished, as *the responsiveness thesis* implies. Getting rid of a duty by violating it is not a morality hack if doing so gives rise to even more burdensome duties.

Weinrib has another response, which consists of two claims: (1) an obligation can require multiple actions and therefore (2) there is nothing amiss

---

[46] Scanlon treats the locution 'is a reason for' as a four-place relation holding between a fact, an agent, a set of conditions, and an attitude or action. The set of conditions includes the time at which the reason supposedly applies, so a given fact may be a reason at one time but not at another. See TM Scanlon, *Being Realistic about Reasons* (Oxford University Press 2014) 30–1.

[47] Weinrib, *The Idea of Private Law* (n 36) 135. Ripstein makes similar claims in *Private Wrongs* (n 27) 12–13.

[48] See also Steel, 'Compensation and Continuity' (n 37) 255 and Goldberg and Zipursky, *Recognizing Wrongs* (n 1) 159.

in thinking the same obligation can require both the avoidance of harm and compensation for that harm.[49] Claim (1) is true. For instance, one can have a conjunctive obligation to do A *and* B. This obligation can be violated in three ways: by doing neither A nor B, by doing A and not B, and by doing B and not A. Alternatively, one can have a disjunctive obligation to do A *or* B. Assuming it is inclusive (ie one can fulfil the obligation by doing A and B), this obligation can be violated in just one way: by doing neither A nor B. There is no conceptual limit to the number of actions that can feature in conjunctive and disjunctive obligations.

The problem for Weinrib is that claim (2) does not follow from claim (1). If the obligation is disjunctive, it might take the form, 'either (don't harm) or (don't harm without compensating)'. This obligation fails to account for the significance of wrongdoing because, if one compensates *ex post*, the obligation is not violated and thus there is no wrong. Alternatively, a conjunctive obligation might take the form, '(avoid harm) and (compensate if you harm)'. Understood in this way, the obligation is contradictory since it is impossible both to avoid harm and compensate for it.

Weinrib has a further response: the multiple actions required by the obligation must be performed at specific times; the obligation is not simply a 'smorgasbord' of actions that the agent can choose when to perform.[50] But this reply doesn't make the problem go away either. If the different elements of the obligation are to be understood in this time-indexed manner, the obligation might be something like this: '(at $t1$ refrain from harming) or (at $t2$ compensate)'. As before, this obligation eliminates wrongdoing from the picture because it can be fulfilled by compensating *ex post*. Alternatively, the obligation might state: '(at $t1$ refrain from harming) and (at $t2$ compensate)'. As before, this obligation is incoherent because it is impossible to perform both actions. This impossibility has to do with the mutual incompatibility of the actions, not the time at which they are performed.

Finally, it might be argued that Weinrib and Ripstein are simply using a different conception of obligation than that which is implicit in the above discussion. Weinrib suggests that an obligation that requires different actions can be identical if both actions share a 'normative ground',[51] whilst Ripstein makes a similar claim about actions with the same 'normative basis'.[52] Like the previous

---

[49] Weinrib, *Corrective Justice* (n 42) 89.
[50] ibid, 93.
[51] ibid, 109.
[52] Arthur Ripstein, 'Reply: Relations of Right and Private Wrongs' (2018) 9 Jurisprudence 614, 618.

manoeuvres, this also does not address the problem. The fact that two mutually incompatible elements of an obligation share the same normative basis does not make them somehow compatible. Furthermore, this move muddies the distinction between obligations and the grounds for those obligations. The grounds of obligations are, roughly speaking, facts that non-causally make it the case that the obligation exists.[53] For example, the fact that some action will interfere with the independence of an autonomous being grounds the obligation not to so interfere. The same grounding fact can give rise to more than one obligation. It might, for instance, give both me and you an obligation not to perform the same action. Still, these are clearly separate obligations; their being grounded in the same fact does not make them identical. It courts confusion to adopt a conception of obligations that makes them a kind of cocktail of actions and grounding facts.

Let's move on to the second version of the objection that *the continuity thesis* eliminates wrongdoing from our understanding of the relationship between primary and secondary duties. This version has been pressed by Victor Tadros.[54] Tadros argues that *the continuity thesis* cannot explain why secondary duties are more stringent than similar duties owed by bystanders. He presents the following cases:

Fix 1: Alice can rescue Cath from serious harm at *t* at some minimal cost to herself and fails to do this. Later, at *t2*, only Alice can fix the harm that resulted at *t* that she failed to prevent.

Fix 2: Beth can rescue Cath from serious harm at *t* at some minimal cost to herself and fails to do this. Later, at *t2*, only Alice can fix the harm that resulted at *t* that Beth failed to prevent.

In both cases Alice can compensate for the harm at *t2*, but only in *Fix 1* does Alice commit the earlier wrong of failing to protect Cath. The reason Tadros constructs the cases around wrongful allowing rather than wrongful doing is to eliminate the distraction that failing to compensate appears to be an instance of allowing harm (although cf our discussion in pt III). Intuitively, Alice has a more stringent duty to repair the harm in *Fix 1* compared to *Fix 2*. The fact that

---

[53] For our purposes, it is not necessary to delve any deeper into the nature of grounding. For discussion of the relation between normative and natural facts as a form of metaphysical grounding, see Gideon Rosen, 'Metaphysical Relations in Metaethics' in Tristram McPherson and David Plunkett (eds), *The Routledge Handbook of Metaethics* (Routledge 2017) 151.

[54] Victor Tadros, 'Secondary Duties' in Paul B Miller and John Oberdiek (eds), *Civil Wrongs and Justice in Private Law* (Oxford University Press 2020) 185, 186–92.

she previously failed to protect Cath means she is required to bear a greater burden to protect her in future. This is evident when we compare this to *Fix 2*, in which Alice is a mere bystander and owes only an ordinary duty of rescue. *The continuity thesis* cannot explain this result because it does not treat Alice's wrong in *Fix 1* as a ground of her secondary duty.

Can *the continuity thesis* survive this objection? John Oberdiek argues it can.[55] On his view, what makes primary and secondary duties distinct is their relationality, and *the continuity thesis* is perfectly capable of accounting for this relationality. The primary duties we owe to others are relational in the sense that the recipient of the duty has a claim to its performance, and secondary duties inherit this feature from primary duties.[56] It is this relationality that explains the distinctive importance of wrongdoing, and why secondary duties are different from those owed by bystanders.

If this is right, we would expect secondary duties arising from relational wrongs and secondary duties arising from non-relational wrongs to function in a very different way. But this does not seem to be the case. Consider this pair of cases, which are similar Tadros' except they involve the non-relational wrong of failing to prevent harm to non-human animals:

Trapped Dog 1: Vic can free a trapped dog at *t1* at some minimal cost to herself and fails to do this. Later, at *t2*, only Vic can free the dog.
Trapped Dog 2: Vic can free a trapped dog at *t1* at some minimal cost to herself and fails to do this. Later, at *t2*, only Wes can free the dog.

It is intuitive that Vic has a more stringent duty in *Trapped Dog 1* than Wes does in *Trapped Dog 2*. The situation mirrors the case of interpersonal duties: Vic's past wrongdoing makes her duty more stringent than that of a bystander who owes the ordinary duty of rescue. Perhaps, though, the duties we owe to animals are relational in the relevant sense, in which case, consider:

Cultural Artefact 1: Vic can prevent the destruction of a priceless piece of cultural heritage at *t1* at some minimal cost to herself and fails to do this. Later, at *t2*, only Vic can prevent the destruction.

---

[55] John Oberdiek, 'Wrongs, Remedies, and the Persistence of Reasons: Re-Examining the Continuity Thesis' in Haris Psarras and Sandy Steel (eds), *Private Law and Practical Reason: Essays on John Gardner's Private Law Theory* (Oxford University Press 2023).
[56] R Jay Wallace also argues that 'the relational structure of the secondary obligation derives from the relational structure of the primary wrong that gives rise to it', see R Jay Wallace, *The Moral Nexus* (Princeton University Press 2019) 94.

Cultural Artifact 2: Vic can prevent the destruction of a priceless piece of cultural heritage at *t1* at some minimal cost to herself and fails to do this. Later, at *t2*, only Wes can prevent the destruction.

Again, Vic's duty to protect the cultural artefact in the first case is more stringent than Wes' duty in the second. Given Vic's previous wrongful failure, she can be expected to bear a greater burden than Wes to correct that failure.[57] Some might doubt Vic acts wrongly in *Cultural Artefact 1*, perhaps on the grounds that violating impersonal values is not wrongful. Still, accepting the assumption that it is wrongful *arguendo*, the same sceptics might well agree that it must make a difference to the stringency of Vic's subsequent duty.

This sequence of cases suggests the switch from relational to non-relational wrongs makes no difference—we see the same effect across all forms of wrongdoing. It is not the relationality of the wrong that explains why secondary duties are generally more stringent than those owed by bystanders. It is the fact that the agent has acted in a way that they were morally required not to act that explains this, regardless of whether this was a directed wrong.

C. In Defence of the Responsiveness Thesis

Recall that *the responsiveness thesis* holds that:

When someone violates a primary right/duty, they pay insufficient regard to the values that underpin it, and thus incur a duty to respond by paying proportionally greater regard than was previously sufficient to those values.

In what sense does wrongdoing pay insufficient regard to the values that underpin the duty? In essence, wrongdoing demonstrates a failure to appreciate the way those values constrain our conduct. The extent of this failure is determined by the severity of the wrong. The severity of wrongdoing is a complex notion, but two considerations are particularly relevant. First is culpability.[58]

---

[57] Some may believe that animal welfare and the value of cultural heritage are not important enough to ground any moral duties. I disagree, but that can be set aside for the moment, as even someone who doesn't think the duties in these cases exist might recognize the intuitive difference between Fix 4 and Fix 5 and between Fix 5 and Fix 6.

[58] Roughly speaking, culpability refers to how the wrong reflects on the actor as a moral agent. The notion of culpability I have in mind is similar to what Gary Watson calls blaming from the *aretaic perspective*, the appraisal of a person's virtue or vice as it is manifested in thought and action, see Gary Watson, 'Two Faces of Responsibility' (1996) 24 Philosophical Topics 227, 231.

A person who intentionally harms another and is thus highly culpable acts more wrongly, all else equal, than a person who recklessly harms another, who in turns acts more wrongly than a person who negligently harms another.[59] The more culpable a person is, the greater their disregard of the values that underpin their duty, and thus the more that can be expected of them as an appropriate response.

Culpability is not the only determinant of the severity of wrongdoing, though. Another is the impact of the wrong, including both the material harm it causes and perhaps any setbacks to non-material values. Setback to non-material values refers to cases of harmless wrongdoing, such as the examples of harmless trespass or discrimination discussed previously. Broadly speaking, a wrong that causes great harm and setback to non-material values is more severe than a wrong that causes less. This is just a sketch of some of the factors I deem relevant to the seriousness of wrongdoing. I do not rely on this sketch, however, and any account of severity can be plugged into *the responsiveness thesis*. The main point is that *the responsiveness thesis* appeals to this familiar idea to explain the category of secondary duties.

There are several reasons to prefer *the responsiveness thesis* to *the continuity thesis*. Perhaps the main one is that it is not vulnerable to the objections previously discussed, and thus better explains the centrality of wrongdoing to secondary duties. It recognizes the secondary duty/right pairing as entirely distinct from the primary duty/right pairing. The distinction between negating and counterbalancing shows us the deep similarity between primary and secondary duties, but similarity is not identity. Also, *the responsiveness thesis* shows why secondary duties are more stringent than primary duties. They are more stringent because they are responses to wrongdoing, and this increase in stringency marks the difference between the burdens a person was required to bear to respect certain constraints prior to violating them and the increased burden they can be expected to bear in light of this violation. Unlike *the continuity thesis*, *the responsiveness thesis* is sensitive to the proportional relationship between the severity of the wrong and the degree of cost the wrongdoer can be expected to bear as a result. It reflects the principle that more severe wrongdoing warrants more significant responses.

It might be objected here that this relationship of proportionality applies to liability to punishment, not to corrective duties. It belongs in the realm of the

---

[59] Although see Seana Valentine Shiffrin, 'The Moral Neglect of Negligence' in David Sobel, Peter Vallentyne, and Steven Wall (eds), *Oxford Studies in Political Philosophy* (vol 3, Oxford University Press 2017) for a different view.

criminal law, not the civil law. Punishment, it might be argued, is focussed on harming offenders in proportion to the severity of their wrongdoing, while the duties enforced by tort law focus on compensation, which is determined entirely by the extent of harm resulting from a tort rather than the defendant's culpability. The reasons adduced in support of this view are also familiar. It is practical to divide labour between the civil and criminal law, since they serve different interests, both for individual victims and society more generally. The two bodies of law protect different, albeit overlapping, rights and adopt different principles of liability. Even those who doubt there is a bright line between civil and criminal law recognize there are good reasons for the distinction.

All of this can be conceded. Our question here is not whether we ought to structure legal systems according to the civil/criminal distinction, but whether the underlying morality of corrective duties reflects this difference. Is the moral duty to submit to punishment fundamentally different from the duty to respond in other ways, such that the former is subject to proportionality but not the latter?[60] There is reason to think not. For one thing, punitive damages are sometimes an appropriate response to non-criminal conduct. One circumstance when they are available is to remove incentives to commit torts in cases where a tortfeasor calculates that they will profit more from committing the tort and paying compensation than not committing the tort. Consider:

> *Car*: A car manufacturer discovers a defect in one of their models. Executives calculate that the cost of recalling the model and fixing the defect is greater than the cost of doing nothing and paying compensation to the inevitable victims and their families. They decide to do nothing.

The executives clearly act wrongly in *Car*, and ought to face punitive damages. Perhaps this can be explained by the fact that we want to remove problematic incentives, but the intuition that punitive damages are appropriate persists even if we imagine that the executives simply miscalculated. Part of the problem is that, without punitive damages, their corrective responses are too

---

[60] There are at least two grounds on which one might deny this. One is that criminal law is concerned with public wrongs while private law is concerned with private wrongs, and The Proportionality Principle applies only to public wrongs. For reasons that have been detailed elsewhere, I doubt appeal to public wrongs offers a principled distinction between criminal and civil law, see James Edwards and Andrew Simester, 'What's Public about Crime?' (2017) 37 Oxford Journal of Legal Studies 105. But even if it does, a further argument is required as to why legal consequences for private wrongs should be unconstrained by The Proportionality Principle. The second is that The Proportionality Principle is moral desert in disguise, and desert is relevant for punishment but irrelevant for remedial responses. Again, for reasons outlined by others (see Tadros, *Ends* (n 43) ch 4). I doubt that desert provides a good basis for the justification of punishment, so I interpret proportionality as resting on other grounds.

easy. They are left no worse off despite their egregious disregard for human life. The imposition of punitive damages allows some degree of proportionality between the seriousness of the wrong and the burdensomeness of the corrective response.

This view also provides a response to a criticism of punitive damages. It has been objected that, though punitive damages may be justified for deterrence-based reasons, there is no reason why they should go to the victim of the tort in particular.[61] According to *the responsiveness thesis*, however, this is too quick. In cases of egregious wrongdoing, victims may be entitled to both compensatory and punitive damages, as this is a way of paying greater regard to the wellbeing of the victim than was required before the wrong.

There are other reasons to prefer *the responsiveness thesis* to *the continuity thesis* too. As a result of its ability to explain the higher stringency of secondary duties, *the responsiveness thesis* does not face systematic problems in explaining how secondary duties are justified even when they are more burdensome and liberty-restricting than primary duties. We acknowledged above that, as a contingent matter, it is often easier to avoid wrongdoing than it is to compensate for it, given that the duty to compensate can be expensive in material terms and prohibits the duty-bearer from doing anything that is inconsistent with compensating. This means most secondary duties are more burdensome to fulfil than their corresponding primary duties. If this is true, it spells trouble for *the continuity thesis*, since according to it, the stringency of the secondary duty must be the same as the stringency of the primary duty. But if it is the same, what justifies the additional burdensomeness of secondary duties? Consider a primary duty where the cost of fulfilment is already close to the stringency threshold. If the secondary duty that follows is more burdensome and liberty-restricting, the cost of adhering to it is likely to exceed the stringency threshold of the secondary duty, meaning that it cannot arise. This is not a problem for *the responsiveness thesis*, since according to it, the stringency of secondary duties is generally greater than the stringency of primary duties, since all the determinants of the initial stringency are still in play, and the fact that the duty has been breached is an additional factor.

Moreover, *the continuity thesis* cannot explain other duties (besides the secondary duty) that arise *post* wrongdoing. Wrongdoing generates duties that cannot be attributed to the continuation of any normative feature that preceded the wrong. For example, a wrongdoer might have a duty to fortify

---

[61] For this argument see Allan Beever, 'The Structure of Aggravated and Exemplary Damages' (2003) 23 Oxford Journal of Legal Studies 87, 107.

themselves against the possibility of similar conduct in future,[62] or simply a weighty duty not to re-offend, which explains the 'recidivist premium', the fact that re-offending is more gravely wrong than the first offence.[63] They might also have a duty to apologize, to atone for their actions, or to reflect more deeply on the values they violated and how they might better adhere to them in future. Admittedly, these duties are not remedial in the sense that they are not owed to the victim in light of the impact the wrong had on their wellbeing, and some of them are not directed to the victim at all. Perhaps a defender of *the continuity thesis* would say they seek to explain only remedial duties rather than the full range of duties arising from breach. If so, this would split an agent's secondary duties into two groups. Remedial secondary duties would be explained by *the continuity thesis* while non-remedial secondary duties—both directed and non-directed—would be explained in some other way. This seems rather *ad hoc* given that both sets of secondary duties arise as a result of the same wrong. *The responsiveness thesis* offers a unified rather than bifurcated account of secondary duties. Although we tend to focus on corrective duties, secondary duties actually cover a broad spectrum which includes both corrective and non-corrective responses. The duty to apologize, to provide an explanation of one's conduct, to make oneself available for accountability processes, to fortify oneself against future wrongdoing, to communicate to others about one's own mistakes, and to reflect on one's transgressions and consider how best to respond to them, are all examples of non-corrective responses that wrongdoers have reasons and sometimes duties to undertake. It is a virtue of *the responsiveness thesis* that non-corrective responses do not need an additional *ad hoc* explanation.

Conclusion

In this chapter, we explored the distinction between negating and counterbalancing, defending the presumption in favour of the former over the latter. We saw that interference with a person's ends is morally significant even if they are left no worse off, and this has relevance for our moral permissions and duties.

---

[62] See Jeffrey Howard, 'Punishment as Moral Fortification' (2017) 36 Law and Philosophy 45.

[63] For discussion of the 'recidivist premium', see Christopher Bennett, 'Do Multiple and Repeat Offenders Pose a Problem for Retributive Sentencing Theory?' in Jesper Ryberg and Claudio Tamburrini (eds), *Recidivist Punishment: The Philosophers' View* (Lexington 2011) and Christopher Bennett, 'More to Apologise For: Can a Basis for the Recidivist Premium Be Found within a Communicative Theory of Punishment?' in Julian V Roberts and Andrew von Hirsch (eds), *Previous Convictions at Sentencing: Theoretical and Applied Perspectives* (Hart Publishing 2010).

One implication is that *ex post* corrective action sometimes makes otherwise wrongful conduct permissible. We defended this claim against a robust insistence on control over property and bodily integrity, and explained why it doesn't collapse into the Holmesian view that what we ordinarily consider wrongs are more like prices, that is, permissible as long as compensation is given.

The distinction between negating and counterbalancing also enlightens us about the relationship between primary and secondary duties, although it should not tempt us to accept *the continuity thesis* over *the responsiveness thesis*. We saw that *the continuity thesis* tends to erase or underplay the significance of wrongdoing in the derivation of secondary duties by implying that the wrong did not occur, that it plays no grounding role, or via its inability to account for the increased stringency of secondary duties. We defended *the responsiveness thesis*, which places less emphasis on trying to make it as if the wrong did not happen, and more on responding appropriately to the failures of one's practical and moral reasoning.

We have now introduced two limbs of the four-fold analysis: conditional permissibility and wrongdoing. In Chapter 4 we explore a form of wrongdoing central to liability for unintentional harm: negligence.

4

Capacity and Cost Sensitivity in Negligence

Introduction

One form of wrongdoing of particular relevance to tort law is negligence. Negligence raises many theoretical questions. Some doubt the very possibility of culpable negligence,[1] and although this is an important debate, we will bracket it in our discussion and assume that negligence, in some form, represents a genuine moral wrong. Instead, we will address a set of questions downstream of that debate, specifically the extent to which the moral wrong of negligence is—and the legal wrong of negligence should be—sensitive to our capacity to avoid negligence, and the cost to us of doing so.

This brief description presents us with two metrics for situating different views about negligence. A view of negligence may be capacity sensitive or capacity insensitive. A view is capacity sensitive if it never deems a person negligent if they lacked the capacity to do otherwise. This is a binary metric. Whilst capacities come in degrees, what we are interested in is whether a person's capacities made it possible for them to avoid some putatively negligent act, and the impossibility of performing that act is not a matter of degree, though it is certainly subject to vagueness. According to a second metric, a view of negligence can be more or less cost sensitive. If a view is cost insensitive, it holds that the costs of avoiding some act are largely irrelevant as to whether that act is negligent. This metric is scalar rather than binary, and different views might defend different degrees of cost sensitivity.

We can define both the moral and legal wrong of negligence in terms of where they are—or ought to be—situated on each of these metrics. We might think the moral and legal wrong should mirror one another as much as

[1] Some deny the possibility of culpable negligence, see Larry Alexander, Kimberly Kessler Ferzan, and Stephen Morse, *Crime and Culpability: A Theory of Criminal Law* (CUP 2009) ch 3; Michael J Zimmerman, 'Moral Responsibility and Ignorance' (1997) 107 Ethics 410; and Neil Levy, 'Expressing Who We are: Moral Responsibility and Awareness of Our Reasons for Action' (2011) 52 Analytic Philosophy 243. I leave this form of scepticism aside in this chapter and assume that negligence can amount to culpable wrongdoing. On this assumption, we could adopt a more or less capacity and cost sensitive account of this moral wrong, and this is our question here.

Wrongs, Harms, and Compensation. Adam Slavny, Oxford University Press. © Adam Slavny 2023.
DOI: 10.1093/oso/9780192864567.003.0004

possible, or alternatively that they should diverge to some extent. The first approach is straightforward. If the legal wrong is justified in part by appeal to the moral wrong, then there is a presumption that the two should not diverge. In Chapter 1 we saw that such divergence generates objections on behalf of both defendants and victims. However, this presumption can be overturned, and these objections might be met by appeal to considerations that arise when we seek to legally enforce standards of conduct across a wide range of situations, especially in the non-ideal conditions in which the law must operate. I will call such considerations 'enforcement factors' and considerations that are relevant to both the moral and legal wrong of negligence, rather than specific to enforcement, 'principled factors'.

Several enforcement factors favour a legal rule that is capacity and cost insensitive. This approach is easier and less time-consuming to apply, since it imposes a more uniform standard across different cases and does not necessitate an interrogation of a defendant's individual capacities; it is less vulnerable to fraud and abuse as people facing the prospect of liability have less incentive to misrepresent their capacities; and it is more predictable and therefore better able to guide conduct and shape expectations. Perhaps the cumulative force of these factors justifies a capacity and cost insensitive approach in law regardless of whether this coheres with the morality of negligence. But, as before, this justification must meet a specific type of challenge. Defendants who do not commit the moral wrong of negligence but are held legally liable can mount the *restricted freedom* and *undue burden* objections, and it must be shown that these objections are overridden, presumably by enforcement factors. This is possible but by no means self-evident, given that the law would then entail the retrenchment of moral freedoms and imposition of burdens for the sake of forward-looking goals such as clarity and cost-reduction.

In this chapter I will argue that defences of a capacity and cost insensitive approach based on principled rather than enforcement factors fail. The moral wrong of negligence is sensitive to capacity and cost because it is fully individualized. It is defined by what can be reasonably expected of a given individual in a given situation, not what can be reasonably expected of some other individual in that situation, or of that individual in some other situation. This means there is a normative presumption that the legal standard should be similarly sensitive. Appeal to enforcement factors might overturn this presumption, but I will offer some tentative reasons why it might not. More importantly, justification of a different legal standard based on enforcement factors creates problems for the widely held view in non-instrumentalist tort theory that the tort of negligence represents a coherent form of wrongdoing.

So far, I have framed the question in terms of our two metrics, deliberately avoiding reference to the legal concept that some might associate with capacity and cost insensitivity—the objective standard of care. This is for two reasons. One is that the language of subjectivism and objectivism is unfortunate, at least insofar as it relates to our two metrics. Capacity and cost sensitive views have nothing to do with subjectivism, at least in the way that term is understood in moral philosophy and metaethics. Second, and more importantly, the extent to which negligence law *does* impose a capacity and cost insensitive standard is unclear, so it is best to separate this interpretive question from the normative questions we are interested in here. However, I will have more to say about the interpretation of the objective standard of care shortly.

I. Clarifying the Two Metrics

A. Capacity Sensitivity

For the purpose of our discussion, I want to tie the concept of capacity to the 'can' term in the maxim, 'ought implies can'. Someone has the capacity to do or avoid doing something negligent if and only if they can do or avoid doing that thing in whatever sense of that term is incorporated in the best understanding of 'ought implies can'. The reason for this will become clear, but of course it merely kicks the 'can' further down the road in terms of our understanding of agential capacities, so it will be useful to say something more about 'ought implies can'.

Interpreting 'can' too broadly might result in the maxim failing to properly constrain the reasons and duties that apply to us. On the other hand, interpreting it too narrowly risks ruling out too much. If it requires that alternative action is possible in a non-deterministic sense, or that action is caused by a decision not subject to causal determination, then 'ought implies can' is true only if determinism is false.[2] The truth of determinism *may* threaten 'ought implies can' in this way, but for the present we will settle on a wider definition of 'can' in the hope that there is a plausible compatibilist conception of ability. For an agent to perform some act, she must be physically capable

---

[2] For discussion of the relationship between 'ought implies can' and determinism, see Dana Nelkin, *Making Sense of Freedom and Responsibility* (Oxford University Press 2011) 100–01 and Derk Pereboom, *Free Will, Agency, and Meaning in Life* (Oxford University Press 2014) 138–46.

of doing it. Rather than trying to adjudicate between different conceptions of physical ability, I will rely on cases like the following:

> *Involuntary Spasm*: Xand suffers an involuntary spasm whilst driving and crashes into Yoona.

Assuming that Xand had no prior warning that they might suffer such a spasm, they are physically incapable of avoiding the accident. Cases like *Involuntary Spasm* are useful for our purposes because, though there are different views of what counts as physical capacity,[3] Xand lacks the capacity to avoid injury on any plausible view.

A person might also be psychologically incapable of doing something. We must be careful with the concept of psychological incapacity as it is difficult to know whether a given action is genuinely impossible or merely very difficult, costly, or stressful. Critics of 'ought implies can' sometimes cite these cases as counterexamples. For example, the compulsive thief ought not to steal even though they cannot avoid stealing, therefore 'ought implies can' is false. These counterexamples are dubious, though, as it is unclear whether the klepto-maniac truly lacks the ability to refrain from stealing. Compulsions often impair our capacities rather than disable them entirely, and compulsive people regulate their behaviour in some situations. These cases don't refute 'ought implies can', then, but they do create problems for defining its scope. Consider:

> *Psychosis*: Xand is in the grip of a severe psychotic episode and tries to light themselves on fire. Yoona attempts to stop this and is burned as a result.
>
> *Agoraphobia*: Xand, who has a severe panic disorder, shops for groceries. Whilst out they have a panic attack and run from the shop, knocking over Yoona.

At what point does psychological impairment constitute psychological incapacity? It seems unlikely that Xand can avoid their actions in the sense that it would be meaningful to impute to them a duty to do so. On the other hand, it is tempting to draw a line between involuntary action such as that in

---

[3] To take one example from the literature on ability, on a simply conditional analysis Xand lacks the ability because it is not the case that if they try to avoid the collision, they will avoid it (either because they lack the ability to try or because their efforts at trying would be fruitless). Although for a well-known counterexample to the conditional analysis, see Keith Lehrer, 'Cans without Ifs' (1968) 29 *Analysis* 29). For the remainder of the chapter, I will work on the assumption that physical incapacity is a paradigm case of inability, and however the 'can' term in 'ought implies can' is ultimately to be interpreted, it will exclude such cases.

Muscle Spasm and voluntary action under extreme compulsion such as that in *Psychosis* and *Agoraphobia*. Perhaps our judgements will depend on further empirical details we cannot investigate here. In the absence of any detailed evidence, we must settle with the hedged conclusion that there may be cases of genuine psychological incapacity in which 'ought implies can' rules out a duty, but these will be difficult to distinguish from those that involve difficulty or high cost rather than genuine incapacity.

A final clarification is that an agent 'can' perform some action only if they have the opportunity to do so. Possessing the physical and psychological capacity to do something is irrelevant if one lacks the opportunity.[4] Consider:

> *Safe*: Xand will die of poison unless Yoona gives them an antidote. The antidote is inside a safe. Yoona does not know the combination to the safe and has no way of finding it.
>
> *Rare Bleed*: Xand, who is a junior doctor, lacks the knowledge required to spot a rare bleed and has no opportunity to seek advice from a superior, and as a result Yoona suffers injury.

In *Safe*, Yoona has the physical and psychological capacity to open the safe but lacks the opportunity to do so without knowledge of the combination. The best understanding of 'ought implies can' rules out her having a duty to open the safe. To see this, imagine the safe has no combination. In this variation, it is physically impossible to open the safe, and so 'ought implies can' straightforwardly applies. But this situation is not materially different from the original. In both cases it is not possible for Yoona to open the safe, and so she has no duty to do so—whether this impossibility results from physical inability or lack of opportunity seems immaterial. Xand's situation in *Rare Bleed* is similar. They lack the knowledge to spot the bleed and cannot take steps to acquire it, so if 'ought implies can' prevents a duty arising in *Safe*, it should have the same effect in *Rare Bleed*.

B. Cost Sensitivity

The notion of cost employed here is the same as that in Chapter 3: any negative consequence of an act that is relevant in determining whether it is reasonable to expect someone to perform it. These costs may be financial or personal,

---

[4] See Peter B Vranas, 'I Ought, Therefore I Can' (2007) 136 Philosophical Studies 167, 169.

that is, costs relating to the pain or stress of doing something. In *Psychosis* and *Agoraphobia,* for example, even if Xand has the capacity to avoid harm, it is costly for them to do so, and this cost is not reducible to time or money.

Cost is also related to difficulty. Actions that agents find difficult are often, for that reason, also costly. We can, though, distinguish between the cost of an action and the likelihood of success. Some actions are not costly in the sense described above but very unlikely to succeed, given an agent's capacities. If an agent is unlikely to be successful if they attempt some action, this affects whether they can reasonably be expected to do it, and should therefore be considered a type of cost for our purpose, although in general we will stick to actions that are costly in the more familiar sense.

As I mentioned above, cost sensitivity is a scalar notion and it is not precise to speak of cost sensitive and cost insensitive duties *per se*, although these terms serve as useful generalizations. There is also a key distinction between two forms of cost sensitivity, which I will call *proportional* cost sensitivity and *threshold* cost sensitivity. The former makes the standard of care owed proportional to the cost of adhering to that standard. The more costly it is for an agent to take care, the less care they can reasonably be expected to take. The latter makes the standard of care uniform until a threshold is reached. A standard level of care can be expected unless the cost exceeds the threshold. This distinction will be important later when we defend cost sensitivity against criticism.

With these clarifications in hand, the rest of this chapter has two aims. First, to critique arguments that favour capacity or cost insensitivity or both; and second, to provide a positive argument in favour of capacity and cost sensitivity and respond to some objections.

II. Is the Objective Standard of Care Capacity and Cost Insensitive?

Although I want to avoid interpretive questions where possible, it will be useful to say something about whether the objective standard of care is capacity and cost insensitive. In this part, we will consider the overlap between the objective standard and capacity and cost insensitivity, and thus the extent to which the arguments of this chapter threaten the legal standard.

Canonical statements of the objective standard certainly suggest that it is capacity and cost insensitive in some respects. For example, in *Nettleship v Weston*, Lord Denning held that the defendant had a duty to drive, 'in as good a manner as a driver of skill, experience and care, who is sound in limb ... and makes no errors of judgment, had good eye sight and hearing, and is free from any infirmity'.[5] Similarly, according to the unanimous decision by the Court of Appeal in *Dunnage v Randall*, as long as the defendant's impairment does not eliminate their voluntariness entirely, they are subject to the objective standard regardless of the difficulty of avoiding their actions.[6]

On the other hand, the law makes many exceptions, such as the one made for children.[7] In the Australian case of *McHale v Watson*, which declined to hold children to the same standard as adults, it was stated that it does not follow from the objective standard that a person 'cannot rely in his defence upon a limitation upon the capacity for foresight or prudence, not as being personal to himself, but as being characteristic of humanity in his stage of development'.[8] Similarly, the approach to cost is somewhat variable, as the personal costs to the defendant in Dunnage did not rule out breach, whilst the financial cost of precautions against injury has been generally recognized as a valid factor.[9]

There is also disagreement about how the objective standard should apply to cases of physical incapacity like *Involuntary Spasm*. For example, in the case of *Mansfield v Weetabix Ltd*,[10] the defendant crashed a lorry into a shop owned by the plaintiffs, causing extensive damage. Although he was unaware of it at the time, he suffered from malignant insulinoma, which caused him to enter a hypoglycaemic state before the crash. The Court of Appeal found the defendant not liable partly on the basis that he had no prior warning of his condition. Consistent with the Mansfield decision, some consider it obvious that the law does not impose duties that defendants are physically incapable of fulfilling,[11] suggesting the objective standard imposes some degree of cost insensitivity but not capacity insensitivity. But others, such as Allan Beever, argue that the court misapplied the standard in *Mansfield* as it allowed the subjective limitations of the defendant to determine the standard of care.[12] According to Beever, the objective standard, properly understood, would have imposed a

---

[5] [1971] 2 QB 691, 699.

[6] *Dunnage v Randall* [2016] QB 639.

[7] *Mullin v Richards* [1998] 1 WLR 1304.

[8] (1966) 115 CLR 199.

[9] *Latimer v AEC* [1953] AC 643.

[10] [1998] 1 WLR 1263, 1268 (CA).

[11] Richard W Wright, 'The Standards of Care in Negligence Law' in David G Owen (ed), *The Philosophical Foundations of Tort Law* (Oxford University Press 1995) 249, 258 (hereafter Wright 'Standards of Care'). Robert Stevens explains this on the grounds that, if an agent is physically incapacitated, we cannot even attribute actions to them. See Robert Stevens, *Torts and Rights* (Oxford University Press 2007) 110 (hereafter Stevens, *Torts and Rights*).

[12] Allan Beever, *Rediscovering the Law of Negligence* (Hart 2009) 80–81 (hereafter Beever, *Rediscovering Negligence*).

duty on the defendant even though the injurious act was committed in a hypo-glycaemic state.[13]

In Mansfield, the defendant avoided liability because he had no prior warning of his condition, and thus no opportunity to avoid placing himself in a situation where he might unavoidably harm others. Similar claims could be made about our hypothetical cases, *Psychosis*, *Agoraphobia*, and *Rare Bleed*. In each of these cases, the injurer could have avoided the harm by refraining from placing themselves in a situation where such harm is unavoidable. In *Agoraphobia*, Xand could have avoided going to the shops. In *Rare Bleed*, Xand could have declined to become a doctor or refused to work without access to a supervisor.[14] But we can then ask: In these cases, what exactly does the breach of duty consist in? Is the collision in *Agoraphobia* an instance of breach? How about the omission in *Rare Bleed*? If these are correctly described as breaches of duty, the 'ought implies can' objection applies even if the *undue burden* objection does not. The possibility of prior avoidance does not make the shopper or junior doctor able to avert impending harm once they are in the relevant position, and that is a position in which their duties should apply to them.

Moreover, the negligent act can consist in a prior failure to avoid only if that failure is unreasonable. Sometimes it is. In *Involuntary Spasm*, as in *Mansfield*, if Xand were aware of their condition, it would be negligent for them to get behind the wheel, just as it is negligent for a person to continue driving if they experience symptoms of drowsiness. Other times it is not so obvious. In *Rare Bleed*, what opportunity does Xand have to avoid placing themselves in a position in which their lack of knowledge might be harmful to patients? On the contrary, they often have a duty to treat patients *despite* the risk of negligence. Of course, the hospital is probably institutionally negligent for failing to provide proper supervision, but this does not operate as an excuse for Xand according to the objective standard. Similarly, in *Agoraphobia*, Xand cannot be expected to remain forever in their house to avoid placing themselves in a position where their panic disorder unavoidably poses risks to others.[15]

---

[13] Peter Birks does not consider the *Mansfield* case but accepts as a general fact that the law imposes duties some individuals cannot adhere to. See 'The Concept of a Civil Wrong' David G Owen (ed), *The Philosophical Foundations of Tort Law* (Oxford University Press 1997) 42.

[14] John Gardner makes a similar point in response to Lon Fuller's objection that strict liability demands the impossible: it doesn't demand the impossible because there are always prior acts that would allow one to avoid harming. See John Gardner, 'Some Rule-of-Law Anxieties about Strict Liability in Private Law' in Lisa M Austin and Dennis Klimchuk (eds), *Private Law and the Rule of Law* (Oxford University Press 2014) 5.

[15] David Miller offers the example of a clumsy person who ought to stay away from a glass shop, see *National Responsibility and Global Justice* (Oxford University Press 2007) 88–89.

Cases like *Rare Bleed* are further complicated by the fact that they arguably involve an assumption of responsibility. This introduces a new ground for liability if things go wrong, as it is fair to hold Xand to the degree of care and skill they hold themselves out as possessing. It is not clear that this justification applies in *Rare Bleed*, though. Suppose Xand informs patients that they are junior doctors and therefore do not present themselves as having a higher degree of skill than they do. In English law, a medical professional is held to the standard of a reasonably experienced person holding that particular post,[16] so mere knowledge that Xand is a junior doctor will not prevent the objective standard from applying. But it is difficult to see how this rule can be justified on the basis of assumption of responsibility. One could argue that simply by occupying this post, Xand is conveying that they possess the skill of a reasonably experienced doctor, but this is hardly convincing given that we know inexperienced people must occupy these posts.

Where does all this leave us with respect to whether the objective standard entails capacity or cost insensitivity? Whether it is truly capacity insensitive is controversial. If a correct understanding of the objective standard would hold Xand liable in *Rare Bleed*, and if the harm in *Involuntary Spasm* itself constitutes a breach of duty (rather than a wrongful failure to take a prior opportunity to avoid), then the objective standard is, in some cases, capacity insensitive and violates 'ought implies can'. Whether it is cost insensitive is also unclear. The statement in Dunnage and other cases suggests a degree of cost insensitivity, but there are other occasions when the costs of taking precautions, especially if these take the form of financial costs, are clearly relevant.

Again, I will not attempt to settle these questions here, as they merit a deeper and more wide-ranging discussion. We will proceed to a discussion of some of the arguments that have been put forward in defence of the objective standard. Since we are interested in capacity and cost sensitivity rather than the objective standard *per se*, we will not engage these arguments in precisely the terms they are intended. But they can all be interpreted as arguments for capacity and cost insensitivity and so are relevant for our purposes. Moreover, if these arguments fail, as I will suggest they do, this is more evidence that, to the extent the objective standard is justified, this is due to enforcement rather than principled factors.

---

[16] *Wilsher v Essex Area Health Authority* [1988] 1 AC 1074.

III. Arguments for the Objective Standard

A. The Fairness Argument

Some argue that each person has a right to expect an equal or consistent level of care from others.[17] If this is true, then capacity and cost sensitivity undermines our right to consistency of care. This argument immediately runs into the problem that it is circular to appeal to a right to consistent levels of care to justify capacity and cost sensitivity when the existence of such a right is exactly what is in question. To make progress, we must explain how this right is grounded. One way of doing this is to give normative reasons why a claimant's interest in an equal level of care should be given priority over a defendant's conflicting interest in not being held to an unattainable standard, or a standard it is very tough to reach, such that only one interest should be recognized as a right.

Why might the claimant's interest be given priority? One answer, or rather a family of answers, appeals to fairness. Without capacity and cost insensitivity, it might be claimed, one injured party would receive compensation while another would be left to bear the burden merely because one of the injurers was more capable than the other—a fact the unlucky victim is not responsible for. This is not an adequate defence of capacity and cost insensitivity, however, since we tolerate this form of unfairness elsewhere. A common critique of tort law in general is that it precludes compensation for most harms: victims of natural diseases and disasters; those harmed by non-negligent accidents who are not covered by strict liability regimes; and those who are unable to prove all elements of negligence. Radical differences in how victims fare are dictated by facts beyond their control. To take the fairness argument seriously, we need to know why it should operate locally to support capacity and cost insensitivity in the content of our duties but ignore the many other instances in which victims fare differently for reasons beyond their control.

A related point is that reducing unfairness between victims creates similar unfairness between injurers. A capacity and cost insensitive approach would yield a more consistent level of care, but at the same time it would make risk imposers fare differently depending on their ability or opportunity to avoid negligence. These abilities and opportunities are partially within a person's control, but not entirely. To the extent that they are not, capacity and cost insensitivity creates unfairness between injurers of precisely the same kind it

---

[17] See, for example, Stevens, *Torts and Rights* (n 11) 109.

mitigates between victims. Mere appeal to fairness, without further argument, does not resolve this tension.

A different type of fairness argument holds that capacity and cost insensitivity is a fair compromise between the interests of injurers and victims considered as distinct groups. In his analysis of the legal standard of care, Allan Beever argues that a subjective standard would be in the best interests of defendants (as a group) while strict liability would be in the best interests of claimants (as a group), and so an objective standard represents a fair balance between these competing sets of interests.[18] Although this argument is directed at the objective standard, it also supports the claim that our moral duties of negligence are capacity and cost insensitive. An objection to it, though, is that it is impossible to strike a fair balance between two broad groups given relevant variations in individual cases. What counts as a fair balance between two parties depends on the features of the particular case and the characteristics of those parties, rather than their membership of a broad, heterogenous group. Where a person is unable to avoid negligence, a capacity insensitive approach is akin to the harshest form of strict liability. Where a person is easily able to avoid it, a cost sensitive approach is akin to applying a subjective standard.

Beever offers a reply to this problem: the characteristics of each party are irrelevant if the other does not know about them in advance.[19] It is unfair for one party to appeal to their own limitations, of which the other is unaware, to escape the burden of liability. Admittedly, there are some situations where information about a person's abilities and limitations changes the character of the interaction in ways that legitimately alter their duties. If a person represents themselves as a professional, for example, they cannot later rely on the fact that they are an amateur to evade liability. But it is difficult to generalize this reasoning. Here the defendant is responsible for creating a reasonable expectation of professional competence, which is not true in the other examples we have considered. In cases where the defendant does nothing to mislead others, why are their limitations irrelevant? Perhaps because we cannot plan around them if we do not know about them in advance. But this answer returns us to an argument we have already disputed, since we frequently expect people to tolerate this form of bad luck and uncertainty.

Similar worries to those sketched previously apply to all attempts to justify capacity and cost insensitivity by reference to an entitlement to expect consistency in our interactions with others. For example, Ripstein argues, again with

---

[18] Beever, *Rediscovering Negligence* (n 12) 81.
[19] ibid, 86.

respect to the legal standard of care, that a subjective standard puts our security too much at the mercy of fate.[20] Similarly, Richard Wright argues that claimants have an interest in sufficiently secure expectations.[21] No doubt Ripstein and Wright are correct that we have such interests, but the question is why should they take precedence over competing interests in being held to a standard that is reasonably attainable for all of the individuals to whom it applies? And why be so concerned about unequally secure expectations amongst victims with respect to the content of the duties that others owe to them when they do not fare equally in so many other ways?

B. The Equality Argument

An alternative argument is offered by Avihay Dorfman. Again, Dorfman is offering a defence of the objective standard of care rather than specifically a capacity and cost insensitive standard, but his arguments lend themselves to both claims. Dorfman's view is also novel because it seeks to justify the objective standard with reference to the interests of defendants as well as claimants, rather than treating it as a burden defendants must bear for the sake of others. His is an equality-based argument consisting of three theses, or facets of equality. The first facet is summarized as follows:

> Treating someone who does not meet the objective standard of care as having acted wrongfully accords with our moral intuitions concerning the respect we owe to our fellow creatures as persons with freestanding claims over their own practical lives, claims for constituting equal worth.[22]

According to the first facet, the objective standard is supported by the respect we owe to defendants given their status as persons with authority over their own practical lives. The second facet indicates that deviating from this standard would undermine this equal respect because it 'communicates the unappealing notions of inferiority and, more generally, hierarchy'.[23] By

---

[20] Arthur Ripstein, *Equality, Responsibility, and the Law* (CUP 1999) 269–70 (hereafter Ripstein, *Equality, Responsibility, and the Law*).

[21] Wright, 'Standards of Care' (n 11), 258–59.

[22] Avihay Dorfman, 'Reasonable Care: Equality as Objectivity' (2012) 31 Law and Philosophy 369, 377 (hereafter Dorfman, *Reasonable Care*). Arthur Ripstein also offers an equality-based argument for the objective standard, though his approach is different from Dorfman's. See Ripstein, *Equality, Responsibility, and the Law* (n 20) 84–87.

[23] Dorfman, *Reasonable Care* (n 22) 391. Stevens appeals to a similar idea to distinguish the law's treatment of children from its treatment of the elderly or those with mental illnesses that affect the level

contrast, adhering to it coheres with tortfeasors' self-conception as able and competent, and avoids patronizing and insulting assumptions about their inadequacies. Of course, this means the disadvantages faced by those with more limited capacities to avoid negligence will be further compounded by a standard of care they are not well equipped to meet. This motivates the third facet of equality, which requires a social effort to neutralize the inegalitarian effects of the objective standard. For example, accessible public transport should be provided to alleviate the harsh consequences on those motorists, such as the sight-impaired, who are unable to reach the standard of a reasonable driver. It is easy to see how this argument could support capacity and cost insensitivity. A standard that expects less of some because they are unable to take the same level of care as others, or because they find it particularly difficult or costly, could be perceived as communicating an insulting message of inequality and inferiority.

There is much to recommend Dorfman's argument, such as the desirability of removing social impediments to meeting a common standard rather than creating exceptions that risk marginalizing disadvantaged groups. We should also note that he does not directly address the two arguments we sketched in the introduction. In fact, on his interpretation of the objective standard, it is not capacity insensitive. It does not demand the impossible, only that those who face disabilities or limitations use whatever means are within their power to meet the standard.

I agree that removing barriers to adherence is preferable to applying a variable standard, but I am less optimistic that these barriers can be eliminated entirely through alterations in the social environment. Also, it is not clear whether Dorfman's claim that the objective standard demands only what is within a person's power is consistent with the rest of his argument. This claim suggests that where some defendant's ability to adhere to the standard is impaired, failing to hold her to that standard violates equality, but where some defendant lacks the ability to meet the standard altogether, failing to hold her to it does not. At least *prima facie*, altering the standard in both of these cases seems to communicate a message of inferiority—in both cases the defendant's physical or psychological limitations or impairments might play a role—so we at least need an explanation of the scope of the principle of equal respect

---

of care they are capable of taking. He says: 'Infantilizing children is acceptable and so we expect less of them. Infantilizing the elderly or the mentally ill is not, and so we expect the same standard of conduct from them as from everyone else.' See Stevens, *Torts and Rights* (n 11) 111.

at play here.[24] Whatever the proper scope of Dorfman's intended argument, one could, in any case, take it further and apply it to both capacity and cost insensitivity.

This brings us to the central question: does Dorfman's equality-based argument justify either of these features? The argument has some affinity with the social egalitarian critique of luck egalitarianism.[25] One strand of this critique is that compensating individuals for their misfortunes amounts to a kind of disdainful pity, which treats the recipients of compensation as inferior to those who give it. Dorfman argues that making exceptions because of defendants' deficiencies fails to recognize them as equals. Conversely, holding them to the same standard respects their self-conception as persons with freestanding claims over their practical lives and avoids subjective judgements.[26]

Dorfman's argument really hinges on whether capacity and cost sensitivity would violate equality-based duties of respect. For this purpose, the claim that deviations from these standards can be disrespectful is insufficient. It must be shown that an injurer's respect-based right to a capacity and cost insensitive standard is not waivable. If the right is waivable, defendants could opt for any relevant limitations to be considered in determining the content of their duty. Surely a rule that gives a defendant the *option* of presenting evidence to demonstrate why they should be held to a lower standard shows greater sensitivity to their self-conception and therefore more respect? Those who find exemptions disrespectful could be measured against an insensitive standard simply by taking no action. But for others, offering such evidence may not be experienced as demeaning. Some of those who are not capable of meeting a higher standard are not members of otherwise marginalized groups, such as junior professionals. Others who are members of such groups may nevertheless not find beneficial exemptions disrespectful. On the contrary, they might think refusing these exemptions is discriminatory as it imposes on them a greater threat of legal responsibility relative to others. Individuals will surely vary, and some may indeed conform to Dorfman's picture, but it seems contradictory to

---

[24] He also emphasizes that 'the fact that people suffer from undeserved deficiency in caring skill does not yield (normative conclusions) concerning how tort law ought to respond to this state of affairs', suggesting that the law might be justified in imposing liability in cases where the defendant truly lacked the ability to meet the standard of care. See Dorfman, *Reasonable Care* (n 22) 398.

[25] Elizabeth S Anderson, 'What is the Point of Equality?' (1999) 109 Ethics 287 and Jonathan Wolff, 'Fairness, Respect, and the Egalitarian Ethos' (1998) 27 Philosophy & Public Affairs 97.

[26] Dorfman suggests that a subjective standard would set the terms of respect according to one's own view of what respect requires, see Dorfman, *Reasonable Care* (n 22) 376. However, it is important to recognize that capacity and cost sensitivity, at least as I understand it here, does not allow each individual's beliefs about what they owe to others to fix the standard of care. The standard is determined by what can reasonably be expected of them given their individual capacities, where the assessment of their individual's capacities is itself an objective matter.

second-guess a person's self-conception. Insofar the standard should be sensitive to it, the argument supports greater optionality, which suggests a waivable right rather than a compulsory insensitive standard.

C. The Mixed Account

So far, we have rejected a number of arguments in favour of a capacity and cost insensitive standard. Despite this, some might remain attached to the idea that those who harm others through blatantly risky activity are wrongdoers, even if they lack the ability to avoid their actions, or if doing so is very costly. Surely the person who drives their car off the road, or blunders a medical procedure, or fails to spot an obvious fire hazard, is guilty of some kind of wrongdoing even if they cannot be reasonably expected to avoid these harms?

Part of this conviction, I think, stems from our unease at allowing victims of dangerous conduct to go uncompensated. However, it does not follow from the arguments above that such victims should go uncompensated, or that their injurers lack duties to compensate them. In fact, according to the four-fold analysis, it is plausible that the negligent and non-negligent alike owe moral duties to compensate for the harm they cause. Since liability is justly imposed on both wrongful and at least some non-wrongful injurers, and the risk-imposing activities of the two groups are outwardly similar, it is tempting to think the source of liability is the same. This is arguably true of the objective standard on the road, which likely encompasses both wrongful and non-wrongful conduct despite being framed in terms of fault.[27]

In light of this, we might adopt a mixed justification of capacity and cost insensitivity.[28] On this view, some injurers who commit negligence are wrongdoers in the moral sense while others are not. Though these others are not wrongdoers, they nevertheless owe conditional duties to their victims. Conditional duties require agents to compensate others *if* certain outcomes

---

[27] See, for example, Mark F Grady, '*Res Ipsa Loquitur* and Compliance error' (1994) 142 University of Pennsylvania Law Review, 887, who argues that the negligence standard on the road is frequently impossible to meet and is therefore a form of strict liability.

[28] Matthew Bedke also criticizes the objective standard of care by appeal to 'ought implies can'. His solution is to defend a wide-scope duty, see 'Explaining Compensatory Duties' 16 Legal Theory 91, 101. This duty explains why both avoidably and unavoidably negligent parties owe compensation but does so in terms of a single duty. This duty mixes importantly different grounds for liability to compensate and is thus subject to the criticisms of the mixed view given here. Moreover, part of the defence of the wide-scope duty is that it protects fungible interests, but this solution will not work for many of the non-fungible interests that negligence protects.

transpire, but do not require them to avoid those outcomes or imply that they were not morally free to do as they did.[29] Taken together, these distinct rationales—wrongdoing and conditional duties—justify a capacity and cost insensitive standard.

The problem with this solution is that it obscures the various sources of liability, buying substantive plausibility at the price of introducing confusion into the way we conceptualize negligence. On the mixed view, the 'wrong' of negligence encompasses both wrongful and non-wrongful conduct (in the moral sense). This makes it highly misleading as it implies that certain acts are impermissible when they are not. Aside from the confusion this would introduce into the 'wrong' of negligence, there is another problem. Although conditional and non-conditional duties have the same outcome in terms of liability, and are therefore similar from an *ex post* perspective, they are crucially different from an *ex ante* perspective. When agents engage in practical reasoning about how they ought to act, reasons and duties feature in their deliberation in different ways depending on whether they occupy an *ex post* or *ex ante* perspective. A non-conditional duty precludes certain action from consideration; a conditional duty imposes a price on certain outcomes that may or may not dissuade the agent from the action in question. This difference in the way these duties should feature in an agent's deliberation is obscured by including them both under the rubric of fault.

Here is another problem with the mixed account. Often, treating one's non-conditional duty as a conditional duty *is itself* a wrong, for it treats an action that an agent is not free to perform as one they are free to perform as long as they are willing to pay the right price.[30] If the legal concept of fault encompasses both types of duty, this further wrong is also obscured. In some cases, this wrong shows sufficient disregard towards the people whose interests ground the non-conditional duty that it might merit a special response such as punitive damages. Consider, for example, the widely discussed case of a manufacturing company that knowingly fails to recall lethally defective products because this is more expensive than paying compensation after the fact. If the company's duty is conditional, there is nothing wrong with this behaviour. If, as is more plausible, the duty is non-conditional, punitive damages may be an appropriate response.

---

[29] See also the description of strict liability as 'conditional fault' in Robert E Keeton, 'Conditional Fault in the Law of Torts' (1959) 72 Harvard Law Review 401, 401.

[30] This is a central criticism of the economic model of torts, which treats all duties as conditional. See Jules L Coleman and Jody Kraus, 'Rethinking the Theory of Legal Rights' (1986) 95 Yale Law Journal 1335.

My critique has rested on the idea that those who violate a capacity and cost insensitive standard but not a capacity and cost sensitive one are not moral wrongdoers. This assumption might be questioned. Even if violating the former standard is not morally wrong independently of the law, we might think, its violation becomes morally wrong once the standard is legally established, in the same way that *mala prohibita* offences do.[31] On this view, the tort of negligence does not encompass wrongs and non-wrongs but rather law-independent wrongs and law-dependent wrongs. Either way, all negligent conduct is morally wrong and so the arguments I have given do not apply.

This argument by analogy with *mala prohibita* offences faces some difficulty. Consider a comparison with possession offences. Suppose a law criminalizing possession of guns is overinclusive in the sense that some people possess guns permissibly. Criminalizing this otherwise permissible behaviour may be legitimate on the grounds that it reduces gun crime overall and those who possess guns permissibly can be expected to give up their guns for the sake of achieving this important aim. The reason why we can expect this is that giving up guns is not particularly costly and therefore it is easy to avoid violating the criminal law.[32] This reasoning is not applicable in defence of a capacity and cost insensitive standard, though, since by definition those who violate this standard (but not a capacity and cost sensitive one) would find it difficult or impossible to avoid violating the law. This makes it more problematic to argue that these individuals commit law-dependent moral wrongs. And this worry is only compounded by the fact that often the impairments that make a person unable to meet a capacity and cost insensitive standard are also the cause of pre-existing social disadvantage.

IV. Defending Capacity and Cost Sensitivity

A. The Undue Burden Argument

There are two main principled arguments in favour of capacity and cost sensitivity. First, depending on a person's abilities and situational limitations, some find it more burdensome to meet a given level of care than others.[33] Some can

---

[31] For this interpretation of *mala prohibita* offences, see Douglas N Husak, 'Guns and Drugs: Case Studies on the Principled Limits of the Criminal Sanction' (2004) 23 Law and Philosophy 437, 476–87.

[32] See Victor Tadros, *Wrongs and Crimes* (Oxford University Press 2016) ch 17.

[33] In this chapter we are concerned with the duties of individuals rather than groups or corporate bodies. Distinct considerations apply to the latter, so it should not be assumed that the arguments in favour of capacity and cost insensitivity apply straightforwardly to them.

do so only through great time or expense; others can do so only with great difficulty or psychological stress. *Psychosis* and *Agoraphobia* are cases in which, assuming it is possible for Xand to avoid causing harm at all, he can do so only at
high levels of cost or difficulty. This means that, if duties in negligence are cost
insensitive, they will sometimes exceed their stringency threshold, and it is not
plausible that duties in negligence are exempt from stringency thresholds. All
duties have a cost that the bearer cannot reasonably be expected to exceed for
the sake of the duty, and duties in negligence are no different. Otherwise, such
duties risk being overly demanding, and avoiding overdemandingness is important for any moral or legal norms that purport to embody a conception of
reasonableness. This argument counts against cost insensitivity, but also capacity insensitivity, since if a person cannot reasonably be expected to bear some
cost to do or avoid doing something, then *a fortiori* that person cannot be reasonably expected to do or avoid doing that thing when they lack the ability to
do so altogether.

It is worth noting that the objection is not just that a defendant may be ex-
cused, but that the burden of performing some action makes it not wrong, or at
least only *pro tanto* rather than all-things-considered wrong. This is important
as it is a response to a common defence of tort against the accusation that the
standards it embodies are not recognizably moral standards. This point is often
made against Holmes' well-known criticism that, though negligence may once
have been bound up with notions of blameworthiness and vengeance, the
moral language of the law is now merely superficial.[34] Holmes' argument relied
on the idea that the objective standard could not properly be understood as
a standard of moral culpability. His critics have emphasized that wrongdoing
can be non-culpable or barely culpable, at least in the sense that it does not
warrant blame or punishment. That the law does not recognize excuses does
not imply that it does not recognize wrongs.[35] The present challenge is not the
same as Holmes', however. The problem is not, as Holmes argued, that the objective standard is divorced from culpability, or that the notion of wrongdoing
is itself a kind of prescientific superstition. Rather, the problem is that the burdens of avoiding certain actions have relevance to the wrongness of those actions, not just their blameworthiness.

This argument in favour of cost sensitivity is motivated by a personalized
conception of reasonableness. We must always ask how much can reasonably
be expected of a particular individual given their capacities and situational

---

[34] Holmes, The Common Law, Lecture III. In *Nettleship v Weston*, Lord Denning notes that a defendant can fall below the objective standard without being blameworthy. See also William Prosser,
Handbook of the Law of Torts (4th edn, West Publishing Company, 1972) s 3.1, at 180.
[35] See John CP Goldberg, 'Inexcusable Wrongs' (2015) 103 California Law Review 467.

limitations. What another individual could do in the same circumstances, or what the same individual could do in different circumstances, is irrelevant to whether that individual commits the moral wrong of negligence. John Gardner offers an objection to 'personalizing' the standard of care in the manner just described: it tends towards logical incoherence. He says:

> Some people, or some people at some times, are incapable of being reasonable. They suffer from severe mental illness, or are in the grip of hallucinogenic drugs, or have worked themselves up into a wild state. If the law attempts to endow the reasonable person with these personal characteristics in the name of compassion, then it ends up demanding that people be judged by the standard of an unreasonable reasonable person, which makes no sense.[36]

This argument about logical incoherence is question-begging, however. It makes no sense to ask what a reasonable unreasonable person would do only because we have already assumed we should apply some independent, depersonalized standard of reasonableness. There is nothing contradictory about rejecting this idea and asking instead what can reasonably be expected of a person in the grip of a psychotic episode. Part of the problem lies in conceptualizing the issue using the framework of a hypothetical reasonable person.[37] It seems contradictory to imagine what a reasonable psychotic person is like, but this apparent contradiction disappears when we reframe the question as what can reasonably be expected of the psychotic person. Clearly such a person is not capable of reaching the standards we associate with an exemplar of reasonableness, but they may be capable of taking more or less care towards others, and the question of what that level of care should be is not a logically incoherent one.

B. The 'Ought Implies Can' Argument

The second argument applies specifically to capacity rather than cost sensitivity. It is that our moral duties cannot violate 'ought implies can' and our legal duties should not violate it either, or at least there is a strong *pro tanto* reason against legal duties violating it. We appealed to a similar idea in our critique of the mixed justification of capacity and cost insensitivity. We can now develop this into a general argument for the claim that 'ought implies can'

---

[36] John Gardner, *Torts and Other Wrongs* (Oxford University Press 2021) 295.
[37] For criticism of personification in legal formulations of the objective standard along feminist lines, see Mayo Moran, *Rethinking the Reasonable Person: An Egalitarian Reconstruction of the Objective Standard* (Oxford University Press 2003).

should constrain the law. Recall that *Muscle Spasm*, *Safe* and *Rare Bleed* are all cases in which Xand lacks the ability to perform some action, and *Psychosis* and *Agoraphobia* might be examples too, depending on the empirical relationship between mental illness and our capacity to be reasonable. Any legal duty that requires Xand to perform the action in question despite this would violate 'ought implies can'.

As this argument rests squarely on the appeal of 'ought implies can', we should begin by considering the rationale behind the maxim, and why it should apply to legal as well as moral duties. One rationale is that it is unfair to require people to do what they cannot, and 'ought implies can' prevents this unfairness. This does not capture the main motivation for 'ought implies can', though. One way to see this is that the maxim constrains reasons as well as duties, yet it is not unfair to posit a reason to do the impossible because not all reasons are binding. It would be odd to interpret the existence of a reason to do something as unfair if one is not required to do it. Relatedly, 'ought implies can' also constrains prudential reasons: there is no reason to turn one's hat into money, regardless of whether the money is for oneself (a prudential cause) or for charity (a moral cause). Fairness cannot explain why prudential and moral reasons alike are ruled out by the impossibility of acting on them. These observations suggest that fairness is, at best, a partial justification.

Some defend the maxim by observing that duties to do the impossible are pointless.[38] One way to understand this claim is that pointless duties have undesirable consequences. Either they will not be fulfilled or, worse, people will waste time with failed attempts to fulfil them. As we will see in Chapter 5, critics of this view have a response: positing a reason or duty does not necessarily require an attempt to fulfil it. But there are other reasons to doubt this view. *Rejecting* 'ought implies can' might have better consequences in certain circumstances. Suppose that imposing duties that people are sometimes unable to fulfil induces them to exercise better care than a duty that imposes lower expectations. If this were true, the instrumentalist justification of 'ought implies can' would have no purchase. But intuitively, 'ought implies can' would still be applicable. The maxim may have some pragmatic value, but this does not explain its deep significance for practical reasoning.

The pointlessness objection should be understood in a different way. It is often pointed out that 'ought implies can' allows reasons and duties to be action-guiding. What motivates this argument is not the worry that people will

---

[38] For this view, see Bart Streumer, 'Reasons and Impossibility' (2007) 136 Philosophical Studies 351, 365.

attempt the impossible, but that the potential for action-guidance is a feature of reasons that allows them to play their proper role in practical deliberation. An agent cannot consult her reasons to decide what to do if they require the impossible. This constraint on what constitutes a practical reason reflects the potential for all reasons to be instantiated in action. For reasons to be practical and function as reasons to act, they must have this potential. If not, the function of practical deliberation as a process geared towards deciding how to act is thwarted. This potential has nothing to do with probability: we can have a reason for an action that is unlikely to be acted upon due to cost, difficulty, or weakness of will. But if an agent has *no* prospect of performing some action, there cannot be a reason to do it if her deliberation is to maintain its function as a process geared towards deciding what to do.

Unlike the fairness argument, this is not a normative defence of 'ought implies can'. A contrast is sometimes drawn between normative and semantic interpretations.[39] On a semantic interpretation, 'ought' presupposes 'can', in the sense that 'ought' questions do not arise regarding impossible actions. The functional argument just sketched does not insist on the validity of 'ought implies can' for purely semantic reasons, however. It is not based on any claim about the meaning of the word 'ought'. Instead, reasons that violate 'ought implies can' lack a feature that is fundamental to their role in practical deliberation. This could be taken as *evidence* that 'ought' semantically implies 'can', since it would be curious if the meaning of the term did not reflect this function, but the argument does not rely on this semantic claim. Reasons to do the impossible are not necessarily *unintelligible* on this view. They are ruled out because they cannot perform their proper function in practical deliberation.

A virtue of this justification is that it answers the argument sometimes made by critics of 'ought implies can', that rejecting the maxim does not require giving up the idea that obligations are action-guiding.[40] According to these critics, unfulfillable obligations can guide us by requiring *ex post* actions such as apology or repair, so the traditional defence that 'ought implies can' is necessary for action-guidance fails. The problem with this view is that impossible obligations cannot offer *ex ante* action-guidance, and *ex ante* action-guidance is integral to the way reasons and duties function in the deliberative sphere. When an agent is deliberating about what to do *ex ante*, it is not enough to

---

[39] Ian Carter, '"Ought" Implies "Practical Possibility"' in Ian Carter and Mario Ricciardi (eds), *Freedom, Power and Political Morality* (Palgrave 2001) 79–80.

[40] Brian Talbot, 'The Best Argument for "Ought Implies Can" is a Better Argument Against "Ought Implies Can"' (2016) 3 Ergo 14 and John Gardner, 'Reasons and Abilities: Some Preliminaries' (2013) 58 American Journal of Jurisprudence 63.

know that their impossible-to-achieve obligation may guide their action retro-spectively once they have inevitably failed to discharge it. On the functional view, duties must be prospectively action-guiding to fulfil their role in practical deliberation.

It might be objected that this rationale applies only to 'ought implies can' as a constraint on *moral* reasons and duties. Why should the maxim constrain legal duties? Here we can refer back to our discussion of the relationship between moral and legal duties in Chapter 2. Legal duties that violate 'ought implies can' cannot be justified in relation to moral duties, which means they are subject to the *restricted freedom* and *undue burden* objections.

There is also a deeper reason why both normative domains should, at least *pro tanto*, respect the maxim. Morality and the law both embody functional roles in our lives as agents engaged in practical reasoning. To perform these roles, it is not necessary that the law enforce all our moral duties or treat mor-ality as an absolute constraint on legal duties, but it is necessary that legal duties, like moral duties, can fulfil their function in our practical reasoning from an *ex ante* perspective. Duties that violate 'ought implies can' cannot do this. Without adhering to the maxim, legal duties are robbed of their potential to feature in practical deliberation the way moral duties do. This divergence is concerning because it threatens the idea that both morality and law address us as deliberating agents.[41]

This guidance function is importantly connected to the rule of law. Joseph Raz describes the rule of law, understood as the standard for measuring the law's ability to guide behaviour, as the 'specific excellence' of the law.[42] Jeremy Waldron says the law 'strains as far as possible' to normatively guide.[43] Legal rules that do not adhere to 'ought implies can' also fuel concerns about the erosion of rule of law values, at least with respect to the subset of defendants who are not able to meet a capacity insensitive standard. Arguments for cap-acity and cost insensitivity based on maintaining the guidance function of the law therefore rest on a central irony: to maintain the ability of the law to guide overall, it is necessary to make it less able to guide for certain individuals.

The problem is not just that a duty that violates 'ought implies can' does not guide action, or does so only *ex post*, but rather that it snarls up the deliberative

---

[41] See also HLA Hart, *The Concept of Law* (first published 1961, 3rd edn, Oxford University Press 2012) 42, 59, 86. Hart aims to refute the general conception of legal obligations as sanction-backed threats or conditional duties. Our argument is slightly different. The problem I am outlining in this sec-tion is with an attempt to mix conditional and non-conditional duties within the rubric of negligence.

[42] Joseph Raz, *The Authority of Law: Essays on Law and Morality* (Oxford University Press 1979) 225.

[43] Jeremy Waldron, 'How the Law Protects Dignity' (2012) 71 Cambridge Law Journal 200, 206.

process itself. Consider a comparison with weakness of will. A duty imposed on the weak-willed agent may not be acted upon, but it can fulfil its function at the deliberative stage. The agent can reason that, considering all relevant factors, this is the action they ought to perform. They can complete this process and decide to act, even if they do not follow this through because they find themselves lacking motivation. The duty that demands the impossible, on the other hand, cannot feature in the agent's deliberation even in this limited way. It is unfit for the deliberative process from the outset.

Of course, agents can consult reasons that violate 'ought implies can' in one sense. They can see them as threats of possible sanctions that they might wish to take steps to avoid. For those who see all legal duties in this way, this is unproblematic. However, for those who think legal duties are genuinely normatively binding, it is a problem if some of those duties cannot feature in the deliberative processes of some of the agents to whom they apply. Perhaps these instances are sufficiently rare to pose no practical threat to the law's functioning. But this should not encourage us to lose sight of how radically a legal duty that violates 'ought implies can' alters the law's understanding of us as deliberating agents.

It might be objected that this understanding of how the law should address us as deliberating agents gives us too much credit. In reality, we are self-interested, biased, and our reasoning is riddled with errors. We are likely to overestimate what others should be doing for us whilst underestimating what we should be doing for others. A capacity and cost insensitive standard might correct for these flaws, demanding more than is morally required of us. If doing this leads to better outcomes, then perhaps this is what the law should do. But then we must recognize that these better outcomes come at a cost. Defending a capacity and cost insensitive standard based on enforcement factors threatens the idea that the tort of negligence can be coherently understood as a form of wrongdoing. Instead, it makes demands and imposes burdens on people that are *pro tanto* morally wrongful. These may be justified by appeal to the need to enforce legal standards in non-ideal circumstances, but if so, this further undermines any claim that the tort of negligence can be coherently understood as a form of wrongdoing.

C. The Variability Objection

There is a worry about capacity and cost sensitivity that is well summed up by Robert Stevens, who states that: 'Our right not to be carelessly injured which is good against the rest of the world is not infinitely variable according to the competence of each person.'[44] The concern is that adopting a capacity and cost sensitive approach to negligence would lead to an overly variable standard in which the content of each person's duty would be different depending on their capacities. This 'infinitely variable' standard would undermine equality of security for potential victims of negligence, which in turn would make it difficult to plan around one's own duties and those owed to us by others.

We addressed this worry earlier in our discussion of the fairness argument. There I responded that a simple appeal to equal security is not dispositive. A critic might push back, arguing that, though a balance must be struck, the more a rule frustrates equal security, the more problematic it becomes. A capacity and cost sensitive standard would be endlessly variable; each defendant would have a different duty, relativized to their particular capacities. The harm that this would cause to potential victims would be extensive enough to outweigh any unfairness such a standard would cause to the occasional injurer.

However, the worry that a capacity and cost sensitive standard would be 'infinitely variable' is overstated. This is because the best understanding of this standard endorses what I called *threshold* cost sensitivity rather than *proportional* cost sensitivity. According to the former, the content of our duty to take care does not vary proportionally with the cost or difficulty of doing so. Cost and difficulty are relevant only when they are so significant as to exceed the stringency threshold of the duty. The duty's content is therefore similar for differently situated and differently able people as long as the cost of fulfilling it falls below this threshold.

This is true of many of our other moral duties. Compare the saint who satisfies their duties gladly and derives gratification from doing so, with the sinner who battles powerful cravings. Clearly the saint and sinner bear different costs in fulfilling their duties—in fact the saint sees them as a blessing rather than a burden—but their most important duties are nevertheless similar in content. For example, they are subject to the same duties not to kill, injure, or steal, though the sinner must bear greater costs to fulfil them, because these costs do not exceed the stringency threshold of their duties. Similarly, rejecting cost sensitivity in negligence does not necessitate tailoring the duty to the capacities of each individual. Rather, it involves determining the maximum cost or burden some individual can reasonably be expected to bear for the sake of taking care not to harm others, and when life and limb is at stake, there is every reason to think this threshold is quite high.

---

[44] Stevens, *Torts and Rights* (n 11) 109. See also Tindall CJ's statement in *Vaughan v Menlove* that inquiring into the capabilities of the defendant would create a rule 'as variable as the length of the foot of each individual' (1837) 3 Bing NC 468 475; 132 ER 490, 493.

Let's make this point about variable standards a little more precise (those put off by crude numerical illustrations, look away now!). Consider two scales, one measuring the extent of a person's ability to take care (A1 ... A10) and another measuring the level of care this person is expected to take (C1 ... C10). Now here are two ways of understanding cost sensitivity. On one version, a person with ability A1 is required to take C1 amount of care, a person with ability A2 is required to take C2 amount of care, and so on. This is proportional cost sensitivity. On the second version, we can stipulate that everyone is expected to take C8 amount of care unless doing so surpasses the stringency threshold of their duties. And let's also stipulate that those with ability A2 and below cannot take C8 amount of care without exceeding this threshold. On this second version, all people with ability A2 and above are expected to take the same level of care, and only those with ability A1 are exempt due to costliness. This is threshold cost sensitivity. As this schema demonstrates, the latter approach does not treat the expected level of care as proportional to a person's ability. Rather, it recognizes that, for some individuals, meeting a given level of care exceeds what can reasonably be expected of them, and therefore implies that, if they fail to meet this level, they have not committed the wrong of negligence.

So far, we have been discussing cases involving agents with lower than average capacities to avoid harming others. What about cases where agents have greater than average capacities? Should we expect more from such agents, and if so, does this resuscitate the variability objection? Consider:

> *Emergency:* Xand and Yoona are assisting in an emergency in which lives are at risk, applying bandages and treating wounds. They can both be expected to give up five hours of their time to do this before the costs to them are high enough to cancel any duty to assist further. Xand is highly skilled and can treat ten patients in this time, while Yoona, who represents the average ability, can treat five patients.

Should Xand treat five patients—the average number—and finish his duties early, or should he treat ten patients and finish at the same time as Yoona? Assuming the only relevant cost to the rescuers is time, it is plausible that Xand should treat ten patients instead of five. His greater capabilities mean that more can reasonably be expected of him before his duties are too demanding. Does this raise the variable standard objection again in a different guise? No, because both Xand and Yoona are subject to the same stringency threshold—five hours of time—it is just that Xand can do more good within this threshold than Yoona.

This means that Xand cannot appeal to his superior capacities to make his duties lighter than Yoona's. We expect individuals to make effective use of the costs morality requires them to bear, and this means that those with higher skills can often be expected to do more or achieve better outcomes within the bounds set by those costs. This also means less capable people must bear costs up to the threshold to 'catch up' with the level of care others can offer at lower cost, just as the more capable person may not free themselves of costs because they are able to do what others can do at low cost. These results are driven by the same factor: the stringency threshold of our duties. When the costs of some action are too high there is no duty for a person to perform it, but when the costs are low, often we can expect a person to do more than they would be required to do if the costs were higher.

There is a kind of equality in operation here. It is not equality in outcome, or equality in the level of care we expect of different people. Rather, it is equality in the burden we can each be expected to bear for the sake of fulfilling our moral duties. Given differences in capacity, resources, and circumstances, this equality inevitably leads to some inequality of outcome, but it is easy to over-estimate this when we ignore stringency thresholds. The less capable are not necessarily expected to take less care, except in those relatively rare cases in which they are unable to do so, or it is too burdensome.

Conclusion

In this chapter I argued that principled defences of capacity and cost sensitivity fail. Principled factors differ from enforcement factors in that they are not solely concerned with the problems of enforcing rules in non-ideal circumstances. Consequently, principled arguments support cost insensitivity in moral negligence duties as well as our legal ones, although the arguments we have considered generally focus on the law of negligence.

There are two arguments in favour of capacity and cost sensitivity. One is that they prevent our duties being overly demanding and another is that capacity sensitivity, in particular, ensures that they function correctly in our *ex ante* reasoning by adhering to 'ought implies can'. We also defended capacity and cost sensitivity against a range of different objections, including the worry that it makes the content of our duties in negligence infinitely variable. The upshot of our discussion is that our moral negligence duties are capacity and cost sensitive, and if capacity and cost *in*sensitivity in law can be defended at all, it must be on the basis of enforcement factors alone.

5

Outcome Responsibility

Introduction

We have seen that harming others through negligent conduct is one of the main grounds of corrective duties. According to *the responsiveness thesis* (Chapter 3, pt IV), we have powerful reasons to respond to our wrongdoing by prioritizing the values our initial duty was designed to serve, and when wrongdoing leads to harm, this response typically includes negating and counterbalancing (Chapter 3, pts I–III). We have also seen that corrective duties sometimes arise independently of wrongdoing when the *ex ante* permissibility of some action is conditional on compensating *ex post*.

In Chapters 6 and 7 we defend two other grounds of corrective duties that don't necessitate wrongdoing, filling out the final two limbs of the four-fold analysis. Consider:

Well: Zelda is blown down a well by a freak wind, crushing Abbas who is at the bottom. Neither Zelda nor Abbas had a better opportunity to avoid placing themselves in this situation.[1]

Truck: Zelda gets into their truck, knowing that even careful driving poses a small but foreseeable risk of serious harm. Abbas, a pedestrian, steps in front of the truck and is injured.[2]

Well and *Truck* differ because, in *Well*, Zelda harms Abbas *non-responsibly*, that is, their agency is not meaningfully involved in the causal chain that leads to Abbas' harm. Zelda does not choose to undertake some act they know, or ought to know, creates a reasonably foreseeable risk of harm to others, but rather finds themselves unexpectedly posing a threat via the operation of external forces. In *Truck*, although Zelda is also at the mercy of external forces, their actions are responsible in the sense that they choose to pose a risk of harm by driving even

---

[1] Robert Nozick, *Anarchy, State, and Utopia* (Blackwell 1974) 34.
[2] For discussion of cases such as *Truck*, see Jeff McMahan, 'The Basis of Moral Liability to Defensive Killing' (2005) 15 Philosophical Issues 386 (hereafter McMahan, *Defensive Killing*) and Bernard Williams, *Moral Luck* (Cambridge University Press 1981) 27–29 (hereafter Williams, *Moral Luck*).

Wrongs, Harms, and Compensation. Adam Slavny, Oxford University Press. © Adam Slavny 2023.
DOI: 10.1093/oso/9780192864567.003.0005

though this choice is justified. Jeff McMahan defends an account of liability to defensive harm based on responsibility understood in this sense.[3] Similarly, Bernard Williams argues that the truck driver's actions generate agent-regret, a species of regret attached to the causal consequences of one's voluntary actions even if one is not at fault.[4]

Despite their differences, *Well* and *Truck* are similar insofar as, in both cases, Zelda harms Abbas without any culpable or impermissible conduct. If Zelda owes corrective duties to Abbas in *Well* or *Truck* or both, it follows that the grounds of these duties are not limited to wrongdoing. They would be conditional duties, that is, duties to compensate if one's action results in harm rather than primary duties to avoid harm, the violation of which would be a wrong. If conditional duties exist, they represent an alternative route to compensatory liability that operates alongside the familiar primary/secondary duty model.

One way to defend conditional duties is by appealing to outcome responsibility. This notion was developed by Tony Honoré and others have since extended and refined versions of it. Broadly speaking, Honoré argues that we are responsible for the outcomes we bring about, or that are properly attributable to us, despite not being fully within our control, and despite our not being blameworthy for them. This does not generate a duty to compensate on its own, but does so in certain circumstances, some of which we will review shortly. In particular, Honoré thinks this idea vindicates legal liability to pay compensation of the kind we typically find in tort law, specifically the objective standard of care in negligence and some strict liability regimes.[5]

'Responsibility' is a notoriously slippery notion, though. Here we are interested in whether outcome responsibility can explain conditional duties to

---

[3] Specifically, his view implies that Zelda is liable to be killed in *Truck* on the grounds that their responsible decision to pose a permissible but foreseeable risk means that it is fairer that they bear the burden of harm than Abbas. See McMahan, *Defensive Killing* (n 2).

[4] Williams, *Moral Luck* (n 2). Two caveats should be made at the outset. First, some distinguish between guilt and remorse. Remorse can be considered a sub-category of guilt that attaches to one's wrongful conduct. Guilt is sometimes understood in a broader way, for example one might feel guilty (but not remorseful) about failing to achieve personal goals. In this chapter I use the term 'guilt' rather than 'remorse', but I am always thinking of cases that involve moral wrongdoing. Second, some argue that agent-regret can follow from our non-voluntary actions too. I am sympathetic to this view but will not commit to it here. For a defence of this claim, see Michael Zhao, 'Guilt Without Perceived Wrongdoing' (2020) 48 Philosophy & Public Affairs 285.

[5] See Tony Honoré, 'The Morality of Tort Law-Questions and Answers' in David G Owen (ed), *The Philosophical Foundations of Tort Law* (Oxford University Press 1997) 73, 78. See also Stephen R Perry, 'Honoré on Responsibility for Outcomes' in Peter Cane and John Gardner (eds), *Relating to Responsibility: Essays in Honour of Tony Honoré on his 80th Birthday* (Hart 2001) 61 (hereafter Perry, 'Honoré on Responsibility').

compensate. We are therefore using 'responsibility' in its allocative sense.[6] To say a person is responsible for a harm in this sense is just to say they have a duty to repair or compensate for it, which implies nothing about whether this person committed a wrong or whether this wrong is the basis of their allocative responsibility. This is not the only sense in which Honoré used the term, but this is the thinnest type of responsibility necessary to vindicate conditional duties.

Any account of outcome responsibility must answer three questions. First, what outcomes that we cause are we responsible for? We might be responsible for all of them, only those we could have foreseen, only those we in fact foresee, or some other subset. An issue of particular importance is whether we can be outcome responsible for harms that do not flow from our voluntarily actions. The contrast between voluntary and non-voluntary actions is exemplified by *Well* and *Truck*. In the former, Zelda has no agential involvement in the threat while in the latter they voluntarily impose a risk, albeit a permissible one. Some writers such as Stephen Perry defend versions of outcome responsibility that apply only to harms the agent could have avoided, while others such as John Gardner defend broader versions that, at least on my interpretation, can encompass non-responsible harms.

Secondly, what form does outcome responsibility take? It might give us reasons to apologize, offer an explanation, feel bad, compensate, or some combination of these. If outcome responsibility is to justify some form of tort liability, it must be shown that injurers have reasons to compensate in the sort of situations in which the law imposes liability, which cannot be taken for granted. Even *reasons* to compensate fall short. We have many reasons to do things we are not required to do, and which it would be unjust for third parties, including the state, to force us to do. Reasons are cheap; enforceable duties are dearer.

The final question is in some respects the most important one. Why are we outcome responsible when we are? Insisting that we must compensate because we are outcome responsible is an empty claim unless we can provide some basis for accepting outcome responsibility as a normative practice that is indispensable or at least worth keeping. We will begin with this question because exploring it will help us answer the first two; understanding why we are outcome responsible should tell us when we are so responsible, and what actions such responsibility entails. With these clarifications made, let's begin by considering some of the arguments that have been put forward to explain outcome responsibility.

---

[6] This is a narrower version of TM Scanlon's concept of 'substantive responsibility'. See his distinction between substantive and attributional responsibility in *What We Owe to Each Other* (Harvard University Press 1998) 248–51.

I. Four Arguments for Outcome Responsibility

A. The Fairness Argument

One argument Honoré gives for outcome responsibility can be called *the Fairness Argument*. This states that outcome responsibility, here understood as a system of allocative responsibility of roughly the kind we find in tort law, is fair if it is 'impartial, reciprocal, and over a period, beneficial'. Honoré recognizes that impartiality and reciprocity are not sufficient conditions for fairness. Take impartiality first. Imagine a system that imposes the burden of repair by lottery but is impartial in its application: those who administer the system are not subject to bias, everyone has an equal chance of being selected, and any other condition we might associate with impartiality is satisfied. Few would dispute that such a lottery is substantively unjust even though it is impartial in its implementation, which shows us that impartiality, by itself, does not ensure substantive fairness.

Reciprocity is also insufficient, since the lottery system described above may be reciprocal in Honoré's sense, which is that 'each … person is entitled to apply it to others and they to him'.[7] As a general matter, it is not clear that reciprocity is even necessary for fairness, though this is a more complex issue that I leave for the next chapter (see Chapter 6 for some criticisms of George Fletcher's Non-Reciprocity Theory). The normative force of *the Fairness Argument*, then, must derive primarily from the appeal to benefit. The system is fair, on this view, because in the long term it benefits those to whom it applies.

There are several problems with *the Fairness Argument* so understood. First, from an *ex post* perspective it is untrue that everyone benefits from a system of outcome responsibility. The workings of chance mean that, like any lottery, there are winners and losers. In response to this problem, the argument might be recast from an *ex ante* perspective, appealing to expected benefits rather than actual benefits. But this variation is also difficult to support. Outcome responsibility is subject to two forms of luck: circumstantial luck (luck in the circumstances in which one finds oneself) and constitutive luck (luck in one's traits, dispositions, and capacities). Bad circumstantial luck bites harder against those who are exposed to a greater risk of liability, such as those with dangerous jobs, those who live in overpopulated areas, those who cause statistically unlikely accidents, and so on. Bad constitutive luck bites harder against those with limited capacities, such as those with physical or mental

---

[7] Tony Honoré, *Responsibility and Fault* (Hart 1999) 26 (hereafter Honoré, *Responsibility and Fault*).

impairments that affect their ability to take care not to harm others. In short, the *propensity* to be negatively affected by bad luck is itself unevenly distributed,[8] so for the unluckiest individuals, it is far from clear that outcome responsibility is beneficial even *ex ante*.

In response to this problem, Honoré says that 'all those who possess a minimum capacity stand to profit from a system of outcome allocation most of the time and, if there is a minority of permanent losers, they teeter on the edge of incapacity'.[9] The idea is that, since the majority of those with capacity to face liability are expected to benefit and most of those who will not benefit lack this capacity, there is only a small minority who will lose out under the system. This reply mitigates but does not eliminate the objection. The group of non-beneficiaries will include those who are less physically and psychologically able to avoid harming, despite being above the threshold for legal capacity. Members of this group are also likely to face pre-existing social and economic disadvantages, and Honoré gives no explanation why these individuals should accept a system that compounds this disadvantage. Any system of allocation that benefits the already advantaged many by concentrating costs on the already disadvantaged few surely requires more in the way of justification.

One could alter the account so that only those who are expected to benefit under the system face liability. This would be a substantial amendment because, although Honoré says those who will not benefit 'teeter on the brink of incapacity', the fact remains that minimum capacity for responsibility and minimum expected benefit are two separate thresholds. But even if liability rules are defined so as to ensure that everyone is expected to benefit, this would not vindicate *the Fairness Argument* because the benefits and burdens of liability might still be distributed unequally. We need an argument for the claim that minimum expected benefit is sufficient for distributive fairness. I doubt any such argument is forthcoming as this claim is not very plausible.

First of all, we need to specify a baseline against which minimum benefit can be measured. Is the idea that people generally benefit from a system of outcome responsibility compared to other systems for allocating the costs of injuries, or no system at all, or what?[10] Before this baseline is specified, it is difficult to know what it means to say that the system benefits most people in the long

---

[8] This is a variation of John Rawls' argument that 'no one deserves his place in the distribution of native endowments, any more than one deserves one's initial starting place in society'. See *Theory of Justice* (first published 1971, Harvard University Press 2005) 104.

[9] Honoré, *Responsibility and Fault* (n 7) 27.

[10] For a similar criticism, see GA Cohen's objection to the 'Lockean proviso' in *Self-Ownership, Freedom, and Equality* (Cambridge University Press 1995) 76–78.

run. The baseline issue brings to the fore that outcome responsibility must be justified against other available options, and this means we need an explanation why it should be preferred to those that distribute the burdens of accidents more equally, or according to moral priority, or some other criterion of distributive fairness. To assume that minimum benefit is sufficient is to bypass one of the problems that motivated the work of John Rawls, Ronald Dworkin, and a generation of scholars of distributive justice, namely that differences in our abilities to secure certain benefits and avoid certain costs are unearned, unchosen, and therefore morally arbitrary, so we should not tolerate a system that allows these features to generate significant inequalities in the way peoples' lives turn out. This is not to say that the distribution of benefits plays no role in justifying corrective duties. We will explore this idea in Chapter 6. But *the Fairness Argument* does not, by itself, justify a general regime of liability that corresponds to pre-existing tort practices.

B. The Consistency Argument

Let's move on to another argument in Honoré's discussion, which we can call *the Consistency Argument*. This is the claim that, if we want to enjoy the good that flows from the exercise of our agency, we must also accept responsibility for the bad. In a social context, this means we cannot enjoy praise for our achievements whilst simultaneously distancing ourselves from our failures. In a tort law context, it means if we want the freedom to engage in risky activities, we must accept responsibility for the unintended but harmful outcomes that flow from them. Liability to compensate is imposed in the name of forcing us to be consistent in our claims to freedom and responsibility.

An initial problem for this argument is that, insofar as allocative responsibility is imposed on people without their having to 'claim' anything, it is unclear how appeal to consistency escapes the objections levelled against *the Fairness Argument*. For those who lose more than they gain from the system, why should receipt of a modest expected benefit bind them, on pain of inconsistency, to accept a much greater expected burden?[11]

Perhaps the idea is that we proactively claim the benefits that flow from our action, and this is why we cannot disclaim the burden of redress when we cause

---

[11] Appeal to hypothetical agreement devices will not help either, since most of these devices attempt to implement choice situations that are, to some degree, insensitive to luck or morally arbitrary features of our identities and circumstances.

harm. This understanding of *the Consistency Argument* ignores the fact that people differ in the extent to which they are willing to accept credit and responsibility for their achievements and failures. Granted, we are suspicious of people who credit themselves for their achievements while blaming others for their failures. But our objection to such people is not based on intrapersonal consistency. After all, we are not affronted by people who take responsibility for their failures while distancing themselves from their achievements, even though they are just as inconsistent as those who do things the other way around. This suggests that disclaiming one's responsibility is objectionable independently of whether it is coupled with taking credit for one's successes. If so, there must be some independent justification for responsibility besides consistency.

Consider someone who recognizes the deep role that luck plays in their endeavours, both good and bad, and limits their responses accordingly. This person accepts neither credit for their achievements nor blame for their failures. They refuse compensation from those who harm them, but equally refuse to compensate those whom they harm. We might respect the integrity of such a person, but I doubt we would be comfortable allowing them to disown their corrective duties. If this is right, it is further evidence that *the Consistency Argument* fails to pick out the correct grounds of outcome responsibility.

C. Duties to Succeed

The third and fourth arguments have been advanced by John Gardner in his development and defence of Honoré's ideas. The third may be called *the Duty to Succeed Argument*. It appeals to Gardner's distinction between reasons to try and reasons to succeed to show how an agent can be outcome responsible for things they not only permissibly bring about but cannot avoid bringing about. We will dwell on Gardner's argument a little longer than the others for a few reasons. First, it is quite complicated and has multiple interlocking claims. Second, it directly contradicts the arguments presented in the Chapter 4 in favour of capacity and cost sensitivity in negligence, especially the 'ought implies can' argument (Gardner rejects the maxim explicitly, or at least the version of that maxim I defended there). Finally, it casts doubt on the claim that we sometimes have conditional duties to compensate, which is a general theme of this book. The *Duty to Succeed Argument* treats fault cases and non-fault cases alike in the sense that duties to compensate are based on the violation of prior duties even if the duty-bearer was unable to fulfil them.

Gardner conceives of strict liability duties as straightforward duties-not-to-harm, and primary duties in negligence as duties-not-to-harm-through-unreasonable-conduct.[12] The common element here is that both types of duties require securing certain outcomes, regardless of the difficulty or possibility of doing so. Gardner motivates his view by appealing to a prior distinction between reasons to try and reasons to succeed. He claims that a reason to try to x is not a reason to x but a reason to act because the act will hopefully bring about x. It is a mistake to assume reasons to try and reasons to succeed are identical. To support the distinction, he first argues that, if acting with a view to x-ing would not contribute to one's x-ing, one may have a reason to x without a reason to try to x.[13] Consider:

> *Truck 2*: As a result of an unforeseeable muscle spasm, Zelda accelerates their vehicle towards Abbas, a pedestrian. Zelda does everything they can to avoid the accident, but they are not in control of their body and the collision is inevitable.

Since no amount of trying will avert the harm, Zelda lacks a reason to try to avert it; however, they retain a straightforward reason not to hit Abbas. Gardner applies the same reasoning to cases of failure to save.

> *Drowning*: Zelda stands on a clifftop looking on helplessly as Abbas drowns below. Zelda flails and waves and sinks to their knees, desperate to find a way to rescue Abbas. Eventually Zelda realizes that nothing they can do will have any chance of saving him.

On Gardner's view, if Zelda does not have a reason to succeed in these cases, they could walk away without compunction. Yet we would expect the opposite of them, regarding them with the utmost suspicion if they did not give their own involvement in the harm a second thought. The situation leaves a 'trace' on Zelda's life and moral agency,[14] and anyone who has read the harrowing testimonies of those who have unintentionally killed others will know that the

---

[12] John Gardner, *Torts and Other Wrongs* (Oxford University Press 2019) ch 5 (hereafter Gardner, *Torts and Other Wrongs*).

[13] Gardner also suggests one may have reasons to try that do not correspond with reasons to succeed. If Zelda's daughter is drowning, for example, Zelda may have a reason to try and save her as an expression of love, even if such an attempt is doomed. See John Gardner, 'The Wrongdoing that Gets Results' (2004) 18 Philosophical Perspectives 53, 57. Since such reasons cannot be the basis of strict duties to compensate, we will not consider them further here.

[14] Gardner, *Torts and Other Wrongs* (n 12) 165.

term 'trace' is an understatement.[15] The responses that agents typically have to cases like *Truck 2* and *Drowning* are explained, Gardner thinks, by their unmet reasons to succeed.

Gardner also argues that reasons to succeed are primary in the sense that the intelligibility of reasons to try depends on the existence of reasons to succeed. The act of trying logically requires something one is trying to achieve. If one has no reason to x, one cannot intelligibly try to x, as one cannot act for the reason that what one does will bring about x. Thus, if there are no non-derivative reasons to succeed, then there can be no derivative reasons to try. Consider:

Accessibility: Zelda is a wheelchair user. They are unable to ride the bus under current circumstances as it is not wheelchair accessible.

On Gardner's view, Zelda has a reason to ride the bus even though it is not wheelchair accessible. Of course, Zelda does not have a reason fruitlessly to attempt to ride the bus (this would be a reason to try), they just have a reason to ride the bus. This reason explains a host of other reasons derived from it, such as the reason to lobby for improved accessibility on public transport, which could not otherwise be explained satisfactorily.[16]

These two arguments are intended to establish the existence of reasons to succeed in bringing about outcomes (or avoiding them), despite having no reasons to try and bring about these outcomes (or avoid them), and despite it being impossible for the agent to bring them about (or avoid them). Gardner claims that such reasons, when agents inevitably fail to act on them, give rise to reasons to respond via *the continuity thesis*, which include reasons to compensate. Once *reasons* to succeed are on the table, it is a short step to the conclusion that sometimes these reasons have mandatory force; that is, they are also *duties* to succeed. Gardner cautions against drawing this inference too quickly,[17] but it is inevitable that some of these reasons will be undefeated some of the time, in which case they must also be duties. In this way, Gardner's argument about reasons to succeed might support some form of allocative outcome responsibility. Not only this, but it does so without accepting conditional duties. For

---

[15] Several powerful testimonies from individuals who have harmed people unintentionally are collected in https://accidentalimpacts.org.

[16] Ulrike Heuer offers a similar argument in defence of reasons to do the impossible. See Ulrike Heuer, 'Reasons and Impossibility' (2010) 147 Philosophical Studies 235.

[17] John Gardner, 'As Inconclusive as Ever' (2019) 19 Jerusalem Review of Legal Studies 204, pt 6.

Gardner, corrective duties that follow these unavoidable harms are neverthe-less grounded in the breach of prior duties.

The two objections discussed in Chapter 4—the *undue burden* objection and the objection based on 'ought implies can'—also apply here. 'Ought implies can' is an important constraint on both moral and legal duties since both address agents when they are prospectively reasoning about what to do. Reasons and duties cannot perform this function if they cannot be acted upon.[18] Similarly, it is unfair to burden people with duties that they are not capable of fulfilling, especially when violation of these duties comes at the serious price of legal liability.

Why then does Gardner embrace this picture of reasons and duties? His ar-gument takes the form of an inference to the best explanation. Gardner thinks positing reasons to succeed is the best way of explaining derivative reasons (as in *Accessibility*) and the phenomenology of moral tragedies (as in *Truck 2* and *Drowning*). However, inferences to the best explanation are convincing only if there are no equally good or better explanations, so it is a problem that Gardner does not examine competing explanations. Take 'derivative' reasons first. Consider the potential for purely evaluative facts to explain these. An evalu-ative statement draws attention to a good or bad feature of a state of affairs, for example 'good people ought not to suffer'. A prescriptive statement, by con-trast, holds that a person has a reason or duty to do or refrain from doing some-thing,[19] for example 'you ought to prevent that person suffering'. Gardner's argument relies on the assumption that only prescriptive claims involving reasons to succeed can explain the relevant phenomena. But in the case of 'de-rivative' reasons, purely evaluative facts provide a better explanation. We do not need reasons to generate new reasons; evaluative facts are perfectly capable of generating them. In *Accessibility*, the fact that it is a frustration of Zelda's basic interests in accessing public services generates reasons both for them and others to lobby for wheelchair-accessible transport. The value to Zelda of doing this, or the disvalue of failing to do it, is enough to explain these reasons without assuming they must be derived from pre-existing reasons.

In fact, far from demonstrating the existence of reasons to do the impossible, the best explanation for Zelda's reasons in *Accessibility* actually *relies* on 'ought implies can'. Whether or not Zelda has a reason to ride the bus, presumably

---

[18] Since I discussed this functional argument in Chapter 4, and since Gardner has a response to it that I discuss below, I will put it to one side for now.

[19] On the distinction between prescriptive and evaluative statements, see Ruth Barcan Marcus, 'Iterated Deontic Modalities' (1966) 75 Mind 580; IL Humberstone, 'Two Sorts of "Oughts"' (1971) 32 Analysis 8; and Gilbert Harman, *The Nature of Morality* (Princeton University Press 1977).

they have *conclusive* reason to do something else, such as get a cab, as this is the course of action they should in fact take. But this is the second-best option from their perspective—the best option is to ride the bus—so why would they have conclusive reason to take the second-best option? A natural explanation is that Zelda has no reason to take the best option since this is impossible.[20] This would then 'promote' their reason to take the second-best option, making it a conclusive reason. Obviously, Gardner cannot avail himself of this explanation, which makes it unclear how his view accounts for the fact that Zelda's reason to ride the bus, if it exists, cannot be conclusive. He could argue that Zelda has conclusive reason to take the next-best-but-possible option while also having *a* reason to take the impossible-but-best option. But then if 'ought implies can' does not preclude a reason in favour of the best option, why not a conclusive reason?

Consider now Gardner's other argument about moral tragedies. Recall that it appeals to the concept of the moral 'trace' or 'remainder', which is familiar in discussions of moral tragedies, but also obscure.[21] We can disambiguate the concept into at least four elements. When we harm others without fault, we might owe (1) an explanation to the victim or their family; (2) an apology to the victim or their family; (3) the expression of an affective or attitudinal response to the victim or their family; or (4) compensation to the victim or their family. Part of the problem with bundling all or some of these ideas into the concept of a moral 'remainder' is that the circumstances in which these responses are owed likely come apart. We might think a bystander owes an explanation to the victim's family just by virtue of being a witness, though the injurer or failed rescuer owes an explanation of *their* conduct in particular. We might think injurers and failed rescuers owe apologies while bystanders do not, or that only those who are at fault owe apologies. We might think injurers but not failed rescuers owe compensation, or that they both owe compensation, or that neither do. We might think injurers and failed rescuers owe attitudinal responses, such as expressions of certain emotions, which bystanders do not, or that injurers but not failed rescuers owe such responses, or that neither do. The point is that reasons to engage in all four responses might come apart, and so it is dubious, without further argument, to appeal to the moral 'remainder' to defend a specific claim about reasons or duties to succeed.

---

[20] For a defence of 'ought implies can' along these lines, see Frances Howard-Snyder, '"Cannot" Implies "Not Ought"' (2006) 130 Philosophical Studies 233.

[21] The concept of the 'moral remainder' was introduced by Bernard Williams and has since been discussed in a variety of different contexts. See Bernard Williams, 'Ethical Consistency' in *Problems of the Self: Philosophical Papers 1956–1972* (Cambridge University Press 1973) 166–86.

Having registered this concern, we can concede that at least some of these responses are intuitively owed by Zelda in *Truck 2* and *Drowning*. We can then ask: can purely evaluative facts explain these responses? Others have appealed to similar ideas in cases of moral tragedies. John Oberdiek appeals to value pluralism to explain the phenomenon of moral 'residue' in moral dilemmas. According to value pluralism, there are irreducibly distinct values that are sometimes incompatible.[22] When one value takes priority over another, something valuable is inevitably lost, and this explains why choices between incompatible values have a tragic quality. There are two important components of Oberdiek's explanation: choice and loss of value. In *Truck 2* and *Drowning*, the effect of the situation on Zelda cannot be attributed to their choice (they have none) but perhaps the great loss of value is enough to explain their response.

This suggestion may work for moral dilemmas, but there is a problem with deploying it in Gardner's cases. Take *Drowning*. Deaths every bit as tragic as Abbas' are a ubiquitous feature of human life. Although we are aware of this, our response to these losses rarely mirrors Zelda's response in *Drowning*. The fact that a valuable life is lost seems insufficient, by itself, to explain the reaction. We may appeal to the purely psychological fact that people are more affected by suffering when it is visible or close.[23] This possibility cannot be ruled out, but we shouldn't be too quick to give up the idea that there is a normative as well as psychological component to the explanation of the phenomenology of *Drowning*. At this point, Gardner may reassert that Zelda has this reaction because they have a reason to succeed in saving Abbas, which gives them a special relationship to Abbas' plight that others lack.

However, there are alternative explanations of the phenomenology that are appropriately agent-centred and do not rely on loss of value *or* reasons to succeed. Zelda's situation is tragic not just because they recognize a loss of value, but because they experience a moral emotion I will call *agent-anguish*. Agent-anguish is the emotional response to the recognition that, if one had done things slightly differently, one could have prevented great loss (and therefore would have had a reason or duty to do so). It is not an emotional response to the loss of life *tout court*. Rather, it represents the intense or desperate reaction to being *close* to averting tragedy. 'If only I had arrived slightly earlier, or was a slightly better swimmer', Zelda might lament, 'I could have prevented disaster'. Like regret, anguish comes in both generalized and agent-centred forms.[24]

[22] John Oberdiek, 'Lost in Moral Space: On the Infringing/Violating Distinction and its Place in the Theory of Rights' (2004) 32 Law and Philosophy 325, 332–33.
[23] See Peter Singer, 'Famine, Affluence and Morality' (1972) 1 Philosophy & Public Affairs 229.
[24] Williams, *Moral Luck* (n 2) 27.

A bystander might feel a general form of anguish. They might think: 'If only the current was slightly weaker, if only Abbas had fallen in slightly closer to the shore, he would have survived.' But Zelda feels a special kind of anguish at the thought that *they* almost saved him.[25] Affectively, their pain is likely to be more intense and is focussed on the thought that *they* came close to averting tragedy but failed to do so, whilst bystanders cannot rationally have such agent-centred reactions.

Agent-anguish offers a plausible alternative to Gardner's appeal to reasons to succeed. It is unclear which of the four duties outlined above it requires, but it is plausible that it at least requires the kind of special attitudinal and emotional response to which Gardner appeals as a basis for positing reasons to succeed. In response, Gardner could argue that agent-anguish is itself based upon a failure to fulfil a reason to succeed. This would parallel his account of agent-regret, since he takes this phenomenon as evidence of reasons to succeed.[26] Given the structure of his argument as an inference to the best explanation, though, it is unclear why he thinks agent-regret is evidence for reasons to succeed rather than an alternative explanation for the phenomenology of his cases and thus evidence *against* them. The original *Truck* can be explained by saying that Zelda is in the grip of agent-regret, and this explanation does not have the downside of invoking duties to succeed in doing the impossible, which are subject to the 'ought implies can' and *undue burden* objections. After all, as Williams makes clear in his original formulation, the constitutive thought of agent-regret does not entail that the agent has reason to do otherwise; it consists in the simple thought that they *did* the thing that grounds their regret. Indeed, the fact that they lacked reason to do otherwise is illustrative of their tragedy: they could not have escaped their fate through greater attentiveness to reasons. The same can be said about agent-anguish. In *Drowning*, the emotion of agent-anguish provides an alternative explanation to the proposition that Zelda has reasons to succeed in saving Abbas rather than a basis for it.

In sum, both 'derivative' reasons and reactions to tragic cases admit of alternative explanations besides positing reasons to succeed in doing the impossible. These explanations are further buttressed by the fact that Gardner's

---

[25] Both agent-regret and agent-anguish are directed at what an agent could have done differently. But it is plausible that they also attach to other facts about agents besides what they do. For example, suppose a cyclist hits and kills a pedestrian through no fault of their own. As well as regretting what they did (getting onto their bike, taking the fateful route) they may regret other facts about who they are that also played a causal role in the death (such as the fact that they are a fast cyclist). Similarly, in *Drowning*, Zelda might feel anguish about what they did or failed to do, but also about the fact that they might have saved Abbas if, say, they had longer reach.

[26] Gardner, *Torts and Other Wrongs* (n 12) 165.

account has implausible implications in other areas. For example, he faces the problem of explaining how reasons are appropriately limited. If reasons to succeed in doing the impossible exist, then 'ought implies can' must be false. This seems to open the door to a range of absurd reasons, such as reasons to save members of past generations, reasons to rescue beings on unknown planets, reasons to rescue people through impossible means like wishing them saved, and so on. Most of those who deny 'ought implies can' do not think we have such absurd reasons.[27] This creates a challenge. Proponents of 'ought implies can' have a ready explanation why such reasons do not exist. Those who reject it are left with the task of explaining why we have reasons to do some impossible things but not others.

To address this problem, Gardner proposes a baseline to determine which impossible actions we can have reason to perform. He argues that, if at least one conceivable human being has the capacity to x and A is a human being, then the impossibility of A x-ing does not preclude A having a reason to x. In other words, 'ought implies a conceivable human can'.[28] Although this solution rules out absurd reasons, it does not prevent an implausible proliferation of reasons. It implies that one could have a reason to reach something on a shelf only the tallest person in the world could reach, or to escape an attacker via a gap through which only a toddler could fit. The force of the absurd reasons problem is not just that we don't have *bizarre* reasons but also that practical rationality is not swamped with limitless reasons to do things that we, as individuals, lack the ability to do, and therefore cannot play a meaningful role in our *ex ante* deliberation.

The proposal is also vulnerable to an arbitrariness objection. Why should conceivable human achievement be the appropriate baseline? To illustrate the problem, consider the following cases:

Truck 3: Zelda is trapped under a truck. Abbas cannot lift the truck, but Cain, the strongest conceivable human, could lift it.

Truck 4: The same as *Truck 3* except the truck under which Zelda is trapped is marginally too heavy for even the strongest conceivable human.

[27] The argument is developed in Bart Streumer, 'Reasons and Impossibility' (2007) 136 Philosophical Studies 351 and also in his response to Ulrike Heuer in 'Reasons, Impossibility and Efficient Steps: Reply to Heuer' (2010) 151 Philosophical Studies 79.

[28] John Gardner, 'Reasons and Abilities: Some Preliminaries' (2013) 58 American Journal of Jurisprudence 63.

Gardner's version of 'ought implies can' implies that Abbas has a reason and perhaps a duty to lift the truck in *Truck 3* but not in *Truck 4*. This is hard to believe. Lifting the truck is equally impossible for Abbas in both cases. The conceivability of a human like Cain has no bearing on what Abbas has reason to do in either case. Of course, one could adopt a wider definition of conceivability and argue that a human with superhuman strength is conceivable, but the same problem can be repeated at a higher level of ability, and to stretch the definition of conceivability in this way would be to reintroduce the absurd reasons problem that this move was meant to prevent.

D. The Effacement Argument

Let's move on to the fourth argument for outcome responsibility. Stephen Perry has pointed out that there are really two forms of outcome responsibility in Honoré's work: the social conception and the personhood conception. The two may be mutually reinforcing[29] but they are nevertheless distinct.[30] The social conception refers to a system of allocation for social benefits and burdens, of the kind *the Fairness Argument* was intended to justify. The personhood conception holds that we cannot give up outcome responsibility without effacing our agency and losing some core component of our identity as persons—an idea that partly supports *The Consistency Argument*. As Honoré states, 'if actions and outcomes were not ascribed to us on the basis of our bodily movements and their mental accompaniments, we could have no continuing history or character.'[31] One might appeal directly to this idea to defend allocative responsibility. Call this *The Effacement Argument*.

Others have offered versions of this argument. Joseph Raz says that to 'disavow responsibility is to be false to who we are', because it is equivalent to renouncing our own self conceptions as agents.[32] John Gardner advances *the Effacement Argument* alongside his *Duties to Succeed Argument*.[33] For him, the argument captures the important idea that that what we *do* as agents is not limited to what is fully within our control. If it were, we would do almost

---

[29] Honoré, *Responsibility and Fault* (n 7) 78 – 9.
[30] Perry, 'Honoré on Responsibility' (n 5) 66.
[31] Honoré, Responsibility and Fault (n 7) 29.
[32] Joseph Raz, *From Normativity to Responsibility* (Oxford University Press 2011) 245.
[33] John Gardner, *From Personal Life to Private Law* (Oxford University Press 2018) ch 2 (hereafter Gardner, *Personal Life*). For Honoré's discussion, see Honoré, *Responsibility and Fault* (n 7) ch 2. Gardner also calls his argument *The Biography Argument* rather than *The Effacement Argument*. I will stick to my terminology here as I think the effacement of agency is an important component of this argument, and also the target of my criticism of it.

nothing; in most of our interactions with the world, we would be mere patients. What we commonly understand as our actions and decisions would no longer be intelligible. A focal point for *The Effacement Argument*, then, is the observation that some outcomes are constitutive of our actions. The death of a living thing, for example, is constitutive of the act of killing. If one fails to bring about a death, one fails to kill. Compare this to the act of shooting: one commits this act by pulling the trigger of a gun irrespective of whether this results in the death of a living thing. Once the nature of these actions is properly understood, we see that outcomes are an important part of what we do as agents. To deny this is to deny that we do almost anything and therefore to efface our agency.[34] From this claim about outcomes as constitutive of action, the argument moves to the claim that we are sometimes responsible for the outcomes we bring about in the allocative sense.

The problem with *The Effacement Argument* is that it posits an implausibly extreme dichotomy: either accept outcome responsibility or embrace the total effacement of our agency. These are not the only two options here. We can recognize limits on our responsibility that nevertheless preserve the fundamental elements of our agency.[35]

The personhood understanding of outcome responsibility is primarily a claim about action rather than responsibility. It holds that certain outcomes are attributable to agents. We cannot deny that agents *do* things, and this includes actions whose outcomes are, to some extent, beyond their control. What must be explained, then, is why mere attribution is insufficient to do justice to this observation; why we should hold agents responsible for the outcomes they bring about in the allocative sense when attribution is all we need to preserve a picture of ourselves as agents, as beings who exercise agential capacities and meaningfully perform actions in the world.

This is not to say it is implausible that agential involvement in harm generates reasons to compensate. As Williams points out, the driver in *Truck* is troubled by his own involvement even though he is not at fault, and offering compensation is one manifestation of this reaction.[36] We can also see the plausibility of the claim that we have more reason to compensate for harms

---

[34] Gardner, *Personal Life* (n 33) 65.
[35] Similarly, Peter Cane argues that it is a large step from saying bad outcomes define our identities to saying that they ground the obligation of repair, see 'Responsibility and Fault: A Relational and Functional Approach to Responsibility' in Peter Cane and John Gardner (eds), *Relating to Responsibility: Essays in Honour of Tony Honoré on his 80th Birthday* (Hart 2001) 94.
[36] Williams, 'Moral Luck' (n 2) 28–29.

attributable to our agency than harms that are not by comparing *Well* and *Truck*. Regardless whether we think Zelda owes corrective duties in either case, it is intuitive that the case for compensation is at least stronger in *Truck* than in *Well*. In *Truck*, Zelda chooses to pose the risk in furtherance of their projects and desires, which then has a catastrophic side effect on the unfortunate Abbas. In *Well*, by contrast, the threat is, in a loose sense, posed by Zelda as it is her body that threatens Abbas, but it is not attributable to Zelda's choice, and thus we cannot say that it is a side effect of Zelda's pursuit of their projects and desires.

In the next section we will question the legitimacy of this distinction between *Well* and *Truck*. For present purposes, what is important is that it is too quick to conclude from the intuitive difference between the two cases that we cannot make sense of human agency unless we recognize allocative responsibility for outcomes. What we need is a further explanation of why we have reasons to compensate for the harms that are attributable to our agency. Why is it that the fact that *I* have harmed rather than someone else gives me special reasons to compensate?

II. Salvaging Outcome Responsibility

A. The Duty to Avoid Harm

We can build an account of outcome responsibility by appealing to the duties we have to avoid harming others. Start with cases of non-responsible threats like *Well*. Some philosophers of self-defence think it is permissible to kill non-responsible threats, though this is controversial. But many accept that those who pose such threats have a duty to prevent the harm they would otherwise cause at some cost to themselves, and this cost is greater than that we can expect a bystander to bear.[37] For example, in *Well*, suppose Zelda can save Abbas' life by diverting their course, but if they do this, they will break their arm. Zelda ought to do this rather than killing Abbas, especially if Abbas has no right to defend himself against the threat. A bystander, on the other hand, is not required

---

[37] See, for example, Francis Kamm, *Creation and Abortion* (Oxford University Press 1992) 47–48; Victor Tadros, *The Ends of Harm: The Moral Foundations of Criminal Law* (Oxford University Press 2011) 255 (hereafter Tadros, *Ends of harm*); Alec Walen, *The Mechanics of Claims and Permissible Killing in War* (Oxford University Press 2019) 146; and Adam Slavny, 'Benefits, Entitlements and Non-Responsible Threats' (2019) 36 Journal of Applied Philosophy 405.

to suffer a broken arm even if this is the only way to prevent Abbas' death. Since the bystander will not cause the death, they are not required to bear the same burdens as the non-responsible threat to prevent it. They owe a duty of rescue, we can assume, but the duty to prevent someone's death is not as stringent as the duty not to kill. This much seems to follow from the doctrine of Doing and Allowing.

To see the plausibility of this idea, consider the following pair of cases.

> *Branch*: A freak wind blows a tree branch towards Abbas, breaking his arm. Zelda is an onlooker.
> *Projectile*: A freak wind blows Zelda towards Abbas, breaking his arm. Cain is an onlooker.

In these cases, what relationship does Zelda have to Abbas' broken arm, and how should they respond? On the view that non-responsible threats are morally indistinguishable to bystanders, Zelda has the same relationship to Abbas in *Branch* and *Projectile*: they are effectively an onlooker, just like Cain. Even when Zelda's body is the instrument of the harm, they are like a third party observing the harm caused by their own presence. On this view, they have no special duty in *Projectile*—distinct from a bystander—to apologize, offer an explanation, or bear some extra burden to alleviate Abbas' suffering, say by taking them to a hospital. This is difficult to believe. Intuitively, Zelda has a different relationship to Abbas' harm in *Projectile* compared to *Branch*. Zelda should do more than a mere bystander in the aftermath, and this adds weight to the suggestion that, if they could have prevented the harm, they ought to have done so even if this would have required them to bear a greater cost than a bystander would have been required to bear under the ordinary duty of rescue.

Why might non-responsible threats bear such duties? The Doctrine of Doing and Allowing holds, roughly, that from a first personal perspective, I have more reason not to cause harm than to prevent it. As well as some distinction between causing and allowing harm, we need to delineate the 'I' to properly elucidate this doctrine. On the view advocated above, the 'I' includes not just the exercise of our agential capacities, but the non-voluntary movement of our bodies.[38] My body is not a mere instrument that I use for

---

[38] On this point, see also Tadros, *Ends of Harm* (n 37) 254.

my purposes (although it is that too) but a part of me, and it would be oddly rationalistic to think that, insofar as the Doctrine of Doing and Allowing is concerned, the only causal upshots that I bring about are those rooted in my agency.

There is a worry about this rationale, though. If it is right, all non-responsible threats have equally weighty duties to prevent themselves causing harm. But this seems unfair given that we do not all benefit equally from our bodies as instruments of our projects and desires. In Kazuo Ishiguro's novel, *Never Let Me Go*, clones are raised for the purpose of donating organs to the public, finally 'completing'—or dying—when they have served this purpose.[39] If the non-responsible threat in *Projectile* was one of Ishiguro's clones, the case for their having a special duty is perhaps diminished. This is because, although their bodies are part of them, those bodies are instrumentalized to the benefit of others. Perhaps, then, what matters is not so much the constitutive relationship between one's body and one's identity, but rather the fact that, usually, one's body plays an integral role, along with one's agential capacities, in the pursuit of one's projects and desires.

We need not commit to any particular rationale here. What matters is that there is some plausibility to the claim that non-responsible threats have duties to avert those threats that are weightier than duties of rescue. It might be objected that no such duties are owed, at least in cases like *Well*, when Zelda has no opportunity to avoid posing the threat, and their agency is not meaningfully involved. This objection tracks the familiar and plausible thought that it is unfair to hold people liable to compensate when they could not have foreseen the outcome of their actions and thus avoided it. However, I want to suggest that, with respect to allocative responsibility (as opposed to defensive liability) lack of a prior opportunity to avoid posing the threat is irrelevant. The distinction between *Well* and *Truck* does not matter for compensatory liability. Consider:

> *Car*: Whilst driving, Zelda suffers a wholly unforeseeable muscle spasm and veers off the road, crushing Abbas' finger. Zelda has two choices: (1) they can keep their foot on the accelerator, which has no cost for Zelda but will crush Abbas' entire arm, or (2) they can remove their foot from the accelerator and have the car pulled backwards. Since the car is stuck, this will destroy the vehicle at serious financial cost.

---

[39] Kazuo Ishiguro, *Never Let Me Go* (Faber and Faber 2006).

What should Zelda do in *Car*? Intuitively, they should take the second option, saving further harm to Abbas but wrecking their car. This intuition serves two purposes. This first is to reinforce the previous claim that Zelda's duty to avoid harming, even non-responsibly, is weightier than the ordinary duty of rescue. If it were not, Zelda would be entitled to crush the rest of Abbas' arm, given that bystanders are not expected to bear great financial cost to rescue others from bodily injury. But, just as Zelda has stronger reason to compensate Abbas in *Projectile* compared to *Branch*, Zelda crushing Abbas' arm in *Car* is not equivalent to a bystander failing to prevent it.

The second purpose of the intuition is to move from the initial claim about the special duties of non-responsible threats to a defence of a limited form of outcome responsibility. A key feature of cases like *Well*, which are often vehicles for discussion of non-responsible threats, is that the falling person has the opportunity to avert the threat she poses. We noted that one objection to using these cases for our purposes is that they show nothing about duties to *compensate*, since most non-responsible threats do not have any opportunity to avert the harm. However, the intuition in *Car*, augmented by the argument set out in Chapter 3, shows us that this is not true (see Chapter 3, pt III). Negating harm after the fact is equivalent to not causing harm (at least for that portion of the harm that can be negated). Counterbalancing harm after the fact is equivalent to ensuring the harm does not cause an overall reduction in wellbeing. In other words, failing to compensate, even when the initial harm was non-responsible, is equivalent to Zelda crushing the rest of Abbas' arm in *Car*. It is a knowing failure to prevent one's previous non-responsible actions from resulting in much greater harm than they otherwise would.

It is worth noting that this argument gives an unexpected cameo appearance to *the continuity thesis*, though not the version intended by Weinrib, Ripstein, or Gardner. While each of these writers employ the thesis to explain the derivation of secondary from primary duties, the present argument applies it only when there is no prior breach, and thus it applies only outside the context of the primary/secondary duty model. When harming constitutes breach of a prior duty, *the responsiveness thesis* tells us that we acquire more stringent duties to further the values that we disregarded by violating the duty. But when the harm is not a breach of duty, as in cases of non-responsible threats, *the continuity thesis* enters the picture because the duty to bear costs to avoid harming survives the initial act of harm and become a duty to mitigate that harm where possible. At both points in time—the *ex ante* and *ex post* perspectives—the non-responsible threat has the same duty to bear costs to prevent themselves harming others. It is just that, in the case of non-responsible threats, this possibility only arises after the initial harm has been caused.

This analysis makes it clear that, even if the initial harm was caused non-responsibly and was therefore unavoidable, the future effects of the harm are plainly foreseeable from the *ex post* perspective. It is easy to be distracted by the fact that non-responsible threats have no opportunity to avert the threat *ex ante*. This fact is important for the question of self-defence where the threat of harm is time-sensitive. However, *ex post*, it is no longer true that a non-responsible threat lacks an opportunity to avoid causing harm. Compensation *is* their opportunity to avoid causing harm. Although they were evidence-relative permitted to act before they knew their action would cause harm, they now know that their action was fact-relative impermissible. This means that, in their current situation, failing to compensate is equivalent to knowingly continuing to cause harm for the sake of an initial end that was—unbeknownst at the time—unjustified in light of the harm it would cause.

Other accounts of outcome responsibility reject the claim that non-responsible threats can be liable to compensate. For example, Stephen Perry argues that the avoidability of the initial harm is necessary for outcome responsibility. For Perry, a person is outcome responsible if she had control over her actions, and this control is cached out in terms of avoidability. According to this account, an agent is outcome-responsible for a harm if and only if she causally contributed to it, possessed the capacity to foresee it, and had the ability and opportunity to take steps, on the basis of what could have been foreseen, to avoid it. Thus, responsible threats are outcome responsible but non-responsible threats are not.

One problem for Perry's account is that he gives no reason why we should focus on an agent's control over the harm only from the *ex ante* perspective. If the agent would have had a duty to bear a burden to avert the injury had they been in control, why does this duty disappear *ex post* once their control is re-established? Though it was not within their power to avert the injury, it is now within their power to substantially mitigate—perhaps even eliminate—the harm resulting from that injury. This control over the victim's fate is no different from *ex ante* control over the threat. In fact, typically the injurer has greater control *ex post* because they have better knowledge of the harm they will ultimately cause if they do nothing.

Our argument, *contra* Perry, suggests that we have some degree of allocative responsibility for *all* the harm we cause. It may be greater in the case of responsible threats, since these individuals take decisions to pose foreseeable risks. Perhaps Zelda has a more stringent duty to avert the threat in *Truck* than in *Well*, given their initial choice to pose the risk. This is an attractive feature of *The Effacement Argument*. Not that we cannot make sense of agency without responsibility for foreseeable harm, but that such responsibility is strengthened by our agential connection to such harm.[40] But if so, this is a difference in degree rather than kind. The basis of outcome responsibility is that we have reason to prevent ourselves causing harm, and though we cannot always do this *ex ante*, we can often do it *ex post*.[41]

On this view, we can have allocative responsibility for both responsible and non-responsible harms. What is the underlying thread that connects these two forms of harm? It is that our being in the world sometimes causes unintended and objectively unjustified costs for others, even when we do nothing wrong. In *Well*, it is Zelda's physical presence that has costs for Abbas.[42] In *Truck*, it is Zelda's voluntary pursuit of their projects that has costs for Abbas. Both our physical presence and our use of our bodies and capacities to pursue our projects are basic features of our being in the world and living amongst others, and one of the tragedies of this form of coexistence is that it inevitably leads to our harming others without objective justification, albeit without ill intent or moral failing.[43] The continuity between responsible and non-responsible harm is also strengthened by the fact that the boundary between the two is, in reality, highly porous. In *Truck 2*, Zelda's muscle spasm is involuntary, but they nevertheless make a prior decision to drive, which poses foreseeable risks. Even in *Well*, Zelda's decision to leave the house means that they will be among others, and whenever we appear in public

---

[40] For an argument to this effect, see Victor Tadros, 'Two Grounds of Liability' (2021) 178 Philosophical Studies 3503.

[41] A possible exception is in cases of fatal harm. Even here, however, if it is possible to harm someone posthumously, it is presumably possible to benefit and thus compensate them posthumously too.

[42] For the view that those who make a victim worse off by their presence are properly considered non-responsible threats rather than bystanders, see Helen Frowe, 'Threats, Bystanders and Obstructors' (2008) 108 Proceedings of the Aristotelian Society 365. A similar idea is deployed by Alec Walen and Gerhard Øverland to replace the Means Principle. See Alec Walen, 'Transcending the Means Principle' (2014) 33 Law and Philosophy 427 and Gerhard Øverland, 'Moral Obstacles: An Alternative to the Doctrine of Double Effect (2014) 124 Ethics 481.

[43] As the personification of delirium puts it in Neil Gaiman's comic series, The Sandman, 'Our existence deforms the universe. That's responsibility.' See Neil Gaiman, *The Sandman* (vol 9, The Kindly Ones, DC Comics 1994–95).

there is a chance we will cause or be the victim of involuntary harm. There is often some degree of choice in the causal chain leading up to harm where it is foreseeable that some injury might occur. In consequence, it should be regarded as a strength rather than a weakness of the present account that it posits a continuity rather than a stark division between responsible and non-responsible harm.

Let's conclude this section by considering an objection based on the indeterminacy of causation. Consider *Well*. Whilst it is true that Zelda's presence is a necessary condition for the harm to Abbas, Abbas' presence is equally necessary. The harm would not occur but for the actions or the presence of either party. Similarly, in *Truck*, Zelda's decision to get behind the wheel and Abbas' decision to step in front of the vehicle are both necessary conditions.[44] Causation is indeterminate as between injurer and victim, so we cannot base any duty to avert harm on judgements about causation.

The answer to this objection is that the simple counterfactual account of causation that it presupposes is false, precisely because it implies that causation is indeterminate in a range of cases in which it intuitively is not. Consider the following case:

> *Corner*: Zelda and Abbas run around a blind corner at the same speed and collide with each other, resulting in a broken arm for Zelda.

In *Corner*, it is difficult to say whether Zelda or Abbas caused Zelda's broken arm, and it is perhaps best to say they both caused it equally. But it is more difficult to believe that *Corner* is identical to *Well* and *Truck* with respect to attributing causation. In these cases, Zelda is intuitively the cause, or at least the primary cause, of Abbas' harm. Ultimately, we need a fully developed theory of causation that vindicates these intuitions as well as solving various problems associated with pre-emption and overdetermination.[45] Obviously enough, that is not something we can accomplish here, but the widespread agreement that simple counterfactual accounts of causation are flawed, as

---

[44] Ronald Coase, 'The Problem of Social Cost' (1960) 3 Journal of Law and Economics 1. Stephen Perry has argued that this problem undermines any attempt to ground liability to compensate in causation. See 'The Impossibility of a General Strict Liability' (1988) 1 Canadian Journal of Law and Jurisprudence 147 and 'Libertarianism, Entitlement, and Responsibility' (1997) 26 Philosophy & Public Affairs 351.

[45] For a detailed treatment of such problems, see LA Paul and Ned Hall, *Causation: A Users Guide* (Oxford University Press 2013).

well as the various attempts to develop alternatives, give us reason to hope it is possible.

B. What Response?

Many discussions of outcome responsibility assume that those who are outcome responsible for harm have duties to compensate.[46] This focus on compensation can have a distorting effect on our understanding of outcome responsibility. Recall that the preventive duty owed by non-responsible threats is not a duty to avert the harm at all costs, but rather to bear a certain degree of cost to avert it. Though the stringency threshold of this duty is greater than that of a bystander, it is plausibly lower than that of a responsible injurer, which in turn is lower than that of a culpable injurer. So, whether compensation is the appropriate response depends on whether forcing the injurer to compensate, in any given case, exceeds this threshold. Since compensating *ex post* is often more burdensome than preventing harm *ex ante*, it may be that forcing non-culpable injurers to compensate fully often exceeds this threshold.

Injurers therefore do not automatically acquire compensatory duties. Rather, they acquire duties to benefit their victims until either they are fully compensated or the stringency threshold of the duty is reached, whichever comes first. Which comes first depends on the precise stringency of the duty to compensate and how costly it is for the injurer to provide it in the circumstances. In light of the general burdensomeness of compensating, at least in the absence of insurance,[47] there is reason to think the stringency threshold will often be reached before full compensation is achieved. If this happens, the duties arising from outcome responsibility are duties of partial compensation.

To illustrate, consider the following schema. Suppose Zelda non-responsibly harms Abbas and full compensation (C) exceeds the stringency threshold (N) of Zelda's duty. What should Zelda do? They have three options: (1) Fully compensate Abbas and pay C, (2) refuse to compensate Abbas and pay nothing,

---

[46] Honoré focussed on duties of compensation given his interest in using outcome responsibility to vindicate features of tort law, such as strict liability and the objective standard of care. David Miller also treats the duty to compensate as a defeasible normative presumption of outcome responsibility. See his *National Responsibility and Global Justice* (Oxford University Press 2007) 87.

[47] We are assuming that no insurance is in place. The presence of insurance raises distinct questions that we will return to in Chapter 8.

and (3) partially compensate Abbas and pay N. (1) is ruled out because it exceeds the stringency threshold of Zelda's duty. They must bear some cost to reduce the harm they cause, but it is unfair to burden them excessively. Since they are non-responsible, they could not have avoided harming Abbas, so the stringency of their duty, though greater than that of a bystander, is limited. (2) is also implausible, though, as it ignores Zelda's duty entirely. If Zelda is not required to do anything, this places them in the same position in relation to the harm as a bystander. But they are not in this position because, unlike a bystander, they are the cause of Abbas' harm. Thus, (3) seems the correct solution. Zelda's outcome responsibility gives rise to a duty to partially compensate Abbas.

Cases like this are difficult to evaluate because I have not allocated any specific values for N and C. The value of N depends on the stringency of Zelda's duty. Some might think this duty is not very stringent, otherwise it places too great a limit on Zelda's freedom, especially since they could not have avoided becoming a non-responsible injurer in the first place. The value of C depends on how burdensome it is for Zelda to fully compensate Abbas, and this in turn depends on their resources and the nature of Abbas' injury. If Zelda has limited means and Abbas' injury is severe, C will be very large. If Zelda has better means and Abbas' injury is less severe, C will be small. The point is that there is a range of cases in which C exceeds N, and they are inevitable given that the cost of compensating varies depending on the two variables above.

Another possibility is that the victim has a duty of rescue towards the injurer. The injurer is also threatened with harm through no fault or choice of their own, specifically the harm of being subject to the burden of repair. The victim is uniquely positioned to prevent this harm because they are the beneficiary of the duty and have the option to waive it. The usual logic of the duty of rescue suggests they have a duty to do this. In *Well*, if enforcing Zelda's duty would make them very badly off, what should Abbas do? On the one hand, Zelda has a duty to bear costs up to threshold N as a result of their outcome responsibility, so surely there is nothing wrong with Abbas demanding that they do this. On the other hand, since Zelda harms non-responsibly, they face a cost (N) through no fault or choice of their own, and Abbas is uniquely positioned to reduce this cost. Abbas therefore has three options here: (1) demand full compensation, (2) waive his right to compensation, and (3) demand partial compensation/partially waive his right to compensation. As before, (3) seems the most defensible option.

It might be objected that this is a form of double counting. If the victim has a duty to assist the injurer in this way, surely this is taken into account when calculating N. We cannot then say the victim has another duty to re-frain from demanding that the injurer bears a burden up to the stringency threshold, N. After all, the stringency threshold is supposed to mark a level of cost beyond which a duty-bearer cannot be made to go without wronging them. It seems inconsistent with this to say that it would wrong the injurer (because the victim would breach their duty towards them) if the victim de-mands that the injurer bear cost up to this threshold. But for our purposes we need not be worried by this. What we are trying to show here is that, in cases of non-responsible injury, the stringency of the injurer's duty is often less than the cost of full compensation ($N < C$). To establish this, it does not matter whether the victim's duty of rescue reduces N or gives her a reason to refrain from demanding that the injurer meets N in full—both routes lead to our desired conclusion.

Next consider responsible threats like *Truck*. In these cases, Zelda takes a small but foreseeable risk of serious harm to others. We should note two cav-eats about these cases, however. First, Abbas, too, might have made a decision that carries a small but foreseeable risk of serious harm to himself. Second, driving often benefits specific third parties, or society generally through trans-portation of goods and services and the like. The distribution of benefits from some activity affects our evaluation of who should pay for it when it causes harm (for further discussion, see Chapter 6) and this is not straightforward in the case of driving.

Despite these caveats, in cases where Zelda does something for their own benefit and imposes a foreseeable risk of harm on Abbas, who does not take a similar decision with respect to his own safety, there is a stronger case for holding Zelda outcome responsible to compensate Abbas. However, while some might think Zelda's responsibility marks a clear line between a duty to compensate and no duty to compensate, a better view is that Zelda's responsibility increases the stringency of their duty to compensate. In prac-tice, this means it is more likely that Zelda will fully compensate Abbas before the stringency threshold of their duty is reached; that is, it is more likely that $N > C$.

Even so, it is possible for the stringency threshold of the injurer's duty to be met before the victim is fully compensated. If Zelda responsibly in-jures Abbas and can compensate him only at high cost, it is doubtful that they should be required to do this. Thus, the responsible/non-responsible dichotomy does not translate to a similar dichotomy in terms of corrective duties. Instead, there is a continuum of corrective duties, with varying strin-gency, with non-responsible threats on one side and culpable threats on the other. The higher the stringency, the more likely the injurer has a duty to compensate fully. But this depends on the stringency combined with circumstantial facts about how costly it is to compensate. These circumstantial facts can mislead us into thinking there is some fundamental distinction between non-responsible, responsible, and culpable threats in terms of the corrective duties they owe.[48]

There are two notable conclusions we can draw from this. One is that, on the version of outcome responsibility presented here, corrective duties are more widespread than many assume. However, when harm is non-responsible or barely responsible, these duties are not very stringent and therefore not worth enforcing through legal institutions. This vindicates Honoré's thought that outcome responsibility justifies legal liability only when further conditions are satisfied. The second conclusion is that widespread low-stringency corrective duties may be more effectively pooled to provide protection for victims of harm rather enforced on a one-to-one basis. We will explore this possibility further in Chapter 8 when we discuss the justifiability of compensation schemes.

Conclusion

At the beginning of the chapter, we defined outcome responsibility in terms of allocative responsibility, specifically the burden of repair. We canvassed a number of arguments that might justify outcome responsibility in this sense even in cases where no wrongdoing has occurred. We rejected *The Fairness Argument*, *The Consistency Argument*, *The Duties to Succeed Argument*, and *The Effacement Argument*. Instead, we appealed to the duties we have to bear costs to prevent ourselves harming others, arguing that these duties require some corrective action *ex post*.

This led to a few conclusions. One was that, although we previously rejected *the continuity thesis* as an unsatisfactory explanation of the derivation of secondary from primary duties, it has a role to play in cases where harm is caused non-wrongfully. Second, an opportunity to avoid the initial harm does not vitiate outcome responsibility, since it is still possible to prevent oneself causing future harm from an *ex post* perspective. Finally, outcome responsibility takes

---

[48] A similar continuum exists with respect to the victim's duty to mitigate the burden of the wrongdoer. For similar arguments, see Victor Tadros, *To Do, To Die: Individual Ethics in War* (Oxford University Press 2022).

the form of a duty to bear costs for the sake of those one has harmed and need not always amount to a full duty of repair. If the arguments of this chapter are on the right lines, we have offered another ground for corrective duties that does not necessitate wrongdoing; or, to put the point another way, another source of corrective duties independent of the primary/secondary duty model. In Chapter 6, we will expand this conclusion to examine distributive fairness as a ground for corrective duties.

6

Fairness and Liability

Introduction

In the last three chapters we saw three distinct moral bases for liability to compensate, encompassing both wrongful and non-wrongful conduct. In this chapter we examine the final limb of the four-fold analysis: distributive fairness.

Here are three views that appeal to distributive fairness:

The Non-Reciprocity Principle: Whenever one party harms another, there is a *pro tanto* duty to let the cost fall on the party who imposed a non-reciprocal risk on the other.

The Benefit Principle: Whenever one party harms another, there is a *pro tanto* duty for the cost to be borne by a party in proportion to how much they benefit from the risk-creating activity, as long as either (a) the benefits are endorsed or (b) the beneficiary lacks the opportunity to endorse them.

The Avoidance Principle: Whenever one party harms another, there is a *pro tanto* duty for the cost to be borne by the party for whom it was less costly to avoid the risk.

All these views trade in *pro tanto* rather than all-things-considered duties. This is because, within the four-fold analysis, they can conflict with each other and with the other bases for liability we have already encountered. If our discussion so far has taught us anything, it is that the normative foundations of corrective duties cannot be reduced to a single master principle. Each of these views offers considerations in favour of liability, but they are not always conclusive.

A version of *The Non-Reciprocity Principle* has been defended by George Fletcher, and we begin the chapter with an analysis of his work, which represents one of the few attempts to articulate a fairness-based account of compensatory liability. According to Fletcher, a person's liability to pay compensation depends on whether they non-reciprocally imposed a risk of harm on others. In Fletcher's words, 'a victim has a right to recover for an injury caused by a risk

Wrongs, Harms, and Compensation. Adam Slavny, Oxford University Press. © Adam Slavny 2023.
DOI: 10.1093/oso/9780192864567.003.0006

greater in degree and different in order from those created by the victim and imposed on the defendant—in short, for injuries resulting from nonreciprocal risks'.[1] This view is founded on a Rawlsian principle of distributive justice, which guarantees equal security for individuals compatible with a like system for all.[2]

Although we will ultimately reject non-reciprocity, this exercise will help us clarify how concerns of distributive fairness affect liability. In the second part of the chapter, we develop an alternative view grounded in *The Benefit Principle* and *The Avoidance Principle*. These principles interlink to form a fairness basis for individual corrective duties which overlaps with other parts of the four-fold analysis but is distinct from it.

The relevance of distributive fairness to compensatory liability is often doubted by those who seek to separate distributive and corrective justice into irreconcilable normative domains. We have already noted Weinrib's well-known claim that introducing distributive concerns into the practice of corrective justice would produce incoherence.[3] This worry is partly driven by the thought that without the relational pairing of injurer and victim, there is no way of picking out any individual who owes a corrective duty. In this chapter we throw doubt on this claim. Exploring the relevance of fairness to compensatory liability will show the reverse: that liability cannot be restricted to the bilateral interaction between injurer and victim.

---

[1] George Fletcher, 'Fairness and Utility in Tort Theory' (1972) 85 Harvard Law Review 527, 542 (hereafter Fletcher, 'Fairness and Utility'). Like many interpretive theories, it has both explanatory and normative ambitions. Fletcher claims it can account for the general relationship between negligence and strict liability, as well as unifying disparate pockets of strict liability. He argues that liability for damage caused by falling aeroplanes or injuries inflicted by dangerous animals, and the rules laid down in *Rylands v Fletcher* (1868) LR 3 HL 330 and *Vincent v Lake Erie* 109 Minn 456 (1910), are motivated by the creation of a non-reciprocal risk. He also notes that principles of negligence typically apply in contexts where people create and expose themselves to equal risk, such as driving on roads and playing in sports fields. In these contexts, the activity only generates non-reciprocal risk if performed carelessly. Finally, he extends the analysis to intentional torts. An intentional blow or assault 'represents a rapid acceleration of risk, directed at a specific victim' which readily distinguishes 'the intentional blow from the background of risk'. These explanatory claims have been questioned. Jules Coleman doubts that non-reciprocity can explain intentional torts. An innocent falling person 'rapidly accelerates' the risk to a person located beneath them but does not thereby commit a battery, see Jules Coleman, 'Justice and Reciprocity in Tort Theory' (1974) 14 Western Ontario Law Review 105 (hereafter Coleman, 'Justice and Reciprocity'). We will bracket these discussions, noting that the interpretive potential of Fletcher's theory is a reason for foundationalists to take it seriously from a normative perspective.

[2] See Fletcher, 'Fairness and Utility (n 1) 550 and Jules Coleman, 'Moral Theories of Torts: Their Scope and Limits: Part 1' (1982) 1 Law and Philosophy 371, 389. Some theorists cite Fletcher's article as paving the way for a proper understanding of the normative basis of tort law. See, for example, Gregory Keating, 'Reasonableness and Rationality in Negligence Theory' (1996) 48 Stanford Law Review 311, 313–14.

[3] For denials of this claim, see Ronen Avraham and Issa Kohler-Hausmann, 'Accident Law for Egalitarians' (2006) 12 Legal Theory 181; Larry Alexander, 'Causation and Corrective Justice: Does Tort Law Make Sense?' (1987) 6 Law and Philosophy 1; and Wojciech Sadurski, 'Social Justice and Legal Justice' (1984) 3 Law and Philosophy 329.

I. Understanding Non-Reciprocity

Let's begin by laying out Fletcher's view in more detail. He does not provide an analysis of risk and I will not commit to any specific conception here, since almost any can be plugged into *The Non-Reciprocity Principle*. We should, however, distinguish the degree of risk from the magnitude of potential harm. Jules Coleman's discussion of non-reciprocity incorporates both concepts by defining non-reciprocity in terms of expected value or disvalue. The expected value of a risk is a combination of the magnitude of a potential harm and the likelihood of its occurrence.[4]

As Coleman also points out,[5] Fletcher's criterion is ambiguous between the size and the social tolerability of risks. Here we will exclude the latter. The social tolerability of a risk has little to do with non-reciprocity and is better understood as an indicator of social value.[6] If a risk-creating activity is socially tolerated, this suggests it is valued by the community. The fact that an activity is socially valued implies a large group of people benefit from it in some way, and this is a reason against holding those who engage in the activity liable if they cause harm. But if so, this reason is not based on non-reciprocity, as the activity may involve the same degree of non-reciprocal risk as some other less-valued activity.

Fletcher claims that non-reciprocity should be measured against a 'community of risk takers' rather than a single party. Hence, 'keeping a domestic pet is a reciprocal risk relative to the community as a whole; driving is a reciprocal risk relative to the community of those who drive normally; and driving negligently may be reciprocal relative to the even narrower community of those who drive negligently'.[7] The notion of a 'community' of risk-takers also needs refining. On Fletcher's view, such a community is constituted by participation in a shared activity. However, this does not guarantee that risks will be reciprocal. Consider:

> *Minis and Hummers*: Dev drives a Mini while Elle drives a Hummer. Due to their weight and strength, Hummers impose much higher risks and have the potential to cause more harm than Minis. Dev and Elle spend an equal amount of time in their cars and drive with equal competence.

---

[4] Jules Coleman, *Risks and Wrongs* (Oxford University Press 1992) 254.
[5] Coleman, 'Justice and Reciprocity' (n 1) 108.
[6] ibid, 111.
[7] Fletcher, 'Fairness and Utility' (n 1) 549.

Both Dev and Elle fall within Fletcher's definition of a community of reciprocal risk-takers as they meet a reasonable standard of care on the road. Nevertheless, Hummer-drivers such as Elle impose non-reciprocal risks on Mini-drivers such as Dev because of their decision to drive a more dangerous vehicle.[8] Fletcher could respond that reciprocity requires only rough equivalence of risk rather than precise equivalence, but it remains the case that a 'community' of reciprocal risk-takers may contain 'sub-communities' of non-reciprocal risk-takers. To keep things clear, we will focus on interpersonal instances of non-reciprocal risk here.

We can analyse non-reciprocity into two core components. The first is that non-reciprocity requires an *unequal distribution* of risk between two parties. If the risk is equally distributed, the principle does not get off the ground. The second is that this risk distribution must exhibit *asymmetrical causality*. Non-reciprocity exists only if one party imposes a risk on the other and not *vice versa*. Note that the two components are distinct. We can imagine cases in which risks are distributed *unequally* between two people and *neither* of them are a causal source of the risk (unequal risk but no asymmetrical causality), and cases in which risk is distributed *equally* between two people and *one* of them is the causal source of the risk (asymmetrical causality but no unequal risk). This distinction will be important when we argue that unequal risk is not only insufficient for *The Non-Reciprocity Principle*, but sometimes militates against it.

II. Some Objections to The Non-Reciprocity Principle

The Non-Reciprocity Principle plausibly implies that negligent actors and those who expose others to extraordinary—even if permissible—risks are liable to compensate if those risks materialize into harm. One worry about the principle, though, is that it yields plausible results in these cases not because it is itself a compelling account of fairness but because it is sometimes co-extensive with such an account. We can investigate this possibility by considering:

> *Life Raft*: Through no fault or choice of their own, Dev and Elle are set adrift in danger of death. Dev's arm has been broken in the wreck but he can climb aboard a life raft and potentially save both of their lives. To do so,

[8] Similarly, see Helen Frowe, 'Risk Imposition and Liability to Defensive Harm' (2022) 16 Criminal Law, Philosophy 511 for the argument that cost/benefit justification of types of risky activity cannot justify individual tokens of risk imposition.

he must clamber over Elle's unconscious body, risking injury. Dev does this, saving their lives, but breaks Elle's arm.

In *Life Raft, The Non-reciprocity Principle* is satisfied as there is both unequal risk distribution and asymmetrical causality. We also stipulate that Dev already has a broken arm so he and Elle suffer the same outcome. This may seem like an arbitrary stipulation, but if only one of them suffers an injury, the inequality of outcome may give Dev independent reasons to compensate Elle.[9] Since this is unrelated to non-reciprocity of risk, we should eliminate it from consideration. We will make the same assumption about subsequent variations of *Life Raft* except for *Life Raft 4*, where our purpose is explicitly to compare the moral relevance of outcomes with *ex ante* risk distribution.

In *Life Raft*, it seems Elle has no convincing claim for compensation against Dev. The fact that Dev acts for their equal benefit overrides any relevance non-reciprocity may have. We can press this objection further by evaluating the two components of non-reciprocity individually. First consider asymmetrical causality. We can test the importance of this feature by comparing two variations of *Life Raft*. In the first variation, Dev and Elle benefit equally from a rescue attempt being performed by Dev *alone*. Dev performs the rescue, imposing an equal risk of harm on both and Elle is injured. In the second variation, Dev and Elle benefit equally from a rescue attempt being performed by the two of them *together*. They perform the rescue, reciprocally imposing an equal risk of harm on each other and subsequently Elle is injured.

Let's review the similarities and differences here. In both variations, the risk imposition equally benefits both parties. Both are subject to an equal risk. The outcomes are identical (they each end up with a broken arm). The only difference between the two is that asymmetrical causality is present in one but not the other. In the first variation Dev is the causal source of the risk, while in the second they impose risks on each other. I suggest there is no morally relevant difference between the two. To conclude this, we need not even commit to a view about the existence or otherwise of compensatory duties, only to the parity of the cases. If Dev owes compensation in the first then he also owes it in

---

[9] For a detailed discussion of inequality and the multifarious ways it might be undesirable, see Larry Temkin, *Inequality* (Oxford University Press 1993). Note that these reasons based on outcome inequality are agent-neutral: they are as applicable to bystanders or other members of society as much as to Elle. The present examples involve two individuals, so agent-relative and agent-neutral reasons coincide. But we should bear in mind that, where costs can be spread across larger groups, reasons to compensate based on distributive factors such as equality of welfare or prioritarianism may support loss-sharing solutions rather than individual liability.

the second, and if he does not owe it in the first then he does not owe it in the second.

What about the second component of non-reciprocity: unequal risk distribution? Unlike asymmetrical causality, the distribution of risk does seem relevant to liability. In *Life Raft*, we assumed that Dev and Elle could be saved only if Dev climbed over Elle's unconscious body. Now consider:

> *Life Raft 2*: The same as *Life Raft*, except Elle is not unconscious and either she or Dev could use the other to climb to safety, imposing a risk of injury. Without Elle's agreement, Dev climbs over her to rescue both of them and in doing so breaks her arm.

Is Elle entitled to compensation in *Life Raft 2*? She could argue that, although her injury is preferable to death, Dev still treated her unfairly. He could have distributed the risk of injury equally, or, if the risk was indivisible, split the chances of undertaking the risk. Unequal risk distribution may be a reason for compensation when the risk was non-reciprocal if the *ex ante* risks were not distributed fairly.

Although *Life Raft 2* demonstrates the relevance of risk distribution, this does not vindicate *The Non-Reciprocity Principle*. This is for two reasons. First, we are assuming equality is the correct criterion for distributive fairness here, yet it is familiar from debates about distributive justice that this is not a secure assumption. In some cases, for instance, we may have prioritarian reasons to give benefits to the worse off rather than distributing them equally.[10] Consider:

> *Life Raft 3*: Dev and Elle are set adrift, in danger of death. There is a chance they can climb to safety, saving both their lives. They can distribute the risks of the rescue attempt equally, or one of them can use the other to climb to safety, imposing the risk on them. Both options have an equal chance of success. Elle has a degenerative disease which means she is generally at high risk of serious injury and death.

In *Life Raft 3*, Dev ought to accept the risk for the sake of the rescue. Splitting the risk would be unfair as Elle is already subject to greater risk of physical injury than Dev, and therefore has priority in avoiding further risk. Dev acts wrongly if he performs the rescue unilaterally, imposing the risk on Elle.

---

[10] On the distinction between priority and equality, see Derek Parfit, 'Equality and Priority' (1997) 10 *Ratio* 202.

Conversely, *The Non-Reciprocity Principle* has the counterintuitive implication that if Elle performs the rescue by visiting the risk on Dev, causing injury, Elle owes him compensation. The problem is partly that *The Non-Reciprocity Principle* ignores background risk distributions, which are relevant in determining the fairness of any particular risk allocation, and partly that it treats equality as the correct criterion of distributive fairness, which is controversial given the availability of alternative criteria such as priority.[11]

Second, even if we assume that equal distributions are fair, the relevance of fairness in the distribution of costs goes beyond the boundaries set by *The Non-Reciprocity Principle*, sometimes in ways that conflict with it. This is because the principle applies the distributional requirement exclusively to *risk*. But the importance of fair distribution applies more powerfully to costs that matter more than risks, if indeed risks are to be counted as costs at all, such as *ex post* harms. This means that variations in outcomes ground compensatory duties *despite* initially equal risk distribution. Gregory Keating makes this point in his defence of strict liability, claiming that 'what counts is not reciprocity of *risk* but reciprocity of *harm* … Risk can be fairly distributed while harm is unfairly concentrated, and it is harm that matters.'[12]

Outcome inequality might confer reasons for compensation or cost-sharing which cannot be picked out by *The Non-Reciprocity Principle* when the initial distribution of risk is equal:

> *Life Raft 4*: Through no fault or choice of their own, Dev and Elle are set adrift, in danger of death. They can save themselves by climbing aboard a life raft but this carries a risk of injury. The attempt will only succeed if they are both involved. They perform the rescue attempt together, imposing equal risks on one another. Dev emerges onto the life raft unscathed while Elle injures herself and loses the use of her legs.

Does Elle have a moral claim against Dev in *Life Raft 4*? *The Non-Reciprocity Principle* implies not, since the *ex ante* risks are equal and there is no asymmetrical causality of risk, but this is at least contestable. As Keating recognizes, risks are only significant insofar as they threaten actual harm or loss (although a known risk might itself cause harm or loss by inducing someone to

---

[11] Besides equality and priority, utility and sufficiency are the two most notable criteria of distributive fairness. For the foundational discussion of sufficientarianism, see Harry Frankfurt, 'Equality as a Moral Ideal' (1987) 98 Ethics 21.

[12] Gregory Keating, 'A Social Contract Conception of the Tort Law of Accidents' in Gerald Postema (ed), *Philosophy and the Law of Torts* (Cambridge University Press 2001) 22, 35.

feel anxious or take precautions).[13] We ought to care about the distribution of real losses much more than the distribution of risk. In *Life Raft 4*, Elle suffers significant harm whilst Dev emerges unscathed. Given that cooperation is required to secure the mutual benefit, Dev has reasons to compensate Elle for the harm caused by their joint enterprise, or at least to divide the costs between them rather than letting them lie where they fall.

III. The Benefit Principle

A. Defending the Principle

Many of the judgements made above in the *Life Raft* cases are motivated by the benefits produced by the various rescue attempts. Just as it is problematic that *The Non-Reciprocity Principle* pays no heed to actual harms, it is also problematic that it pays no heed to actual benefits. We might then accept:

> *The Benefit Principle*: Whenever one party harms another, there is a *pro tanto* duty for the cost to be borne by a party in proportion to how much they benefit from the risk-creating activity, as long as either (a) the benefits are endorsed or (b) the beneficiary lacks the opportunity to endorse them.

The *Life Raft* cases show *The Benefit Principle* and *The Non-Reciprocity Principle* can conflict. As a starker example of conflict between these principles, consider:

> *Unconscious*: Elle, a doctor, happens upon Dev, who is unconscious and in danger of death unless Elle acts quickly. There is no one around who might give consent to any treatment on behalf of Dev. Elle can perform a procedure that will probably save Dev's life, but also carries a small risk of paralysis. Elle does this, and Dev loses the use of his right arm.

In *Unconscious*, *The Benefit Principle* rather than *The Non-Reciprocity Principle* gives the most plausible result. The non-reciprocal risk that Elle imposes on Dev should be disregarded given that she acts for his benefit.[14]

---

[13] Adam Slavny and Tom Parr, 'What's Wrong with Risk?' (2019) 8 Thought 76.

[14] In acting for the benefit of another, it is sufficient that one acts for their prospective benefit. A surgeon is not liable to compensate a patient if they act for the patient's benefit, even if their efforts are not successful. On this point, see also Jeff McMahan, 'The Just Distribution of Harm between Combatants

It is important to note an immediate limitation of this argument. It does not apply when one party has a duty to obtain consent before acting for another person's benefit. A surgeon is liable to compensate a patient for operating on them in the face of explicit refusal, even if the intervention saves the patient's life. In other work I have claimed that wrongful paternalism also generates duties to compensate despite not causing objective harm.[15] But where it is not possible to obtain consent, or where there is no duty to seek it, and the prospective benefit justifies the risk, *The Benefit Principle* rather than the *Non-Reciprocity Principle* yields the most plausible result.

It might be objected that Elle acts permissibly in *Unconscious,* not because Dev is the beneficiary, but because he most likely would have consented. Perhaps we should give hypothetical consent some weight here, but if so, it does not follow that *The Benefit Principle* is inert. Suppose there is a slightly better than 50 per cent chance Dev would not consent. I doubt Elle would be acting impermissibly by performing the rescue. Suppose there is a 90 per cent chance Dev would not consent. Still, the 10 per cent chance that Elle, by doing nothing, would leave Dev to suffer an unwanted death is enough to make the rescue permissible. In situations of uncertainty, though hypothetical consent should not be disregarded, at least some weight—perhaps most weight—should be placed on the benefit of intervention, suggesting it bears on the question of compensatory liability independently of consent.

One might also object that Elle has a duty to assist in *Unconscious* and therefore it would be unfair to force her to compensate Dev merely for doing her duty. This is the real reason why Dev cannot later demand compensation. This observation does not get to the heart of the matter, though. Suppose the assistance is not obligatory but supererogatory, perhaps because Dev is lying in the middle of a busy road, creating a risk for Elle. If she assists nevertheless and Dev suffers the same outcome, the judgement that he has no moral claim against her to compensate is just as strong.

It is also important to note that the question of who benefits is not merely a relational matter between injurer and victim. This is often obscured by the fact that, typically, the injurer benefits most from the risky activity. But cases like *Unconscious* show that this is not always true. Third parties who are completely uninvolved in the interaction may also be beneficiaries. Consider:

and Noncombatants' (2010) 38 Philosophy & Public Affairs 342, 360 and Victor Tadros, *The Ends of Harm: The Moral Foundations of Criminal Law* (Oxford University Press 2011) ch 10.

[15] For an argument to this effect, see Adam Slavny., 'On Being Wronged and Being Wrong' (2017) 16 Politics, Philosophy & Economics 3.

Life Raft 5: Dev is set adrift, in danger of death. Elle can save him but will have to clamber over Farrah's body, imposing a small risk of harm. Elle does this and Farrah is harmed.

In *Life Raft 5*, *The Benefit Principle* plausibly implies Dev should compensate Farrah for the injury although he is not involved in the interaction at all. In cases where the beneficiary and the risk imposer are different individuals, the independent significance of benefit distribution is more evident.

Another virtue of *The Benefit Principle* is that it provides some normative basis for liability to compensate in cases of joint enterprise and vicarious liability. Recall:

Joint Enterprise: Ove and Pia own a roofing business. Ove does the books while Pia repairs the roofs, though they both benefit equally from their joint activities. While fixing a roof, Pia negligently injures Quints.

And here is a generic instance of vicarious liability:

Vicarious Liability: Ove runs a business that requires Pia to use roadside machinery. After a moment of carelessness, Pia loses control of the machinery and it injures a pedestrian, Quints.

In both *Joint Enterprise* and *Vicarious Liability*, *The Benefit Principle* implies that Ove has a duty to bear some of the costs of compensating Quints. Some reject the idea that appeal to benefits could support vicarious liability, at least as the legal doctrine is usually understood.[16] Three reasons for this are that (i) in law, charities and the state are vicariously liable even though they do not proceed for their own benefit; (ii) *The Benefit Principle* cannot explain why employers are only liable for the *torts* of their employees, rather than for all harm caused by employees; and (iii) *The Benefit Principle* does not explain the joint and several liability of Ove and Pia, implying instead that there is some reason for them to share the costs of compensation in proportion to how much they benefit.

Though all these points would have merit if *The Benefit Principle* were proposed as an interpretive account, they are less forceful from a foundationalist perspective. First, the argument for making charities vicariously liable for the torts of their employees is, if not insupportable, at least weaker than the

---

[16] See Rob Stevens, *Tort and Rights* (Oxford University Press 2007) 259.

equivalent argument for commercial enterprises. *The Benefit Principle* captures this difference in plausibility. With respect to the state, the situation is also complicated. When employees of the state commit torts in the course of providing services of substantial benefit to the public, *The Benefit Principle* implies there is reason to ensure that the public, via the state, bear the costs of compensation. Thus, vicarious liability for the state might be defensible even though the state is not a profit-making entity in the same way as commercial enterprise.

The Benefit Principle also supports some degree of vicarious liability for the non-tortious conduct of employees. Consider a variation of *Vicarious Liability* in which Pia's loss of control of the machinery is not attributable to negligence but to a reasonable mistake. This does not change the fact that she is engaged in a project at Ove's instruction and for the benefit of the enterprise that Ove runs. *The Benefit Principle* yields some reason for liability in this case, but this is not necessarily a strike against it, as it does not follow that vicarious liability for non-tortious conduct is all-things-considered justified. There are other reasons for limiting vicarious liability to tortious conduct. One is that otherwise it would be prohibitively expensive for employers, which would then have knock on effects for employees and consumers. Another is that it is more difficult to control tortious than non-tortious conduct which may affect the incentives created by liability to take cost effective precautions. I take no position on whether the current law of vicarious liability strikes the correct balance between these and other considerations. The point is rather that, if the restriction of vicarious liability to tortious conduct is indeed justified, this does not show *The Benefit Principle* is wrong or inapplicable, only that it is outweighed.

A similar point can be made about the fact that *The Benefit Principle* implies a degree of costs-sharing rather than joint and several liability. In *Joint Enterprise*, the best outcome is for Ove and Pia to share the costs of compensating Quints, since they equally benefit from the enterprise and initiate it together. In *Vicarious Liability*, it is arguable that Ove should bear greater costs than Pia for the sake of compensating Quints, in proportion to the extent to which Ove is the primary beneficiary of the project. In any case, it is not very plausible that Pia should be liable for the full extent of Quints' injuries if Ove is the primary beneficiary.[17] Again, these considerations might be outweighed by the practical difficulty of seeking contributions from multiple parties. Where it

---

[17] It may be pointed out that in practice Pia would be judgement proof given her inability to pay substantial damages and the obvious advantages of suing Ove, the employer, instead. But this is not an adequate defence of a legal rule. An unjust law that is never enforced due to practical constraints is still an unjust law. This assumption is shared, I think, by many tort apologists who think of core legal rules as justified in principle as well as in practice.

is costly, difficult, or impossible to do this, we have reason to ensure victims of torts are not left to bear the burden. A better solution is to impose joint and several liability and permit defendants to seek contributions from other responsible parties in third party proceedings. But, as before, this shows not that *The Benefit Principle* is wrong or inapplicable, only that it is outweighed by competing factors.

B. Unwanted Benefits

Arguments that ground cost-sharing duties in the receipt of benefits face a more serious objection made famous by Robert Nozick. He asks, 'if each day a different person on your street sweeps the entire street, must you do so when your time comes?'[18] In a similar vein, Ronald Dworkin remarks, 'suppose a philosopher broadcasts a stunning and valuable lecture from a sound truck. Do all those who hear it—even all those who enjoy and profit from it—owe him a lecture fee?'[19] Surely these imposed benefits cannot ground an obligation to contribute to sweep the street or pay the lecture fee.

Subsections (a) and (b) of *The Benefit Principle* are designed to deal with this objection. As we saw in *Unconscious,* when it is uncertain whether a person would accept some benefit, and there is no duty to obtain consent, we should place some weight on that benefit even if we can make an educated guess regarding hypothetical consent. This situation is covered by subsection (b). Subsection (a) rules out the kind of cases envisioned by Nozick and Dworkin. The complaint against foisted benefits is substantially weakened, if not eliminated, when those benefits are endorsed. The notion of endorsement is intended to track a person's values and desires whilst being broader than consent. Where there is no duty to obtain consent, endorsement of the benefit suffices to ground cost-sharing duties.

What exactly is meant by endorsement of a benefit? Of course, one endorses a benefit if it is explicitly consented to or voluntarily acquired. In both *Joint Enterprise* and *Vicarious Liability*, for example, Ove acquires the benefit by

---

[18] Robert Nozick, *Anarchy, State, and Utopia* (Blackwell 1974), 94.

[19] Ronald Dworkin, *Law's Empire* (Harvard University Press 1986), 194. *The Benefit Principle* has a wide range of potential applications. For a Dworkinian argument that third parties who benefit from the positive externalities of procreation are not required to share the costs with those who decide to reproduce, see Paula Casal and Andrew Williams, 'Equality of Resources and Procreative Justice' in Justine Burley (ed), *Dworkin and his Critics* (Blackwell 2005) 150–69.

initiating, running, or authorizing the risky activity that confers that benefit. The situation is more complicated in cases where consent is not explicit or the beneficiary has not done anything to bring about the benefit. Nevertheless, when benefits accrue independently of consent or voluntary acquisition, they are sometimes endorsed. Take the example of a system of public transportation. Such a system benefits most or all citizens, either through the facilitation of personal projects or the provision of goods and services. Most of those who benefit from this system endorse it even though they have not explicitly consented to it or voluntarily acquired it.[20]

The kind of endorsement I have in mind has both behavioural and psychological dimensions. For example, most of us seek to enjoy or maximize the benefits that depend on transportation, to protect them and complain when they are interfered with and to lay claim to the moral rights that protect us against these interferences. The agents in Nozick and Dworkin's examples passively receive benefits, performing no positive actions with the intention of maximizing or using them. Nor do they seek to protect those benefits by laying claim to moral rights that prohibit interference by others. By contrast, we typically engage in this behaviour with respect to many benefits that depend on transportation, and we can plausibly infer endorsement from this, without insisting that a person endorses a benefit merely by failing to disgorge or avoid it. These behaviours are usually indicative of a pro or valuing attitude towards the benefits that are sought, used, and protected. Generally, this implies that an individual would have voluntarily acquired them given the choice.

When endorsement of this form is present, the 'enforced benefits' objection is not plausible, for two reasons. First, the fact that the beneficiary has no reasonable opportunity to avoid being benefitted no longer seems decisive. We have no opportunity to avoid the benefits of transport infrastructure, but endorsement distinguishes this case from Nozick's street sweeper and Dworkin's lecturer. In those cases, the actions of those who create benefits are objectionable even if the beneficiary would have consented to pay for the benefit, since actual consent could have been obtained. When actual consent to a transaction is possible, it is often wrong to rely on hypothetical consent.[21] As the

---

[20] See also Aaron James' argument that those who do not benefit from voluntarily assuming risks can nevertheless be expected to bear burdens for the sake of preventing similar burdens to others, Aaron James, 'Contractualism's (Not So) Slippery Slope' (2012) 18 Legal Theory 263, 271.

[21] Victor Tadros, 'Orwell's Battle with Brittain: Vicarious Liability for Unjust Aggression' (2014) 42 Philosophy & Public Affairs 42, 67–68.

transportation example makes clear, it is often not possible to obtain prior consent, which makes it more plausible that endorsement suffices to generate reasons to compensate when the beneficial activity results in harm.

Second, unlike Nozick and Dworkin's cases, duties created by *The Benefit Principle* do not involve the subjection of one person's will to another. One reason why Nozick's street sweeper cannot create duties for the beneficiaries, or why Dworkin's lecture cannot give him a right to demand payment, is that these actions subject the beneficiaries to someone else's will. They cannot prevent themselves experiencing or enjoying the benefit and therefore have no way of opting out of the arrangement. But on the view defended here, compensatory duties cannot be engaged merely by imposing a benefit. The recipient must also endorse it, and we have more voluntary control over whether we endorse some benefit than we do over whether we experience or enjoy it. One's own will remains the ultimate arbiter of whether the potential for compensatory liability is engaged.

IV. Avoidance Costs

A. In Defence of The Avoidance Principle

The Benefit Principle does not exhaust the range of distributive fairness considerations relevant to corrective duties. Another important factor is the avoidance costs of the risk. Recall:

> *The Avoidance Principle*: Whenever one party harms another, there is a *pro tanto* duty for the cost to be borne by the party for whom it was less costly to avoid the risk.

In cases of negligence, often the victim of the injury would have to bear greater costs to avoid it by virtue of the fact that control over the outcome lies mainly with the injurer. *The Avoidance Principle* thus underpins the wrongfulness of negligence. *The Benefit Principle* does too, since parties are usually the primary beneficiaries of their own negligent actions. That these two principles are often co-extensive with negligence can mislead us into thinking they have no independent significance, but this is not true. In fact, they both form part of a broader set of concerns grounded in distributive fairness, which overlaps with but is separate from negligence.

Consider:

Trolley 1: Dev must take a trolley to a well to get clean water. Elle likes to stroll along the track as it is picturesque, though she knows the trolley passes through. The trolley injures Elle while she is on one of her strolls.

Trolley 2: Dev takes a trolley to enjoy the picturesque view. Elle must brave the track to obtain clean water, though she knows the trolley passes through. The trolley injures Elle while she is retrieving water.

In *Trolley 1*, *The Avoidance Principle* plausibly implies there is some reason to let the loss lie where it falls since the cost to Dev of refraining from using the track is much greater than the cost to Elle. This is true even though Dev imposes a non-reciprocal risk on Elle. Thus *The Avoidance Principle*, like *The Benefit Principle*, conflicts with *The Non-reciprocity Principle* and when it does the former gives the more plausible result.

The relevance of avoidance cost is especially evident when we compare *Trolley 1* with *Trolley 2*. The case for letting the loss lie where it falls is greater in *Trolley 1* than in *Trolley 2*. Even supposing the injury is negligently caused in *Trolley 1*, *The Avoidance Principle* is not completely overridden. The high cost of refraining from using the trolley means Dev has little choice but to do so despite the risk to Elle. Moreover, negligence is statistically unavoidable over time, though each instance of negligence may be avoidable. As we saw in Chapter 4, negligence may be unavoidable in some individual instances too, depending on the capacities of the agent in question. When combined with the ease with which Elle can avoid subjecting herself to the risk, there is an argument to let the loss lie where it falls (or at least share the costs of compensation) rather than imposing the full burden on Dev.

When we hold other things constant, avoidance becomes more clearly relevant. Consider:

Life Raft 5: Dev, Elle, and Farrah are set adrift in danger of death. Elle has a broken arm. Farrah can climb aboard a life raft and potentially save them all. In order to do so they must climb over Dev's unconscious body, risking injury. Farrah does this, saving their lives, but in doing so breaks Dev's arm. Elle could have chosen a safer seat on the raft, where Farrah could have saved them without clambering over anyone, but she made an informed choice not to do so because it was more inconvenient. Dev, being unconscious, had no choice over which seat he took.

In *Life Raft* 5, three factors are held constant. The outcomes for Dev and Elle are the same (they both have a broken arm); neither imposes a non-reciprocal risk on the other (Farrah is the one who performs the rescue); and they benefit equally. However, it is not plausible that the cost of compensating Dev should be divided between them. Dev could not have chosen the safer seat, while Elle had the opportunity to do so at low cost but refused. The relative costs of avoiding the risk as between Dev and Elle make a difference to who should bear the burden of compensating the harm.

It is worth pausing here to clarify the relationship between *The Avoidance Principle* and the legal defences of *volenti non fit injuria* and contributory negligence. *The Avoidance Principle* provides a degree of support for these defences. If a person could easily have avoided some harm, we may infer that they consented to the risk or that their own fault was a contributory factor. On the other hand, *The Avoidance Principle* is not reducible to either of these defences. Though easy avoidance might be evidence of consent, it is not identical to it. Contributory negligence is a closer fit, but there are two key differences between it and *The Avoidance Principle*. One is that the latter does not require that a person contribute to their injury in the sense of playing a causal role. The second is that the 'fault' component of contributory negligence, with all the moral symmetry between injurer and victim that it implies, is highly misleading. The person who could easily have avoided an outcome might fall short of ordinary standards of prudence or self-preservation, but they are not negligent in the sense of being a wrongdoer. Finally, *The Avoidance Principle* is comparative. It invites us to consider, as between the relevant parties, who could most easily have avoided the outcome. Unlike the defences of *volenti* and contributory negligence, it is not focussed only on the conduct of the victim.

B. Choice and Opportunity

The Avoidance Principle is part of an implicit account of distributive fairness because it captures the idea that we are sometimes required to pay for our choices in relation to activities that create burdens and benefits. TM Scanlon defends a similar view. Scanlon argues that the existence of prior choice can weaken a person's complaint against being responsible (in the allocative sense we employed in Chapter 5) for harms they could have avoided. He claims that responsibility depends on 'the value of the opportunity to choose that the person is presented with. If a person has been placed in a sufficiently good position, this can make it the case that he or she has no valid complaint against what results.'[22]

So far, our discussion of *The Avoidance Principle* has been ambiguous between two interpretations. The first is a *choice-based* interpretation, according to which what matters is the way avoidance costs figure in a person's choice to expose themselves to risk. The second is an *opportunity-based* interpretation according to which what matters is the quality of a person's opportunity to avoid some outcome, regardless of how it figures in their actual choices.

Though Scanlon defends an opportunity-based account in his discussion of substantive responsibility,[23] there are three reasons to favour a choice-based interpretation of *The Avoidance Principle*. To illustrate the first reason, consider Scanlon's example in which hazardous waste threatens to contaminate a water supply and must be removed. He stipulates that the officials managing the removal take extensive precautions, including fencing off dangerous sites and wetting the material to mitigate the risk. They also put up signs warning people of the potential danger. Scanlon argues that, at some point, the officials can say they have done enough to prevent harm to the wider population and the opportunity to avoid incurring harm by heeding the warnings means that those who failed to heed the warnings cannot complain if they suffer harm. On the opportunity-based interpretation, the officials fulfil their obligations because the warnings give people a fair opportunity to avoid harm. It does not matter whether any individual actually sees the warning and thus makes a conscious choice to disregard the risk.[24] On the choice-based interpretation, a conscious choice to undergo the risk is required, at least in the sense that a person undergoes the risk knowingly, even in the absence of explicit or implicit acceptance.[25]

---

[22] TM Scanlon, *What We Owe to Each Other* (Harvard University Press 1998) 258 (hereafter Scanlon, *What We Owe*).

[23] Emmanuel Voyiakis develops Scanlon's account into a fully fledged theory of private law in *Private Law and The Value of Choice* (Hart 2017) (hereafter Voyiakis, *Private Law*).

[24] Scanlon, *What We Owe* (n 22) 258.

[25] Scanlon calls this the Forfeiture View. The rationale for this view is that 'a person who could have chosen to avoid a certain outcome, but who knowingly passed up this choice, cannot complain of the result: *volenti no fit iniuria*'. See Scanlon, *What We Owe* (n 22) 259. The choice-based interpretation of *The Avoidance Principle* that I favour does require consent or acceptance of a risk, whether implicit or explicit.

The opportunity-based interpretation is subject to the following objection, pressed by Andrew Williams, Alex Voorhoeve and Zofia Stemplowska.[26] Consider a modification of Scanlon's hazardous waste example in which two policies are available.[27] The first (call it Inform Everyone) involves a widespread information campaign, warning inhabitants of the dangers. If this policy is adopted, we can predict that one person whom we cannot identify will be impetuously curious and ignore the warnings, incurring lung damage (call them Curious). The second policy (Vivid Warning) involves using vivid warnings that will be more convincing but will cost more and thus reach fewer people. If this policy is adopted, we can predict that one person whom we cannot identify will not receive the warning and incur lung damage on their daily walk (call them Walker). Intuitively, Inform Everyone should be chosen over Vivid Warning because although it will lead to the same amount of harm, it will give people an equal opportunity to *choose*. Walker can complain that under Vivid Warning they are not given a choice, whereas Curious has no such complaint about Inform Anyone. This difference matters even though we know in advance that Curious will choose badly. The opportunity-based interpretation is only concerned with the opportunity to avoid, not whether a choice is actually made, and therefore cannot distinguish between the complaints of Curious and Walker.

There are a few things that can be said in response to this critique. First, one reason why Scanlon thinks the opportunity-based interpretation is preferable to the choice-based one[28] is that only the former can explain why a person who hears the warning and forgets about it has no complaint (call them Forgetful). Second, Scanlon has responded that the opportunity-based interpretation *does* have the resources to explain why Inform Everyone should be selected over Vivid Warning. A warning is a benefit, he thinks, and although the value of this benefit is reduced by the likelihood that a person will not act on it, those who receive the warning still have a weaker objection than those who do not.[29]

---

[26] Andrew Williams, 'Liberty, Liability and Contractualism' in Nils Holtug and Kasper Lippert-Rasmussen (eds), *Egalitarianism: New Essays on the Nature and Value of Equality* (Clarendon Press 2006) (hereafter Williams, 'Liberty'); Alex Voorhoeve, 'Scanlon on Substantive Responsibility' (2008) 16 Journal of Political Philosophy 184 (hereafter Voorhoeve, 'Scanlon on Substantive Responsibility'); and Zofia Stemplowska, 'Harmful Choices: Scanlon and Voorhoeve on Substantive Responsibility' (2013) 10 Journal of Moral Philosophy 488.

[27] This modified example is from Voorhoeve, 'Scanlon on Substantive Responsibility' (n 26).

[28] Or in Scanlon's terminology, the Will Theory, see TM Scanlon, 'Responsibility and the Value of Choice' (2013) 12 Think 9, 9–10.

[29] TM Scanlon, 'Reply to Zofia Stemplowska' (2013) 10 Journal of Moral Philosophy 508, 511.

Taking the second point first, it is unclear why the warning is a benefit if a person will not act upon it. Quite the opposite. For Curious, the warning is a burden because their curiosity would not have been piqued had there been no warning.[30] We could respond by varying the case so that Curious has prior opportunities to curb their curiosity. Suppose, for example, that they understand their curious nature and recruit friends and family to help them overcome it.[31] There is a worry that this move shifts the goalposts, and we can shift them back by imagining cases where Curious has no such prior opportunities. Suppose they have no one to help them overcome their curious nature, or their nature is intractable. The judgement that Inform Everyone is preferable to Vivid Warning remains just as intuitive.

On the first point, it is important to distinguish between different ways in which the warnings fail to take effect. For Curious, the warning fails because they choose badly. For Forgetful, the warning fails because, though it registers with them, they subsequently forget it. For Walker, the warning fails because they never receive it. The cases of Forgetful and Walker are a little underspecified. One reason we tend to think Forgetful has no complaint is because we assume they are responsible for their forgetfulness. If we suppose they forget because of a medical condition that impairs their memory, on the other hand, it seems their position is materially similar to Walker's, who never receives the warning.

With respect to Walker, if they overhear their neighbours talking about a potential hazard and can find out about the warning by asking them, but fail to do so because they are reckless, we might be inclined to treat their complaint as no stronger than that of Curious, or at least as weaker than the intuition in the original case. Conversely, if Walker would be prepared to incur significant costs to avoid lung damage but never gets to make the choice because they are unaware of the risk, this suggests more strongly that Inform Everyone is the right policy.

This analysis indicates that choice is relevant because it reveals how people weight their interests in avoiding risks with their other desires, values, and goals. The basis of *The Avoidance Principle* is not so much that a person's safety can be disregarded once one has given them sufficient opportunity to protect themselves, but that principles of liability should incorporate a degree of ambition or choice-sensitivity. We are free to make a range of choices regarding

[30] Williams, 'Liberty' (n 26) 254.
[31] For this solution to the problem, see Emmanuel Voyiakis, *Private Law* (n 23) 91.

the degree of risk we are willing to expose ourselves to in pursuit of our chosen ends, and these choices affect the costs we can force others to bear for us if those risks materialize into harm. If some place less weight on their security relative to their other interests, for example, this weakens their claim to common resources compared to someone who does not. Curious makes an explicit choice whilst Walker is denied the opportunity. This is why the background information in the hazardous waste example is so important. If Forgetful forgets because they are more interested in other things, their behaviour is closer to Curious' than Walker's. If they forget as a result of a memory impairment, their position is closer to Walker's. Our shifting attitudes towards Walker, Curious, and Forgetful in these variations track the intuition that principles of compensatory liability should be choice-sensitive.

Let's return to the second reason to favour the choice-based interpretation of *The Avoidance Principle*, which is that it allows it to remain plausible in the face of the objection from prior causes. The objection from prior causes states that a person's choice is either determined, or caused non-deterministically, by prior events over which the agent has no control. If these prior causes make it inevitable or random that an agent will decide in a certain way, we cannot appeal to the protective value of choice to explain why agents such as Curious have weaker claims than others. Once Curious has entered the site, we know that it was inevitable or random that they would choose to do so. Thus, the sign did not provide them with any actual protection, and we cannot now appeal to the protective value of the sign to explain why their claim to being rescued or compensated is weaker than Walker's.[32]

The choice-based interpretation sidesteps this objection because, according to it, the reason why Curious' claim is weaker than Walker's is not based on the protective value of choice. Instead, it depends on the Dworkinian idea that Curious must pay for his choices rather than foisting them onto others.[33] Curious is entitled to prioritize their curiosity over their safety. Indeed, this is a crucial freedom which enables them to lead a more autonomous life. But when Curious exercises this choice, their claim to common resources is weakened relative to those who do not.

---

[32] For this way of putting the objection, see Victor Tadros, *To Do To Die, To Reason Why: Individual Ethics in War* (Oxford University Press 2022) 154 (hereafter Tadros, *To Do, To Die*).

[33] *The Avoidance Principle* does not adopt Dworkin's hypothetical insurance model wholesale but has a clear debt to its approach to choice-sensitivity. See Ronald Dworkin, *Sovereign Virtue* (Harvard University Press 2000) (hereafter Dworkin, *Sovereign Virtue*).

V. Choice Sensitive Fairness

The Benefit Principle and *The Avoidance Principle* interlink to form a fairness-based account of liability to compensate. This account allocates liability so as to effect a fair distribution of the burdens and benefits of risky activity, but in a way that is suitably choice-sensitive. A few additional points are worth making about this account. First, it is not a complete account of fairness, as it leaves many issues unresolved, including what definition of benefits and burdens we should adopt and whether this definition should be purely objective. Similarly, it does not take into account background distributions of burdens and benefits, which, as *Life Raft 3* suggests, are relevant to all things considered judgements about liability. We will investigate this issue further in Chapter 7.

Second, our account overlaps with and is mutually supportive of the wrong of negligence, without being reducible to it. Often, when one commits negligence, the action is done for one's own benefit and the negligent actor could have avoided the risk at a lower cost than others. The fairness rationale therefore buttresses negligence as a ground for corrective duties. This might lead us to adopt a reductive attitude towards negligence, as Fletcher does. On his view, negligence grounds compensation because it is a variety of non-reciprocal risk. However, the view defended here is non-reductive; negligence and the fairness basis for liability can come apart. Consider the case of the volunteer ambulance driver who hits someone with their vehicle whilst rushing a patient to hospital after a cardiac arrest. We might imagine two variations of the case: one in which the driver is negligent and one in which they are not. If they are not negligent, they are still outcome responsible for the injury, but the case for holding them liable to compensate seems weak. The driver is a volunteer and others are the primary beneficiaries of their actions; it is fairer to distribute the costs of compensation amongst the beneficiaries. In the negligent variation, the case for holding the driver liable is perhaps stronger. But the fact that they were acting for the benefit of third parties is surely relevant. Those who think the driver should compensate the victim might accept that their reasons to do so are weaker compared to the person who is negligently joyriding, even if those reasons are still strong enough to ground a corrective duty.

This is one of the features of this account that makes it superior to *The Non-Reciprocity Principle*. The latter attempts to unify negligence and strict liability, and this ambition makes it vulnerable to the kind of criticisms that we made against *the continuity thesis*, namely that it fails to give wrongdoing its proper role in grounding corrective duties. *The Benefit Principle* and *The Avoidance Principle*, on the other hand, provide some support for the view that negligent actors should compensate those they harm, but do not seek to reduce the wrong of negligence to an instance of distributive unfairness.

Third, *The Avoidance Principle* is motivated not by the idea that we forfeit rights of protection by failing to take opportunities to avoid harm, but by the idea that our choices reveal or are constitutive of the way we value our own protection relative to other values, including our own goals and desires and the importance of others. For this reason, the principle encompasses both moral and prudential costs. Return to the case of the volunteer ambulance driver. If they have a moral duty to drive quickly to increase the chance of saving lives, the risks they impose are unavoidable without breaching this duty. And duties are not the only relevant moral costs—supererogatory costs should also be taken into account. If some act is supererogatory, this is a reason against holding a person liable to compensate for harm caused in doing that act. In both cases, the moral costs of avoiding some action show that their weighting of their own safety compared to their other ends does not weaken their claim to common resources.

In this way, *The Avoidance Principle* is impervious to an important objection to views that incorporate some form of the option luck/brute luck distinction. In Dworkin's original formulation, 'option luck is a matter of how deliberate and calculated gambles turn out—whether someone gains or loses through accepting an isolated risk he or she should have anticipated and might have declined', whilst 'brute luck is a matter of how risks fall out that are not in that sense deliberate gambles'.[34] The risks taken by the ambulance driver are a matter of option rather than brute luck. On a strict application of the option/brute luck distinction, the case for holding the ambulance driver liable to compensate is just as strong as the case against the person who drives for their own benefit.[35] This is not plausible: the moral costs of not driving the ambulance mean that it is unfair if the driver also internalizes the risks it imposes.

Finally, another important feature of our account is that the question of compensatory liability is not a purely relational matter between the injurer and victim. The wrong of negligence is relational, but the fairness account is not. A complete theory of the grounds of corrective duties must therefore

---

[34] Dworkin, *Sovereign Virtue* (n 33) 73.
[35] See also Tadros, *To Do, To Die* (n 32) s 7.2.

incorporate both relational and non-relational elements. It is often true that *The Benefit Principle* and *The Avoidance Principle* connect the injurer and victim. But this is a contingent matter and does not always hold. Sometimes the victim will benefit more from the risk than the injurer (as in *Unconscious*) and sometimes they will benefit equally (as in many of our *Life Raft* variations) and sometimes individuals other than the victim and injurer may benefit (as in *Joint Enterprise* and *Vicarious Liability*). Similarly, sometimes the victim can avoid the risk at the lowest cost, and sometimes they can avoid the risk at equal cost, and sometimes individuals other than the victim and injurer may be the ones who can avoid the risk at the lowest cost. Consider:

> *Life Raft 6*: Farrah goes swimming in choppy waters and starts struggling. Dev and Elle can rescue Farrah with their life raft but to do so Dev must impose a risk of injury on Elle. Dev does so, rescuing Farrah but breaking Elle's arm in the process.

Intuitively, Farrah should compensate Elle for the injury, despite that fact that Farrah was not party to the injurer/victim relationship. Farrah could have avoided this situation at the lowest cost (the costs of doing nothing are high, since Dev and Elle are required to save Farrah, or at least there is a substantial moral loss in not saving them), and Farrah is the primary beneficiary of the risk. Even if Dev wrongs Elle in performing the rescue, say by imposing a greater risk than is necessary to rescue Farrah, it is still plausible that Farrah should bear all or some of the cost of compensating Elle.

Conclusion

In this chapter we discussed the final limb of the four-fold analysis, arguing that considerations of distributive fairness have a direct impact on individual corrective duties. We evaluated three distributive principles, *The Non-Reciprocity Principle*, *The Benefit Principle*, and *The Avoidance Principle*. While we cast doubt on the independent significance of *The Non-Reciprocity* principle, the other two interlock to form a fairness-based rationale for corrective duties.

By this point in the book, the breadth and diversity of the grounds of corrective duties should be evident. They arise as a result of wrongful harming, as in the case of negligence, but also as a result of causing harm via the Doctrine of Doing and Allowing. They arise in the form of conditional permissibility, and also as a result of a fair distribution of the benefits and burdens of risky activity. All these factors play some role, and any attempt to reduce the grounds of corrective duties to a single idea or principle is destined to fail. In Chapter 7, we expand the scope of our enquiry beyond the grounds of corrective duties to focus on the impact of distributive injustice on these duties.

7

Corrective and Distributive Justice

Introduction

The relationship between corrective and distributive justice has been much discussed. Often, the focus is on the relative independence of the two spheres of justice, with some insisting they are irreducibly separate and others arguing they are more porous. On one end of the spectrum is Weinrib's view that corrective justice is strictly limited to the bilateral relationship between the doer and sufferer of harm,[1] and on the other end is the position that a single ideal—such as equal protection from bad luck—should be realized in both spheres.[2]

One problem with thinking about the relationship between corrective and distributive justice in general terms is that the tension between them can be unpacked in different ways. Here are seven questions that will help us disambiguate the relevant issues.

(1) Should agents prioritize fulfilling their corrective duties over their distributive duties?

(2) Should the state prioritize redressing corrective injustice over distributive injustice?

(3) Can corrective justice survive anti-luck objections?

(4) Do corrective duties arise when the victim is above the threshold for distributive justice?

(5) Do corrective duties arise when the injurer is below the threshold for distributive justice?

---

[1] See Ernest Weinrib, *The Idea of Private Law* (first published 1995, Oxford University Press 2012) 71 (hereafter Weinrib, *The Idea of Private Law*).

[2] See Ronen Avraham and Issa Kohler-Hausmann, 'Accident Law for Egalitarians' (2006) 12 Legal Theory 181. Some adopt a more moderate position. Stephen Perry accepts that enforcing corrective justice irrespective of the prior allocation of wealth may not be permissible but argues that there are different justificatory bases for claims in corrective and distributive justice. See 'On the Relationship between Corrective and Distributive Justice' in Jeremy Horder (ed), *Oxford Essays in Jurisprudence* (Oxford University Press 2000) 237. Others have criticized specific legal rules from a distributive justice perspective, particularly in relation to recovery for lost earnings, noting that this rule re-entrenches inequalities in earning capacity, and that the pricing of liability insurance is regressive, effectively forcing low-earners to subsidize high-earners. On the regressive cross subsidy, see Tsachi Keren-Paz, 'Private Law Redistribution, Predictability and Liberty' (2005) 50 McGill Law Journal 327, 337–38.

Wrongs, Harms, and Compensation. Adam Slavny, Oxford University Press. © Adam Slavny 2023.
DOI: 10.1093/oso/9780192864567.003.0007

(6) Do corrective duties arise when the victim is above the threshold for distributive justice *and* the injurer is below the threshold?

(7) What implications do these answers have for how courts should decide cases and the justification of tort law more generally?

None of these questions should be conflated with any of the others. We will try to address them, inevitably in a non-exhaustive way, in this chapter. We will find that there is no straightforward generalization to be made about the priority or independence of the two spheres of justice. In some respects corrective justice has priority, in others distributive justice has priority, and in others there is parity. This mixed picture should bring no comfort to tort apologists. Although corrective duties are not reducible to deviations from distributive justice or always overridden by them, interference effects between the two spheres present systemic problems for the justification of tort in conditions of background injustice.

To explore the relationship between corrective and distributive justice, I make a number of simplifying assumptions that I spell out here. First, we assume wellbeing is the currency of distributive justice, focussing on cases in which different individuals in a group are better or worse off than others, or where we have reasons to move towards a more just distribution. This choice is for ease of framing more than anything else, and the cases we discuss could be reframed in terms of any other currency such as resources, primary goods, opportunities, utility, capabilities, etc.

Second, I will sometimes refer to the threshold of distributive justice. Again, this is mainly for ease of exposition. It clarifies that, whatever theory turns out to be correct, there will be some who have more than their fair share (above the threshold) and some who have less (below the threshold). Where this threshold lies depends on the correct criterion for distribution, which is a hotly contested matter.[3] Four familiar criteria are equality, priority, sufficiency, and utility. To my mind, the two most plausible distributive criteria are equality and priority, and these will be my focus in this chapter. In the cases we discuss, their implications are co-extensive, so the difference between them need not concern us. The general arguments do not rely on these criteria, however, and could be reformulated in terms of sufficiency or utility.

---

[3] On equality, see Larry Temkin, *Inequality* (Oxford University Press 1993); on priority, see Derek Parfit, 'Equality and Priority' (1997) 10 Ratio 202 (hereafter Parfit, 'Equality and Priority'); and on sufficiency, see Harry Frankfurt, 'Equality as a Moral Ideal' (1987) 98 Ethics 21. There are other criteria for distribution including utility, the difference principle, maximin, and so on, but at present we will restrict our attention to a narrower range of principles.

Third, many theories of distributive justice incorporate some degree of responsibility or ambition sensitivity. That is, deviations from fair distributions are acceptable if they can be attributed to some form of fault or choice. We will assume any such conditions are met. When we speak of people being above or below the threshold, we are assuming this is an unjust distribution, rather than one that is just because it is traceable to a responsible choice on behalf of either of the parties.

Finally, what we must assume about the scope of distributive justice is more complicated. We will be concerned with the impact of distributive injustice on the moral corrective duties owed by injurers to their victims. Does this presuppose that duties of distributive justice are owed by individuals and have identifiable beneficiaries? Not exactly. We must assume that individuals at least have duties to contribute to systems of redistribution, even if they do not have duties to take distributive justice into their own hands, or to take it into account in all their choices.[4] This is enough to generate the conflict between corrective and distributive duties in terms of the duties of individuals rather than group entities like states. Although I do think duties of distributive justice arise independently of mediating group entities like states—when parents deal with children, when private organizations distribute benefits and burdens among members, when states fail to enforce their citizens' duties—we do not need this assumption to generate tension between corrective and distributive justice. It is possible to have individual duties to contribute to group projects which have specific beneficiaries. One might have a duty to contribute to a distributive project run by the state or some other organization like a charity rather than a duty to benefit some individual directly, but the difference between these group mediated duties and duties of direct transfer is not relevant for our purposes because it does not remove the conflict between corrective and distributive justice.

I. The Priority of Corrective over Distributive Justice

Sometimes, fulfilling corrective duties can exacerbate distributive unfairness. Consider:

---

[4] GA Cohen, 'Where the Action Is: On the Site of Distributive Justice' (1997) 26 Philosophy & Public Affairs 3.

> *Wrongful Harm*: Gil and Hara are neither too badly off nor too well off according to distributive justice. Gil becomes less well off in an accident that is no one's fault. Hara loses the same amount of wellbeing as a result of being wrongfully harmed by Ibra. Ibra can either fully compensate Hara or divide the same resources between Gil and Hara, making them each as well off as each other but neither as well off as they were before.

Since neither Gil nor Hara are responsible for their losses, the best result from a distributive justice perspective is for Ibra to divide their resources between them. Consider how equality and priority views would apply to this case. If we have reasons to realize equal welfare, then Ibra has some reason to divide resources. By doing this, they make Gil and Hara equally well off whereas the alternative exacerbates the inequality between them. According to prioritarianism, we ought to maximize moral value defined as weighted wellbeing, where the value of improving wellbeing for someone is greater the lower their lifelong level of wellbeing.[5] Prioritarianism also favours Ibra dividing resources between Gil and Hara. This would maximize value because the value of incremental benefits to Hara would start to diminish once she is better off than Gil as a result of compensation. Egalitarians and prioritarians therefore have some reason to think Ibra should divide their resources rather than compensate for their wrong. More generally, we might think it unfair if Hara ends up better off than Gil given that (1) they are both below the threshold for distributive justice, (2) this is through no fault or choice of their own, (3) Ibra can improve the situation in terms of distributive justice, and (4) if Ibra compensates Hara instead, they will exacerbate the situation in terms of distributive justice.

One response to this claim is that Ibra is linked to Hara via their wrongdoing, whereas they have no such link to Gil, and thus there is no reason why they should focus on Gil's wellbeing rather than anyone else's. This response does not get to the heart of the problem, though. In *Wrongful Harm*, we assume there is no other way Ibra can make improvements in terms of distributive justice, and this why they should focus on Gil. It might be pressed that, in a more realistic setting where Ibra could benefit any number of victims of distributive injustice, no individual could have a claim against them. But this does not follow. There are plausible ways of framing such a claim. Any individual within a group of eligible victims of distributive injustice may claim either (1) that Ibra owes it to them to benefit some of a group of which they are a member, or (2) that Ibra owes them a conditional duty to benefit them *if* they

---

[5] Parfit, 'Equality and Priority' (n 3).

do not benefit other eligible members of the group.[6] We would still have to explain why wrongdoers should prioritize their corrective duties over these more complex distributive duties.

Nevertheless, there are several reasons why Ibra should compensate Hara instead of dividing resources. First, if Ibra does not compensate Hara, Ibra will have harmed her, whereas if Ibra does not give resources to Gil, Ibra will merely have failed to benefit him. The Doctrine of Doing and Allowing gives Ibra reason to prioritize Hara over Gil. This reason would apply even if Ibra's action were not wrongful, as Ibra would still be outcome responsible. However, this argument would not apply if Ibra's corrective duty was grounded in a wrongful omission rather than a positive act, so this cannot be a general reason to favour corrective justice.

The fact that Ibra wrongs Hara also means that, second, *the responsiveness thesis* applies (see Chapter 3). Recall that this thesis states that:

> When someone violates a primary right/duty, they pay insufficient regard to the values that underpin it, and thus incur a duty to respond by paying proportionally greater regard than was previously sufficient to those values.

The responsiveness thesis also supports the claim that Ibra should prioritize Hara. Ibra must give Hara's wellbeing extra weight in their practical reasoning in proportion to the extent to which they disregarded her wellbeing through their wrongdoing, and this tips the balance in Hara's favour although it undermines distributive justice.

Third, Hara and Gil have equal claims in distributive justice, since they are both below the threshold to which they are entitled through no fault or choice of their own. But Hara has an additional claim against Ibra in corrective justice. Given that the claims in distributive justice are equally weighty, Hara's claim in corrective justice also tips the balance in favour of compensating her. To think otherwise implies that the normative force of corrective justice is inert or excluded. Perhaps distributive justice *outweighs* corrective justice, but it is not plausible to think it excludes it entirely.

Finally, Ibra has already fulfilled their distributive duties. The only reason they can now be expected to give up further resources is because of their wrong to Hara. Some of their resources are *morally unlocked*, in the sense that, by virtue of their wrongdoing, they can now be expected to give up further

---

[6] For this second way of understanding similar duties, see Victor Tadros, 'Refuge and Aid' (2023) 31 *Journal of Political Philosophy* 102, 123.

resources for certain purposes. Their wrongdoing is the only reason the tension between corrective and distributive justice arises—if not for this wrong, Ibra would owe no duty to either Hara or Gil. In light of this, it is not plausible that the resources that have been morally unlocked by Ibra's wrongdoing can be put to *any* use, or indeed the best use from an impartial moral perspective. They are unlocked *in order* to compensate Hara and cannot be diverted from that end simply because they can be used to serve other morally valuable ends such as improving distributive justice.

These considerations suggest that when all else is equal, agents should fulfil their corrective duties even when this results in patterns of wellbeing that are suboptimal from the perspective of distributive justice. This means corrective justice is independent in two senses. First, corrective duties are not reducible to duties to fix deviations in distributive justice. This is unsurprising given the four-fold analysis developed in the last four chapters. If this analysis has any plausibility, it entails, at the very least, that correcting deviations from distributive justice is not the only ground of corrective duties. Second, corrective duties are not always overridden by considerations of distributive justice, or indeed reasons to realize the best state of affairs from an impartial point of view. Corrective duties—at least those that arise from wronging or harming others—form part of that sphere of non-consequentialist morality that are not merely conduits for the impartial good.

Let's conclude this part by noting two limitations on the priority described above. First, it is weighted rather than lexical. Suppose Gil is made very badly off by the accident and Hara is made only slightly less well off by Ibra's wrong. Then the difference in wellbeing seems more decisive. If Ibra can lift Gil from misery and destitution, they ought to do this rather than provide a modest benefit to Hara who is much better off. There comes a point at which the need to improve the wellbeing of others, even those with whom one has no relationship, overrides the priority of corrective duties.[7] Second, this argument suggests only the first personal priority of corrective duties. It does not show that third parties or the state have any reasons to prioritize assisting victims of corrective injustice over victims of distributive injustice. This is because, from the perspective of the state (or any other third party) it is failing to benefit

[7] One reason for this is that Hara might have a duty to authorize Ibra to divert the resources to which she would otherwise be entitled to Gil, based on her duty of rescue. Tadros appeals to this idea to explain how a general deterrence justification for punishment can be derived from the protective duties wrongdoers owe their victims. See Victor Tadros, *The Ends of Harm: The Moral Foundations of Criminal Law* (Oxford University Press 2011) ch 12.

either way. The situation is different, of course, if the state itself is implicated in a wrongful failure to achieve distributive justice, but we will return to that possibility and its implications in pt V.

II. The Parity of Corrective and Distributive Injustice

A crucial feature of *Wrongful Harm* is that Gil's lowered wellbeing is not the result of distributive injustice. It is the result of an accident that is no one's fault rather than some past failure by Ibra or anyone else. This fact supports the case for Ibra fulfilling their corrective duty although doing so makes the relative wellbeing of Gil and Hara worse from a distributive justice perspective. The situation is more complex when we reverse this assumption. Suppose Ibra commits two wrongs: the wrong of failing to benefit Gil as per their duties in distributive justice and the wrong of harming Hara. Perhaps Ibra wrongfully avoids making their contribution to a just scheme that benefits Gil, and also negligently injures Hara. Suppose also that Ibra can now benefit either Gil or Hara but not both. Which should they choose?

Some of the considerations given above no longer favour corrective justice. *The responsiveness thesis* applies to both duties. Ibra's disregard of both Hara and Gil's interests—albeit in different ways—gives them a duty to pay more regard than was previously sufficient. Hara and Gil's claims in distributive justice against Ibra are also no longer equally weighty, since although they are both below the threshold for distributive justice, Gil's claim results from Ibra's previous wrongful failure and is therefore stronger. And whatever resources are morally unlocked by Ibra's wrongdoing, they can legitimately be put to either purpose, since Ibra has violated duties in both domains of justice. One consideration still favours Ibra's corrective duty, though: the Doctrine of Doing and Allowing. It is better for Ibra to prevent themselves continuing to wrongfully harm Hara than it is to prevent themselves continuing to wrongfully fail to benefit Gil. There is thus some reason to think Ibra should prioritize their corrective duty.

However, as we saw, this feature of Ibra's corrective duty is contingent, unless we adopt the view that there are no wrongful omissions, or that corrective duties never arise from such omissions. Suppose Ibra sees Hara struggling in the water and can save her life at no risk or cost to themselves. Intuitively, Ibra acts wrongly if they walk blithely by. Suppose further that Hara manages to pull herself out of the water but is in urgent need of medical attention which either Ibra or Gil, a bystander, can provide. Ibra rather than Gil should provide the assistance, suggesting they owe some special duty towards Hara that Gil lacks. This duty is best understood as a corrective duty grounded in Ibra's prior wrong, which is weightier than Gil's ordinary duty of rescue. Note that arguments as to why the law does or should not impose a duty of rescue are irrelevant on this point since such arguments bear on the enforceability of such moral duties rather than their existence. If duties of rescue exist, the Doctrine of Doing and Allowing does not provide any general way of demonstrating the priority of corrective over distributive duties. This means that fulfilling corrective duties arising from prior wrongdoing has no priority over fulfilling distributive duties arising from prior wrongdoing.

III. The Anti-Luck Objection

One objection to affording any priority to corrective over distributive duties is that the benefits and burdens of corrective justice depend on bad luck. Two distinctions are relevant here: between the victim and injurer's perspectives, and between brute and option luck. From the victim's perspective, it is a matter of brute luck whether one is harmed by another person or a natural event. Gil has an accident while Hara is wronged by Ibra. Should their access to compensation and therefore their comparative wellbeing depend on these facts, over which neither of them have any control?

This objection is considerably tempered by the following factor, though. That the recipient of a corrective duty has an advantage that another equally badly off person lacks does not preclude the possibility that the latter person is owed distributive duties by others. If some general version of luck egalitarianism is the right distributive view, victims of natural harms are entitled to the same level of wellbeing as victims of wrongful injury—it is just that, in this instance, compensation is owed by everyone as a collective rather than specific injurers. And since the state has no reason to prioritize redressing distributive injustice over corrective injustice, these victims would not be systematically disadvantaged relative to victims of wrongful injury in a society in which both sets of duties are properly fulfilled. This puts the anti-luck critic of corrective justice in something of a bind. If outcome inequality resulting from bad brute luck is truly objectionable across the board, this logic leads to a universal compensation scheme. If such a scheme is justified, however, victims of natural misfortunes would have no objection against the first personal priority of corrective justice, since it affects only who pays compensation rather than eligibility for compensation itself.

A more powerful objection is evident when we turn to the injurer's point of view. To see this objection, note that sometimes the same risks have drastically different outcomes in terms of liability for those who impose them. Consider Jeremy Waldron's example of two drivers, Fate and Fortune. Both briefly take their eyes off the road in a moment of carelessness, but while Fortune continues unnoticed, Fate veers into oncoming traffic and causes a disastrous accident. It seems unfair that Fate should be saddled with burdensome liability while Fortune gets away scot-free, given that their culpability is identical.[8] There are two concerning features about this case. One is that Fate and Fortune face vastly different liability despite their parity in terms of culpability, and the second is that Fate's liability is totally out of proportion to their wrong.

Here are two responses to this objection. The first is that the difference in outcomes between the two drivers is due to option luck rather than brute luck. Option luck, recall, is luck attributable to a person's fault or choice, and contrasts with brute luck, which is luck that is not so attributable.[9] By appeal to option luck, it can be argued that the difference in liability between the drivers is justified because they responsibly took the same risk. This risk was attributable to their choice or fault, and one of them cannot now complain that the risk turned out worse than they had hoped.

The second is that Fate and Fortune have not committed the same wrong. John Goldberg and Benjamin Zipursky reject the application of moral luck to this case on the grounds that Fortune breaches a duty of *non-injuriousness* while Fate breaches a duty of *non-injury*.[10] We have seen that causation makes a difference to liability, so it is not arbitrary to distinguish between the drivers on this basis. If we can vindicate the idea that causing harm grounds corrective duties independently of imposing risk, it follows that some degree of luck must affect liability.

Neither response eliminates the objection entirely, however. The problem is that both responses assume the objection is binary: either it is justified or unjustified for luck to play a role in liability. One reason for this framing is that the debate about *moral* luck is binary, in the sense that some argue that there is

---

[8] See Jeremy Waldron, 'Moments of Carelessness and Massive Loss' in David G Owen (ed), *The Philosophical Foundations of Tort Law* (Oxford University Press 1995) 387.

[9] This is a more pared down notion of option luck than Dworkin's original formulation. According to Dworkin, option luck is a matter of how 'deliberate and calculated gambles turn out—whether someone gains or loses through accepting an isolated risk he or she should have anticipated and might have declined', see Ronald Dworkin, *Sovereign Virtue: The Theory and Practice of Equality* (Harvard University Press 2000) 73. We dispense with the 'deliberate and calculated' requirement, since non-calculated risks that an agent chooses to impose are plausibly a matter of option luck.

[10] John CP Goldberg and Benjamin C Zipursky, *Recognizing Wrongs* (Harvard University Press 2022) 186–87.

moral luck (ie that certain forms of luck legitimately affect moral blameworthiness) while others argue there is not. A single example in which blameworthiness is legitimately affected by luck is enough to disprove the view that moral luck does not exist. This framing of the problem of moral luck has influenced the way the anti-luck objection is considered in the tort context. Goldberg and Zipursky, for example, explicitly address themselves to the problem of moral luck even though they are referring to liability rather than blameworthiness.

It may be appropriate to think of the moral luck problem in this binary way, but it is misleading when considering the relationship between luck and compensation. Given the arguments based on option luck and the grounds of corrective duties, it is true that some difference in liability is justified as a matter of luck. But this type of luck is not as counterintuitive as moral luck. We are more attached to the idea that we cannot be blameworthy due to factors beyond our control than we are to the idea that we cannot bear burdens due to factors beyond our control. Consider:

> *Parenthood 1*: Two men are warned not to smoke around their pregnant partners. Both ignore the warnings. One baby is born with brain damage while the other is healthy.
> *Parenthood 2*: Two men are given advice about contraception. Both ignore the advice. One gets his partner pregnant while the other does not.

Parenthood 1 is a paradigm case of moral luck. Philosophers will split on whether the two fathers are equally blameworthy, but those who think the father of the brain damaged child is more blameworthy should at least see the intuitive pull of the opposite view. In *Parenthood 2*, I suspect there would be more general agreement that the man who becomes a father owes the usual duties to his child, and there is no problem with the fact that the other man avoids these duties as a matter of luck. At the very least, any objection to the unequal outcome in *Parenthood 2* is much less weighty than the objection in *Parenthood 1*.

Equally, however, this does not mean the anti-luck challenge in tort has been answered. We should instead think of the challenge in a scalar way:

> *The Scalar Anti-Luck Objection*: The greater the luck-based discrepancy in terms of liability between individuals based on factors beyond their control, the stronger the objection to the role of luck.

Once we understand the challenge in this way, we can see that the arguments above do not provide a general defence of tort liability. For example, even if

Goldberg and Zipursky are right that Fate breaches a different duty to Fortune, and that this duty should have more serious consequences, the anti-luck objection has not been answered until we can show that this difference is commensurate with the *extent* of the difference in outcome attributable to luck. Similarly, appeal to option luck is not dispositive, as Waldron shows, because the difference in liability between Fate and Fortune is not commensurate with the significance of their decisions, which were merely fleeting moments of carelessness. Only a harsh and grudging adherence to the option/brute luck distinction would rationalize any degree of inequality of outcome on the basis of option luck. The anti-luck objection, then, is not best understood as challenging the mere fact that Fate and Fortune face differential liability due to factors beyond their control, but as challenging the scale of this difference.

One implication of this understanding of the anti-luck objection is worth drawing out. That the presence of luck is not a decisive objection to tort liability does not imply that we lack reasons to mitigate luck-based inequalities where possible, or that luck should have no bearing on a choice between multiple justified principles. One option, discussed by Waldron, is to replace tort with a compensation scheme that dispenses with the need to prove causation. We will consider such schemes in Chapter 8, and so shelve that discussion for now. Another is liability insurance. Some corrective justice theorists think of insurance as a permissible means of fulfilling one's corrective duties, not part of the justification or the normative structure of those duties. But here is one respect in which it is normatively significant: it mitigates the effect of outcome luck and thus reduces the objection that individuals like Fate can mount against compensatory liability. In many cases, I suspect, this makes the difference between the justified and unjustified enforcement of corrective duties.

IV. The Priority of Distributive over Corrective Justice

A. Just and Unjust Holdings

Consider:

> *Billionaire*: Jill, who is neither above nor below the threshold for distributive justice, negligently crashes into Kiki, a billionaire.
> *Single Mother*: Jill, a single mother who is well below the threshold for distributive justice, negligently crashes into Kiki, who is neither above nor below the threshold.

Billionaire and Single Mother: Jill, a single mother who is well below the threshold for distributive justice, negligently crashes into Kiki, a billionaire.

Does Jill have a duty to compensate Kiki in any or all of these cases? *Single Mother* raises the question of whether victims of distributive injustice owe duties in corrective justice. One thing to note here is that, even if Jill *does* owe a corrective duty to Kiki, this duty is more likely to exceed its stringency threshold because Jill is the victim of distributive injustice. When measuring the cost of fulfilling a corrective duty, we must take into account the injurer's pre-existing wellbeing. If it is already low, then giving up further resources will, for that person, have a greater impact than an equivalent loss would have for a better off person. This already gives us reason to doubt the legitimacy of imposing burdensome corrective duties on the worst off.

In *Billionaire*, the argument against compensation is different. We should take care to distinguish different elements of Kiki's loss. Let's grant that Kiki is entitled to be free of physical pain and suffering, and also to a good car and a decent salary. The question, then, is whether she has a moral right to compensation beyond these things, which, let's suppose, includes the difference between the value of a good car and the value of her luxury car, and the difference between a decent salary and her exorbitant salary. Does Jill have a moral duty to compensate Kiki for the loss of these additional goods? The problem is that Kiki has no moral entitlement to what she possesses above the threshold for distributive justice. They are unjust holdings, and therefore, in a sense, not really *hers*. As Jules Coleman puts the point, 'if you have no right to your wealth, how can you have a right to have it restored when I reduce it?'[11]

The argument is yet stronger in *Billionaire and Single Mother*. This is partly because the argument against liability incorporates both the previous points. There is a good chance the additional cost of Kiki's unjust holdings will exceed the stringency threshold of Jill's duty, and Kiki has no moral right to her unjust holdings in any case. But the argument is also greater than the sum of its parts. It is not just that full compensation is too burdensome for Jill and not within Kiki's moral entitlement. There is something distinctively objectionable about Kiki demanding full compensation *from* Jill. There are two reasons for this. One is that Jill is a victim and Kiki a beneficiary of distributive injustice, and

---

[11] Jules Coleman, *Risks and Wrongs* (Oxford University Press 1992) 304. Coleman poses this question as a challenge that corrective justice can overcome, while I take it as a fundamental problem with the practice of corrective justice in distributively unjust societies.

there is something objectionable about a legal mechanism that allows beneficiaries of injustice to extract resources from victims of that same injustice.
Consider:

Stolen Goods: Jill's car is stolen, and she has no legal recourse. She then negligently destroys Kiki's car. Kiki bought the car at a huge discount because it was stolen. The law permits Kiki to keep her stolen car. Kiki brings a claim against Jill and is awarded full compensation.

In *Stolen Goods* it is unjust, let's assume, both that Jill's car has been stolen and that Kiki should be allowed to keep a stolen car. But there is something additionally unjust about the fact that Kiki—a beneficiary of injustice—is permitted to extract compensation from Jill—a victim of the same type of injustice—for the loss of the car. The analogy between *Stolen Goods* and *Billionaire and Single Mother* should be clear: they both involve the beneficiary of a legally tolerated injustice extracting resources from a victim of that same injustice. Many argue that beneficiaries of injustice owe duties to disgorge those benefits, at least under certain conditions.[12] Anyone sympathetic to these views will surely look askance at a principle that allows beneficiaries to extract benefits from victims of that injustice.

A second distinctive objection to full compensation in *Billionaire and Single Mother* is that it violates considerations of narrow proportionality. Narrow proportionality refers to the assessment of harms imposed on individuals who are liable to suffer some harm.[13] We conceded at the outset that Jill is liable to suffer some cost by virtue of her wrong, but this cost must be proportionate. We have already encountered one feature connected to narrow proportionality: stringency thresholds. The stringency threshold focusses on the burden imposed on the wrongdoer individually, but another principle emerges when we compare Jill and Kiki. This is that each increment of harm to Jill must generate sufficient value for Kiki. Consider the following case (those turned off by crude numerical illustrations, look away again):

[12] Daniel Butt, 'On Benefiting from Injustice' (2007) 37 Canadian Journal of Philosophy 129; Göran Duus-Otterström, 'Benefiting from Injustice and the Common-Source Problem' (2017) 20 Ethical Theory and Moral Practice 1067; Tom Parr, 'The Moral Taintedness of Benefiting from Injustice' (2016) 19 Ethical Theory and Moral Practice 985; and Haydar Bashshar and Gerhard Øverland, 'The Normative Implications of Benefiting from Injustice' (2014) 31 Journal of Applied Philosophy 349.
[13] For the distinction between narrow and wide proportionality, see Jeff McMahan, *Killing in War* (Oxford University Press 2009) 20–21.

Narrow Proportionality: Jill wrongs Kiki and Kiki suffers 10 units of harm. Jill can either suffer 1 unit of harm, which will give Kiki 9 units of wellbeing or suffer 15 units of harm, which will give Kiki 10 units of wellbeing.

Bracketing issues of distributive justice, it can be argued that narrow proportionality favours Jill suffering 1 unit of harm rather than 15, even though this leaves Kiki with less than full compensation. The reason is that Jill can almost fully compensate Kiki at the cost of only 1 unit of harm, and suffering an additional 14 units just to raise Kiki a single further unit—thus reaching full compensation—seems disproportionate. This is true despite the fact that Jill is liable for up to 15 units of harm to compensate Kiki; that is, Jill *would* be required to suffer 15 units if the alternative was to do nothing. In *Narrow Proportionality*, the presence of a much better outcome for Jill and an almost-as-good outcome for Kiki makes full compensation disproportionate.[14]

Applying this principle, we can see that stark asymmetries in terms of distributive justice between injurers and victims are likely to make full compensation disproportionate. In *Billionaire and Single Mother*, it is already quite difficult to justify the first increment of harm to Jill. Jill is badly off and Kiki is well off, so the first increment is more burdensome for Jill and less beneficial for Kiki compared to a similar exchange between two individuals who are equally well off. Moreover, each subsequent increment only gets harder to justify, since each increment makes Jill yet worse off and Kiki yet better off. It is therefore difficult to believe full compensation is narrowly proportionate in *Billionaire and Single Mother*. There may well come a point before full compensation is reached when further transfer of resources from Jill to Kiki is so harmful for Jill and so negligible for Kiki that it is disproportionate to inflict this harm on Jill.

It might be pointed out that considerations of proportionality would apply as much to just inequalities as to unjust inequalities. This may be true, but if the inequality is unjust, this plausibly makes it more likely that the burden of repair is disproportionate. This is because unjustified inequalities should at least be given greater weight than justified inequalities (if the latter should be counted at all) in proportionality calculations. This practice is familiar from proportionality in other contexts. For example, punishing a wrongdoer who is badly off as a result of bad luck is harder to justify than punishing a wrongdoer who is badly off as a result of a previously justified punishment. The justified

---

[14] For another argument that proportionality is relevant to compensatory duties, see Todd Karhu, 'Proportionality in the Liability to Compensate' (2022) 41 Law and Philosophy 583.

punishment, if it is to be counted in proportionality calculations, counts less than an equivalent amount of unjustified harm.

B. Hypersensitivity

Let's consider some objections to the argument of the previous section. The first is not so much an objection to our conclusion as to the basis on which it is reached. James Penner agrees that there is something awry with tort law allowing the rich to extract compensation from the poor but argues that this anxiety has a different explanation to the one given here.[15] Penner suggests tortfeasors should not have to compensate the financially hypersensitive.[16] In *Billionaire and Single Mother,* by driving her expensive car and drawing her huge salary, Kiki exposes Jill to much greater liability. She is financially hypersensitive in the sense that a wrong against her is likely to result in much greater losses than a similar wrong committed against almost anyone else. Note that this explanation makes no appeal to background injustice. We need take no stance on whether Kiki is entitled to her wealth to see why her hypersensitivity undermines her claim to compensation.

Perhaps hypersensitivity has some role in explaining the intuitive objection to compensation here, but I doubt it is the full story. Background injustices cannot be eliminated from the picture. One way to see this is to observe that protecting hypersensitivity becomes less problematic the further we move down the scale of wellbeing. Consider:

> *Eggshell Skull*: Jill negligently injures Kiki. Kiki is a haemophiliac and suffers a severe injury.

In *Eggshell Skull*, Kiki's hypersensitivity imposes extra burdens on Jill because Jill's liability would be less extensive if she had injured a non-hypersensitive person. Nevertheless, Jill should take Kiki as she finds her and compensate for the full injury.[17] What distinguishes *Eggshell Skull* from

---

[15] James Penner, 'Don't Crash into Mick Jagger while he's Driving his Rolls Royce: Liability in Damages for Economic Loss Consequent upon a Personal Injury' in Paul B Miller and John Oberdiek (eds), *Civil Wrongs and Justice in Private Law* (Oxford University Press 2020) 253 (hereafter Penner, *Economic Loss*).

[16] Penner, 'Economic Loss' (n 15) 266–69.

[17] The legal picture with respect to hypersensitivity is complicated. Often, losses attributed to hypersensitivity are not recoverable, even if other elements of a tort are made out, one example being the rule in *Robinson v Kilvert* that there is no liability in nuisance where ordinary use of land damages an 'exceptionally delicate trade'. (1889) 41 Ch D. 88. An exception to this is the eggshell skull rule. As Mackinnon

the billionaire cases is that, in the former, Kiki's vulnerability renders her worse off in an absolute sense and therefore it is a type of hypersensitivity that merits special protection. Some might think the salient difference is rather that the billionaire's hypersensitivity is financial instead of physical, but this is doubtful. Consider:

> *Empty Wallet*: Jill negligently damages Kiki's car. Kiki is impecunious and cannot afford a replacement car, which she needs for work and to transport her family. She is forced to borrow money at a high interest rate to hire one.[18]

It is plausible that, like in *Eggshell Skull*, Kiki's hypersensitivity merits special protection and Jill should compensate her for paying the high interest rate. It makes no difference that the hypersensitivity is economic rather than physical. What matters is that it reflects Kiki's lower wellbeing. She should not be disadvantaged relative to others simply because she is economically worse off than they are.

This does not mean that Kiki's hypersensitivity in *Empty Wallet* is greater than that of the billionaire. Probably the opposite is the case—harm to the billionaire will cause much greater financial loss than harm to the impecunious. Nevertheless, we cannot explain the difference between the billionaire cases and *Empty Wallet* solely by reference to the degree of hypersensitivity involved. Background considerations of wellbeing play an important role in determining which hypersensitivities are deserving of protection. Protecting the interests of less well-off people, even if they are hypersensitive to harm, is less objectionable because they are entitled as a matter of distributive justice to what little they possess. What makes the billionaire hypersensitive—her wealth and extremely high income—are holdings to which she is not entitled as a matter of distributive justice and thus less deserving of legal protection.

LJ states it, this holds that 'one who is guilty of negligence to another must put up with idiosyncrasies of his victim that increase the likelihood or extent of damage to him: it is no answer to a claim for a fractured skull that its owner had an unusually fragile one.' *Owens v Liverpool Corp* [1939] 1 KB 394, 400–01.

[18] For a legal case with similar facts, see *Lagden v O'Connor* [2003] UKHL 64; [2004] 1 AC 1067. In this case, the House of Lords rejected the rule that a defendant cannot be held liable for damage attributable to the claimant's impecuniosity. Lord Hope stated that, 'The wrongdoer must take his victim as he finds him ... This rule applies to the economic state of the victim in the same way as it applies to his physical and mental vulnerability' (at [61]).

C. Let's Hang on to What We've Got

Robert Goodin and John Gardner both argue that sometimes people should be compensated for what they have lost, regardless of whether they are entitled to it as a matter of distributive justice. Wrongful interferences in the status quo should be corrected, even if the status quo is unjust, and even though improvements in terms of distributive justice *can* permissibly be pursued through other channels such as tax reform.

Let's begin with Goodin's version of this argument. Goodin argues that the rationale for compensation is that it underwrites reasonable expectations, allowing people to live their lives, form plans, and pursue projects without the threat of sudden frustration. Compensation cannot always prevent harm (although it has some deterrent effect) but it can ensure that those who are harmed have access to resources that allow them, as far as possible, to continue with their prior way of life. Since the frustration of a person's projects does not depend on whether a previous distribution is just or not, their expectations to continue with these projects justify the practice of compensation with respect to unjust holdings.

Goodin is right that compensation plays an important role in mitigating frustration with a person's ends and projects—we made similar arguments in Chapter 3. Nevertheless, there are problems with the view. Goodin argues that, when we look at the range of our compensatory practices, we see it is a mixed bag. In the law of torts damages seek to right wrongs, but compensation in other contexts such as that paid by statutory compensation schemes does not have this aim. Thus, we cannot explain all our compensatory practices with reference to the aim of redressing wrongs.[19] Goodin thinks his favoured rationale (underwriting reasonable expectations) is superior precisely because it highlights what is common to all our compensatory practices rather than just a subset. It is unclear, though, in what sense a rationale that explains more cases is superior to one that explains fewer. Scope is not the only relevant evaluative criterion for normative explanation. More important is that a given explanation accurately captures the grounds for compensatory liability in the domain in which it applies. We have seen in the last three chapters that there is a plurality of grounds for corrective duties, and it would be misleading to search for a single idea that explains all of them.

---

[19] Robert E Goodin, 'Compensation and Redistribution' 33 Nomos (1991) 143, 151 (hereafter Goodin, *Compensation and Redistribution*).

The main problem with Goodin's rationale, though, is that not every expectation should be underwritten by the promise of compensation. Goodin recognizes this and argues that only *reasonable* expectations merit compensation.[20] Otherwise, people could make themselves eligible for compensation merely by having unreasonable expectations. The concept of reasonable expectations Goodin employs is moralized. It is reasonable to expect others not to steal from me even when this expectation is not epistemically reasonable in the sense that I have evidence that people will steal. But this means the tension we have been investigating between corrective and distributive justice simply reappears under a different guise. Is it reasonable or unreasonable to expect to continue to pursue projects that depend on the possession of unjust holdings? If the holdings are unjust, all the arguments offered above can be harnessed to show that expectations founded on them are unreasonable and we are back to where we started. Until we have a substantive argument that shows why projects based on unjust holdings are reasonable, Goodin's account offers no further guidance.

Let's turn to Gardner's version of the argument. Gardner argues, in a similar vein, that sometimes we have reason to hold on to what we have despite having no moral entitlement to it. In support of this view, he notes that we cannot help but see the goals we have chosen to pursue as more valuable than alternatives we could have chosen.[21] Part of this value derives from the general value of our having goals at all. In addition, from the internal perspective, we cannot help but see our chosen goals as more valuable than others.[22] Again, we expressed a similar thought in Chapter 3: the value of our ends depends partly on the features they possess that make them worthy of being valued and partly on the fact that they are *ours*. For Gardner, this makes the desire to hold on to what one already has rationally intelligible, and this rational intelligibility in turn helps to explain the principle of full compensation and its insensitivity to distributive justice. Compensation in tort does not exist to sort through the rights and wrongs of acquisition and possession; it fulfils the rational purpose of helping people pursue the plans and projects that are valuable to them.

To assess this idea, compare:

Art Studio 1: Kiki uses her unjust holdings to build her own art studio, which she would not be able to do given the resources to which she is entitled

---

[20] ibid, 154.

[21] John Gardner, *From Personal Life to Private Law* (Oxford University Press 2018) ch 5 (hereafter Gardner, *Personal Life*).

[22] Gardner, *Personal Life* (n 21) 174–75.

as a matter of distributive justice. Jill crashes into the studio, destroying it and devastating Kiki. Jill can fix the damage at reasonably low cost.

And:

Art Studio 2: Kiki uses her unjust holdings to buy an art studio. It is an impulse buy and she forgets about it, leaving it in her garage to gather dust. Jill crashes into the garage, destroying the studio. Jill can fix the damage at reasonably low cost.

Some might think Jill has a moral duty to compensate in both cases, and some that Jill lacks a duty in both cases. But I suspect many will agree that the case for compensation is stronger in *Art Studio 1* than it is in *Art Studio 2* because in the former case, Jill's wrong interferes with an end that is central to Kiki's life. Gardner is right, then, that we can acquire interests in the continued pursuit of projects that are dependent on unjust holdings. This is partly explained by the fact that, if Kiki is not compensated in *Art Studio 1*, she suffers *transitional harm*, that is, the harm of having a project she has already grown attached to taken away from her.[23] This is another reason why we cannot dismiss her claim on the grounds that she was never entitled to the resources that built her studio. Now that she has built it, she is vulnerable to suffering a special harm if it is taken away.

The significance of transitional harms should not be underestimated, but this does not provide a general justification for the insensitivity of corrective duties to distributive justice. First, as the comparison between *Art Studio 1* and *2* suggests, the extent to which a person's projects depend on unjust holdings is contextual. When a loss is purely financial, and is suffered by one who is extremely wealthy, it is unlikely that the plans and projects that structure that person's life are dependent on those resources. Second, the transitional harm of having one's projects frustrated must be balanced against the benefit of having been able to pursue that project in the first place, when those without unjust holdings lacked similar opportunities.[24] Third, even if we give the interest in holding on to what we have some weight, it does not follow that it trumps the various considerations that militate against compensating the unjustly wealthy. Finally,

---

[23] As Francesca da Rimini says in *Dante's Inferno*, 'There is no greater pain/Than to remember happy days in days/Of misery'. Dante Alighieri, *Inferno* (Harvard University Press 2013) 59.

[24] As Alfred Lord Tennyson wrote in *In Memoriam*, ''Tis better to have loved and lost/Than never to have loved at all.' Alfred Tennyson, *In Memoriam*, eds Susan Shatto and Marion Shaw (eds), (Oxford University Press 1982) 59.

we have been assuming so far that Kiki is blameless for her unjust holdings. If we imagine that she bears some culpability—even partial culpability—for her unjust wealth, her claim to compensation looks much weaker. Otherwise she would effectively be able to acquire entitlements to resources by virtue of her own culpable acquisition or possession of them. Overall, then, whilst it is possible to acquire interests in unjust holdings that generate duties on others not to interfere with them, and to compensate for them if they do, these interests are not powerful enough to justify the general independence of corrective from distributive justice.

V. The Division of Labour Argument

We have seen that in some respects corrective justice has priority over distributive justice, in others distributive justice has priority, and in others there is parity. What do these conclusions tell us about the justification of compensatory liability in tort law more generally? Our mixed picture provides little comfort for tort apologists, since if it is correct, courts routinely make judgments in conflict with the underlying moral rights and duties of the parties. It does not follow that such practices are all-things-considered unjustified, but they must be justified by some other reasons, and these reasons must be strong enough to overcome the undue burden and other objections.[25]

One such argument is that accepting the above conclusions in relation to the parties' moral claims is consistent with the view that corrective and distributive justice should remain separate domains of institutional practice. Several writers who defend some form of separation between corrective and distributive justice have a claim like this in mind. One reason to hold it is that there are different justificatory bases for claims in distributive compared to corrective justice. As we have seen, Weinrib argues that it is incoherent to mix the rationales of corrective and distributive justice. Specifically, he is concerned with appeal to 'loss spreading' as a ground for awarding compensation in tort cases.[26] The reasoning behind loss spreading is quintessentially distributive. Damages paid by insurance companies can be spread across the pool of policy holders whilst victims of torts are unlikely to be insured for their losses, and it is better that many people pay a small cost than a single person bear a huge one. This

---

[25] Though not the *restricted freedom* objection. Our argument does not imply injurers are morally free to wrong people because they are below, or their victims are above, the threshold of distributive justice.

[26] Weinrib, *The Idea of Private Law* (n 1).

reasoning, Weinrib argues, cannot be deployed to justify damages in any given case because, if we follow the rationale to its natural conclusion, it recommends dispensing with a juridical approach entirely and replacing tort law, or large sections of it, with a compensation scheme that more thoroughly implements the logic of loss spreading.

A related objection is that if we accept the balancing of corrective and distributive justice in principle, it would still be undesirable to try and implement this result in practice as there are strong reasons to maintain a division of labour at the institutional level.[27] These reasons include the fact that judges are not well qualified to incorporate distributive justice reasoning into their decisions; introducing such reasoning would make the application of the law more complex and unpredictable; it would muddy the relationship between different limbs of the state; it would be undemocratic to vest unelected judges with the power to make decisions on contentious issues of public policy; and so on.[28] There is also a path dependency element to this argument. The division of labour just described is deeply ingrained and it would be undesirable to ask individuals and institutions that have traditionally restricted themselves to practising corrective justice fundamentally to alter their roles.

This is certainly a forceful argument, but it is important to be clear about what it shows and what it does not show. It shows there is a powerful presumption against judges transgressing their roles, not that distributive considerations can never be taken into account whilst respecting the division of labour. There is some debate over the extent to which tort law can further distributive goals. Some argue that there are a variety of ways courts might introduce distributive considerations without obliterating the division of labour between institutions that practice corrective and distributive justice.[29] These are not debates for us, except to say that different options for taking distributive justice into account, such as capping recovery for lost earnings or acknowledging financial vulnerability as a relevant factor for liability, must be considered on a case-by-case basis rather than dismissed with reference to the general division of labour.

We should accept, however, that imposing corrective duties on the unjustly badly off, especially within the framework of liability insurance and

---

[27] See Stephen R Perry, 'On the Relationship between Corrective and Distributive Justice' in Jeremy Horder (ed), *Oxford Essays in jurisprudence (Fourth Series)* (Oxford University Press 2000).

[28] For objections to this 'division of labour' argument, see Hanoch Dagan and Avihay Dorfman, 'Justice in Private: Beyond the Rawlsian Framework' (2018) 37 Law and Philosophy 171.

[29] Lous Kaplow and Steven Shavell, 'Why The Legal System is Less Efficient than Income Tax in Distributing Income' (1994) 23 Journal of Legal Studies 667. For criticism, see Tsachi Keren-Paz, *Torts, Egalitarianism and Distributive Justice* (Routledge 2007) 43.

bankruptcy law, is not so egregious that judges should refuse to apply the law as they should in some rare cases.[30] This means that legal institutions do not act wrongly all-things-considered when they enforce legal rights and duties that conflict with moral rights and duties.

However, once we recognize that the division of labour argument is not germane to our *moral* rights and duties but rather the enforcement conditions of those rights and duties, we see that it offers little support for the justification of tort law, and thus little reason to preserve tort over alternative institutions and practices more sensitive to distributive justice.[31] If anything, the division of labour argument *adds* to the case against tort, for it means that, not only does the law consistently ride roughshod over moral rights and duties in unjust conditions, it is also unable to permissibly correct its own unjust practices.

This reveals one of the fault lines between interpretivist and foundationalist approaches to tort theory (see Chapter 2). On an interpretivist view, if Weinrib is right that loss spreading and other forms of distributive justice reasoning are inimical to the logic of corrective justice, the matter is settled: loss spreading cannot play a role in an interpretive account of tort law. On a foundationalist approach, this inconsistency leaves the matter wide open. For all that has been argued to the contrary, it may be taken as a critique of the tort system rather than a defence of it. There is plenty more to say about this, and in Chapter 8 we will address the various distinctive features of tort that, it is argued, justify its existence over alternative institutional arrangements.

Conclusion

Corrective duties have first personal priority over distributive concerns. We should fulfil our corrective duties even if this generates inequalities in wellbeing that are objectionable from a distributive justice perspective. This shows that corrective justice has some independence from distributive justice. Corrective justice does not merely correct wrongful deviations from distributive patterns, and corrective duties are not straightforwardly overridden by considerations of distributive justice. But this is a limited form of independence and falls well

---

[30] See Joseph Raz, 'On the Autonomy of Legal Reasoning' in *Ethics in the Public Domain: Essays in the Morality of Law and Politics* (Oxford University Press 1995) for the view that courts should sometimes resort to moral reasoning when deciding whether to apply legal rules.

[31] Patrick Atiyah makes a similar point: even though it is impossible for the courts to remove the principle of full compensation, this does not provide a logical defence of the principle. See Peter Cane and James Goudkamp, *Atiyah's Accidents, Compensation and the Law* (9th edn, Cambridge University Press 2018) 154.

short of the conclusion that background distributions do not affect the corrective duties we owe to each other. Background distributive injustice directly impacts corrective duties because there is no moral right to be compensated for unjust holdings, except in limited circumstances. Tort apologists may retreat behind the idea that, if this is true, it is another example of the morality of corrective justice being irrelevant to its institutional practice, since the division of labour argument shows that it would be wrong for courts to incorporate distributive concerns into their adjudication. This argument, however, should be no consolation to tort apologists, and in Chapter 8 we will confront directly the choice between tort and alternative systems of compensation.

8

Compensation Schemes

Introduction

The tort system—which encompasses not just tort *law* but also the institutional framework within which tort actions are brought, settled, and adjudicated—has been subject to some penetrating objections. Patrick Atiyah, one of its fiercest critics, argues that the system is inefficient, ineffective, and insensitive to the needs of victims.[1] In response to challenges of this kind, interpretivists have rejected the underlying assumption that tort should be viewed as a mechanism for loss compensation,[2] holding instead that it embodies distinctive normative structures and principles. Two familiar and overlapping interpretivist views already encountered in this book are that tort implements corrective justice and that it provides citizens with civil recourse.

Both sides have a valid point. I argued in Chapter 2 that articulating the normative structure of the law falls short of justifying it, as the costs of the system and its relation to underlying moral duties are part of what needs justifying. On the other hand, if interpretivists are right that tort embodies a distinctive and valuable normative practice, then reform also has its costs, and treating the system as nothing more than a convoluted loss compensation scheme defines this problem away.

The disagreement between apologists and reformists seems to have reached something of an impasse. One reason for this is that it is often framed as a collision of irreducibly distinct paradigms. It is said that tort reflects a conception of individual responsibility that compels us to redress the wrongs we commit against others, while compensation schemes reflect our collective responsibility for statistically inevitable accidents. This distinction between irreducible paradigms is implicit in Weinrib's claim that, however sensible loss spreading may be from a distributive justice perspective, it is incoherent in private law

---

[1] Atiyah's classic work is now under the editorship of Peter Cane and James Goudkamp, see *Atiyah's Accidents, Compensation and the Law* (9th edn, Cambridge University Press 2018) ch 7 (hereafter Cane and Goudkamp, *Atiyah's Accidents*).

[2] Robert Stevens calls this the 'loss compensation' model of tort, and rigorously defends its alternative, the 'rights-based model' in *Torts and Rights* (Oxford University Press 2007).

Wrongs, Harms, and Compensation. Adam Slavny, Oxford University Press. © Adam Slavny 2023.
DOI: 10.1093/oso/9780192864567.003.0008

which operates according to corrective justice. Reformists, too, often frame their attacks on the tort system in terms of distributive justice or collective responsibility.[3]

Unlike Chapter 7, my purpose here is not to try and adjudicate between these paradigms. I have argued that we have moral duties that overlap with—but are not identical to—many of the primary and secondary duties or liabilities imposed by tort law. My aim here is to show that these moral duties are consistent with institutional arrangements other than tort, specifically some types of compensation schemes.[4] Rather than appealing to the superiority of an alternative paradigm of justice, I aim to show that moral corrective duties are more complex and flexible than we might believe were we to focus too rigidly on their legal correlates.

I. Three Arrangements

Let's sketch three institutional arrangements we might adopt for personal injury claims. According to the first—tort law—the injured party has a right to bring a legal action against the wrongdoer. If that action is successful, the victim is entitled to a remedy, typically compensation. According to the second—the at-fault scheme—those who impose wrongful risks, whether they cause harm or not, pay a fee into a centrally administered fund. Those who are harmed as a result of wrongful risks apply for compensation from the fund rather than bringing actions against their injurers. And according to the third—the no-fault scheme—victims receive compensation from a centralized fund without having to prove they were harmed because of another's fault (although other eligibility requirements are imposed).

There are, of course, many further details to be filled in, especially in relation to the compensation schemes. The at-fault scheme requires fault while the no-fault scheme does not, but beyond this we leave the conditions of entitlement

---

[3] Jonathan Morgan claims that tort is based on corrective justice and compensation and loss spreading are based on distributive justice. Jonathan Morgan, 'Tort, Insurance and Incoherence' (2004) 67 Modern Law Review 384, 392.

[4] On the view sketched here, both tort and the compensation schemes can be justified by appeal to underlying corrective duties, and other considerations have the final say as to which is preferable. It is worth noting that some corrective justice theorists adopt a similar view. See Jules Coleman, *Risks and Wrongs* (Oxford University Press 1992) 306–18. Even Weinrib says that formalism 'does not itself choose between distributive and corrective arrangements; it requires only that whatever mode of ordering a jurisdiction adopts conform to the rationality immanent in that mode of ordering'. Ernest Weinrib, *Idea of Private Law* (first published 1995, Oxford University Press 2012) 228 (hereafter Weinrib, *Idea of Private Law*).

unspecified. The at-fault scheme is, in principle, paid for by wrongdoers, while the no-fault scheme could be funded in a variety of ways, including contributions from wrongdoers, permissible injurers, permissible riskers, taxpayers, and others. Both schemes envisaged would replace corresponding sections of tort, although it would be possible to retain some claims, for example for punitive or vindicatory damages. In addition, the schemes need not replace the primary norms of tort,[5] especially if these norms have some deterrent effect in the absence of the threat of legal action. To keep things simple, we suppose that all schemes seek to offer the same levels of compensation.

Two initial points are worth emphasizing. One is that our aim is not to assess the feasibility, practicality, or cost-effectiveness of the two compensation schemes, or to offer any guidance as to their specific design. Our purpose is to consider the normative justifiability of their core features compared with tort, specifically in relation to our moral corrective duties. Of course, empirical factors bear on their ultimate justification. Assessing their deterrent effect, operational costs, and efficiency is vital. For example, at-fault schemes may turn out to be unfeasible given the operational costs of determining fault. We will return to some of these empirical factors later, but our present task is to consider whether there is any decisive normative, non-instrumental reason to prefer tort law to either scheme.

The second point is that the scope of all three systems, at least as they are understood here, depends on the underlying moral duties involved. The at-fault scheme is funded by those who commit wrongs, at least ideally. It may be possible to use proxies such as risk profiles to predict who will commit a wrong and raise contributions accordingly, but in principle compensation is not funded by those who are not at fault. Similarly, the no-fault scheme is funded by those who owe duties to contribute. We know wrongdoers have corrective duties, but the four-fold analysis tells us that those who harm others permissibly sometimes also have such duties. In Chapter 6, we saw that other parties such as beneficiaries of risky activity may owe duties, and broader public subsidies to 'top up' the scheme may be justified with reference to general duties of assistance. One's attitude towards these arrangements will therefore depend on one's beliefs about the existence of the underlying corrective duties. One who thinks that corrective duties do not arise in the context of permissible harming or that there are no general duties of assistance may reject the possibility of a

[5] Gregory Keating, 'The Priority of Respect over Repair' (2012) 18 Legal Theory 293.

no-fault scheme on this basis. The point to remember is that the at-fault and no-fault schemes are not generalized compensation systems for all accident victims, or indeed all victims of life's misfortunes. This is important as it wards off a common objection to such schemes, that there is no reason to prioritize those eligible under the scheme over other victims. The reason to prioritize beneficiaries of either scheme is that they are owed corrective duties, either from specific individuals or groups, even if they do not recover compensation directly from those who owe it.

That each of these schemes might be permissible in light of our underlying corrective duties will not be surprising given the four-fold account of the moral basis of corrective duties defended in previous chapters. It means that those who are compelled to contribute to the scheme cannot make the *restricted freedom* or *undue burden* objections, since all three systems would require them to bear burdens for the sake of compensating others only when they already have duties to do so.

II. Compensation Scheme vs Tort without Insurance

Compare the at-fault and no-fault schemes with tort in the absence of insurance. If defendants were required to pay compensation from their own pockets, many would be unable to pay and a proportion of those who would be able to pay could not be morally required to do so because this would exceed the stringency threshold of their duties. A system of law that routinely made people destitute by forcing them to compensate for their mistakes would be difficult to defend, to say the least.[6]

A reason to prefer the at-fault scheme has been set out by Jeremy Waldron. Waldron argues that it would be permissible and rational for potential injurers to agree, *ex ante*, to share the costs of compensation to mitigate the effects of luck on their liabilities.[7] Injurers can find themselves saddled with huge

---

[6] As Tony Honoré puts the point, loss spreading in this way is not an objective of tort law but a mechanism that 'is essential if a system of corrective justice is to operate fairly in modern conditions'. Tony Honoré, 'The Morality of Tort Law-Questions and Answers' in David G Owen (ed), *The Philosophical Foundations of Tort Law* (Oxford University Press 1997) 73. Peter Cane suggests that 'liability insurance may be seen not only as a necessary pre-condition of the achievement of tort law's reparative function, but also required in practice, in some cases at least, to redress distributional injustices generated by tort law'. Peter Cane, 'Retribution, Proportionality and Moral Luck' in Peter Cane and Jane Stapleton (eds), *The Law of Obligations-Essays in Celebration of John Fleming* (Clarendon Press 1998) 141, 164.

[7] Jeremy Waldron, 'Moments of Careless and Massive Loss' in David G Owen (ed), *The Philosophical Foundations of Tort Law* (Oxford University Press 1995) 387 (hereafter Waldron, 'Moments of Carelessness').

liabilities due to minor moments of carelessness, while those who are negligent but lucky enough to avoid injury escape this fate. Under these conditions,
Waldron says, it would be rational for potential injurers to agree to share the
costs of their future liabilities. Victims might be dissatisfied that they are unable to recover from the specific individuals who harmed them, but this objection could be met by emphasizing the arbitrariness of causation or by insisting
that any significance it has is outweighed by wrongdoers' interests in mitigating
huge differences in their liabilities.[8]

Taken together, I think these arguments count decisively in favour of both
schemes against tort without liability insurance. They are also a response to
the claim that the presence of insurance is irrelevant to liability. Far from
being irrelevant, any normative defence of tort liability in roughly its current
form *depends* on the possibility of loss spreading mechanisms like insurance.
This is not to say insurance should be taken into account in individual decisions about liability, but rather that the system as a whole could not be justified
without it. If we compare the scheme to insurance-backed tort law, however,
these arguments lose a lot of their force. In theory, in conditions of perfect
uptake (ie when all meritorious claims lead to compensation) the outcomes
would be the same: all beneficiaries of corrective duties would receive what
they are owed. Also, the actual burdens suffered by tortfeasors would be drastically reduced, so they would likely have no complaint of the kind described
by Waldron.

The main difference between the compensation schemes and insurance-
backed tort—at least on these idealizing assumptions—is that only tort em-
powers victims to recover the resources they are entitled to from the people
who caused them injury. The link between victim and injurer the civil suit
embodies is often thought to possess normative significance. Let's test the
significance of this link by considering three objections to the way compensation schemes sever it. The first objection is that there are limits on which
duties can be discharged by third parties, and the scheme violates these limits
while tort does not. The second is that tort offers a process whereby victims
can hold accountable those who have wronged them while the schemes do
not. And the third is that the normative significance of causation supports
tort law over the schemes.

---

[8] ibid.

III. Compensation Schemes vs Insurance-Backed Tort

A. Dischargeability

When one person owes a corrective duty to another, it seems incumbent on the duty-bearer to perform it. We generally expect wrongdoers not to ask others to perform their duties for them, even if the outcomes are the same; that is, even if the victim is placed in the same position they would be in had the wrongdoer personally performed the duty. One objection to the compensation schemes, based on this idea, is that they systematically prevent victims from ensuring those who wronged them personally perform their corrective duties. Under the schemes, the actions that should be performed by wrongdoers are instead performed by the administrators of a central fund. To explore this objection, it is worth taking a step back to consider what makes a duty dischargeable by a third party more generally.

Let's begin with a couple of clarifications. First, the question I am interested in here is whether it is morally permissible for a third party to perform the actions required by the duty. To say a duty is dischargeable by a third party is to say it is morally permissible to delegate the performance of that duty.[9] Second, it may be that multiple actions are required by the same duty, or there are multiple duties to perform different actions. It is possible that some elements of a duty can permissibly be delegated while others cannot. For our purposes, the relevant duty is that of compensation, though I will discuss other duties such as apology in the interests of thinking about dischargeability more holistically.

Two important factors that bear on dischargeability are (1) moral hazard and (2) whether delegating increases the chance that future duties will be fulfilled. A reason in favour of permitting (and indeed requiring) delegation is that it might be necessary to ensure that a future duty is performed, typically through insurance. A reason against delegation is that it might incentivize further wrongdoing, that is, it is subject to moral hazard. It is important to note these points; however, they will not be our main focus. Instead, I will explore a different idea that will help us explain the scope of dischargeability independently of the goods it is instrumental in bringing about.

---

[9] It should be noted, then, that a duty that is not dischargeable by a third party is not the same as a non-delegable duty of care in tort, where the latter implies that one can be legally responsible for its breach despite the performance being delegated to a third party. I am interested in whether it is permissible to delegate the action itself rather than responsibility for breach. My usage is closer to John Gardner's in *From Personal Life to Private Law* (Oxford University Press 2018) 113 (hereafter Gardner, *Personal Life*).

It is often permissible for an agent to delegate a corrective action if the value of that action is not impaired by the agent's non-performance. Put differently, it is often impermissible to delegate a corrective action if the duty is grounded in what I will call its *performance value*. Performance value is value attached to the performance of actions by specific persons. This captures the intuitive idea that duties must sometimes be performed by the person whose duties they are, on pain of impairing the value that underpins those duties.[10]

We can identify three general types of performance value. The first is when performance of the duty by the wrongdoer is constitutive of the value that the duty aims at. This can be illustrated with an example discussed by John Gardner, in which a parent breaks a promise to take their daughter to drama rehearsals. If the promise was made to demonstrate commitment to the daughter's interests, the duty cannot be discharged by others. If the promise was made for the pragmatic reason that the daughter needs a lift, then sending a taxi is permissible.[11] The performance value in this example consists in maintaining a good relationship. The parent's commitment to their daughter's interest is constitutive of the shared attitudes and activities that make their relationship valuable. If the parent distorts this value by treating it as mere practical necessity, they act wrongly. There are similar cases outside the context of relationships, particularly in relation to apologies. Usually, the performance of an apology by a wrongdoer is constitutive of the value of that apology because it communicates the recognition of that person's own wrongdoing. This is most obvious when people apologize on behalf of themselves, but it is also the case when they apologize on behalf of other people or institutions with whom they are associated. For example, many argue that current members of the British royal family should apologize for Britain's historical role in European colonialism and the transatlantic slave trade. The identity of members of the family as representatives of the monarchy, and by extension Britain itself, would be constitutive of the value of such an apology.

A second type of performance value concerns the connection between action and reasons for action. Consider:

Careless Millionaire: Lee, a careless millionaire, negligently hits Mike with their car. They could get out and help but this would make them late for lunch. Instead, they ask their assistant, Niamh, to tend to Mike,

---

[10] Andrew S Gold also suggests that personal performance by the wrongdoer may be preferable to enforcement by victim, see *The Right of Redress* (Oxford University Press 2020) 194 (hereafter Gold, *Right of Redress*).

[11] John Gardner, *Personal Life* (n 9) 116.

promising to pay her double for the inconvenience. Niamh, who is more tactful and sympathetic than Lee, happily accepts.

Intuitively, Lee acts wrongly in this case. However, this judgement is not easy to explain. Lee has no prior relationship with Mike; it is more costly for Lee to delegate than to perform the duty themselves; Mike benefits from Niamh's superior capacity for sympathy; and Niamh too is financially enriched.

So what explains the judgement of wrongdoing? One explanation draws from Bernard Williams' classic 'one thought too many' critique of utilitarianism.[12] Lee ensures Mike receives the help he needs, but devising this solution is itself wrongful, or perhaps displays vice or lack of virtue, because Lee should not be thinking about their lunch appointment. They should respond directly to what they have done by helping Mike. Their practical reasoning, though it yields a solution that ensures Mike gets what he is entitled to, involves 'one thought too many'. Of course, personal performance does not necessarily denote a morally healthy willingness to exclude irrelevant or distasteful considerations from one's reasoning, and one can fall foul of the 'one thought too many' problem in cases of personal performance too. However, the connection between good reasoning and personal discharge of one's duties, albeit a contingent one, helps explain performance value in some cases.

Finally, there is an expressive dimension to performance value, based on what personal performance indicates about the priority of the end in the wrongdoer's practical reasoning. Sometimes personal performance indicates one is prioritizing the end over others, perhaps because of the greater opportunity costs of personal performance, or because it suggests sympathy and regard, or because it is a conventional way of indicating concern. There is a sense in which Lee sets assisting Mike as their end, yet they treat the end as insufficiently important by being uninvolved in it. The level of involvement someone has in their own ends often reflects their value to that person. By being less involved, Lee fails to value this end more than other ends such as attending lunch. If instead Lee was rushing to their sick parent's bedside, delegation would be permissible as they are entitled to have greater involvement in this end. Prioritizing it does not imply a failure to give proper weight to their other

---

[12] See Bernard Williams, 'A Critique of Utilitarianism' in JJC Smart and Bernard Williams (eds), *Utilitarianism: For and Against* (Cambridge University Press 1973) and 'Utilitarianism and Moral Self-Indulgence' in Bernard Williams, *Moral Luck* (Cambridge University Press 1981) 40. Many have doubted whether this objection is fatal to consequentialism, or impartial moral theories more generally, but this is irrelevant for our purposes as most agree with the intuitive judgement that having 'one thought to many' is wrong or inappropriate in the relevant circumstances.

ends. Alternatively, suppose Lee wants to assist Mike but knows they would make the situation worse. In this case, it would also be permissible for tactful Niamh to discharge the duty. Common to both variations is the fact that, unlike the original case, Lee appropriately prioritizes Mike's wellbeing. They delegate either because performance by Niamh would be better for Mike or because they have other priorities that justifiably outweigh their personal involvement. Performance value creates a presumption against the delegation of corrective duties, but this presumption can be overridden.

Hopefully, this sketch provides some guidance for thinking about when dischargeability by others is permissible. The next question is, what does this imply about compensation schemes and insurance-backed tort law? They both involve delegation in the sense that third parties make the payment of damages, so are they both equally objectionable? Or does the type of delegation involved in compensation schemes undermine performance value more than that involved in insurance-backed tort law? Or are neither objectionable from the perspective of dischargeability?

I suggest neither are objectionable. When compensation takes the form of monetary damages, relatively little is gained in performance value terms by ensuring that the wrongdoer compensates with their own money. The most important value underpinning compensation is the negation or counterbalancing of harm. Unlike an apology or other forms of interpersonal redress, this value is affected little, if at all, by who ultimately foots the bill. One implication of this is that the reliance of the tort system on insurance does not undermine the relational structure of the duties imposed by the law. Indeed, corrective justice theorists insist on this. Weinrib says that: '[c]orrective justice goes to the nature of the obligation; it does not prescribe the mechanism by which the obligation is to be discharged ... Nothing about corrective justice precludes the defendant from anticipating the possibility of liability by investing in liability insurance.'[13] Similarly, Richard Wright holds that there is no problem with another person or entity discharging the obligation through payment.[14] But if so, there is also no problem with compensation being discharged by the administrators of a centralized scheme rather than a private insurer.

It might be objected that there is an important difference between these two options. When a person purchases an insurance policy, they take responsibility for protecting future victims of their negligence by ensuring they will be

---

[13] Weinrib, *Idea of Private Law* (n 4) 135–36 (n 25).
[14] Richard W Wright, 'Substantive Corrective Justice' (1992) 77 Iowa Law Review 625, 703–05.

compensated,[15] whereas a compensation scheme removes that responsibility from potential injurers entirely. This objection is not very convincing, though, for two reasons. First, insofar as this responsibility consists in the choice to protect victims of one's future conduct, it is non-existent for most tort defendants for whom liability insurance is mandatory. Perhaps this is why Wright claims liability insurance should be voluntary rather than mandatory. But this claim is untenable. We should not be permitted to imperil our future victims by failing to take reasonable precautions against the possibility that we will be unable to fulfil our duties towards them. This would itself be a wrong, a form of unreasonable risk imposition not unlike the kind involved in negligence. Given this, we cannot appeal to the voluntariness of liability insurance as the distinguishing factor between insurance and compensation schemes.

Once this is clarified, it is not clear why the act of purchasing mandatory insurance is of any special significance. It is merely a legally required action that enables the victims of one's future wrongs to be compensated. In this respect, it is no different from being required to contribute to a compensation scheme. In both cases, potential injurers are doing what is required of them to ensure their potential victims are compensated. It might be pressed that we have not been clear enough about precisely what elements of a duty are delegated when one purchases liability insurance. A third party pays the compensation, but the defendant purchases the premiums,[16] and this is the essence of the duty. So the duty, or the part of the duty that matters, has not been delegated after all. However, if this is true of purchasing insurance, it is also true of supporting compensation schemes. Wrongdoers ensure protection for their victims by contributing to the scheme. The crucial element of the duty is not delegated, but rather fulfilled through participation. What's important in both cases is that participants bear the burdens they are morally required to bear to achieve the ends they have duties to achieve.

The second reason is that performance value can be achieved by other means, such as an admission of liability or an apology. There are many ways a wrongdoer can personally be involved in responding to their actions besides purchasing insurance. Some argue that apology and other reconciliatory processes should play a greater role in tort law.[17] For now it suffices to note that

[15] For discussion see John W Keeler, 'Thinking Through the Unthinkable: Collective Responsibility in Personal Injury Law' (2001) 30 Common Law World Review 349.

[16] For example, Goldberg and Zipursky argue that tort can be understood as a law of wrongs despite the fact that potential wrongdoers can contract with third parties to help them bear the burden of repair. See John CP Goldberg and Benjamin C Zipursky, *Recognizing Wrongs* (Harvard University Press 2020) 274–75 (hereafter Goldberg and Zipursky, *Recognizing Wrongs*).

[17] Linda Radzik, 'Tort Processes and Relational Repair' in John Oberdiek (ed), *The Philosophical Foundations of the Law of Torts* (Oxford University Press 2014) 231.

the possibility of these alternatives, whether they form part of a legal process or not, further diminishes the argument that corrective duties cannot be discharged by compensation schemes.

B. Accountability

A second objection to the schemes is that they fail to give victims an institutional framework in which to hold defendants accountable for their actions. Each stage of the civil justice process, from issuing a claim to negotiating settlements to litigating a dispute, gives claimants opportunities to state their grievance, receive responses and explanations, and potentially obtain a judgment and remedy in court. Some argue that these procedures and opportunities are valuable, especially as a replacement for private reprisals which are prohibited by the state.[18]

There is no denying that both compensation schemes dispense with the kind of accountability practices that some litigants might find attractive. However, there are several points that limit the significance of this argument. First, as previously mentioned, the schemes need not replace the primary norms of tort, which might play a role in reinforcing social practices of accountability by themselves. Moreover, the schemes do not purport to replace all of tort. Tort claims could remain in place in areas where accountability is more central such as libel and intentional torts. Ripe for replacement would be those areas where accountability is more peripheral such as road and workplace accidents, where serious injuries can make compensation the more important goal. We should therefore not consider accountability a general virtue of tort law or private law, but one that depends, in part, on the nature of the claim.

Second, accountability is valuable only in respect of non-conditional duties, where the victim can allege that the injurer has acted impermissibly. Otherwise, there is nothing to be held accountable for (except perhaps the failure to offer compensation *ex post*).[19] When one's duty to compensate is

[18] Goldberg and Zipursky, *Recognizing Wrongs* (n 16) 130–35. Andrew Gold argues that other areas of private law such as contract and unjust enrichment do not embody virtues of accountability, see Gold, *Right of Redress* (n 10) 182. Stephen Darwall also offers an accountability-based justification for civil recourse theory that distinguishes it from retaliation and revenge, see 'Civil Recourse as Mutual Accountability' (co-authored with Julian Darwall) *Morality, Authority, and Law: Essays in Second-Personal Ethics* (Oxford University Press 2013) 179.
[19] See Gregory C Keating, 'Strict Liability Wrongs' in John Oberdiek (ed), *The Philosophical Foundations of the Law of Torts* (Oxford University Press 2014) 292–311.

conditional, demanding or legally compelling compensation from them is often permissible, but doing so on the basis that they have acted wrongly, or holding them accountable for the actions that resulted in harm, wrongs them. As I argued in Chapter 4, this is a problem for tort law because it often enforces both conditional and non-conditional duties without distinguishing between them. At least when it comes to conditional duties, loss of the law's accountability function is a benefit rather than a problem. Admittedly, the reverse is also true. With respect to non-conditional duties where there is a prior duty violation, loss of the accountability function is a problem, although this is tempered by the fact that the schemes can implement other forms of accountability. In at-fault schemes, contributions are compelled from those who act wrongly. Criminal fines for such conduct may also buttress this form of accountability. Even with respect to the no-fault scheme, it is possible to imagine various forms of funding patterns, including greater contributions from wrongdoers than those who harm permissibly to maintain some degree of accountability.

Nevertheless, apologists might insist it is important for the victim to have the opportunity to hold the wrongdoer accountable themselves. Perhaps so, but again this value must be placed in perspective. The institutional mechanism commonly associated with holding wrongdoers to account is litigation. Since few claimants get to litigate their complaint, this form of accountability is relatively rare. This is not to say that the right of action itself is not a tool of accountability, since one can use it to threaten or initiate proceedings without ever seeing the inside of a courtroom. Nevertheless, these options, if they result in pre-court settlement, are a shadow of the ideal of holding wrongdoers accountable via making one's case in a court of law and obtaining a judgment of liability.

These points are intended to limit rather than eliminate the significance of the accountability defence of tort law over the schemes. To buttress this argument, note that we must consider the institutional virtues of the schemes too—something advocates of the accountability value of tort rarely do. These institutional virtues must be balanced against accountability to form an all-things-considered judgment. This is the same point we made against interpretivism in Chapter 2: justification is inherently comparative, so pointing to positive reasons in favour of a system of law in isolation makes little progress towards justifying this system with respect to alternatives.

There are two important institutional virtues of compensation schemes, which are in some respects the converse of accountability: ease of claim and non-litigiousness. Victims can often obtain compensation more easily and smoothly through a scheme than by filing a civil action. This may be a considerable boon for those struggling with serious injury,[20] or for those who want to avoid the stress and hassle of a lawsuit. This is all the more valuable in no-fault schemes where the fault of the injurer is not at issue. There is also evidence that many victims of torts decline to bring meritorious claims because they want to avoid litigiousness, particularly when the victim and tortfeasor have a prior relationship, for example employer–employee.[21] Those who advocate the accountability value of tort seldom consider that it might be a virtue of compensation schemes that they do *not* require victims to hold their injurers to account, with all the time, stress, bitterness, and financial risk this may involve.

This point is undergirded by the fact that, as Anita Bernstein argues, private law benefits those socialized to make demands and assert rights rather than those socialized to support and make sacrifices, such as women.[22] Accountability practices may benefit victims of wrongs, but they do not benefit them equally, and these inequalities in access to legal accountability break down along problematic gender lines. Perhaps this objection can be overcome by changing socialization practices and the legal environment to ensure all victims are equally likely and able to press their claims. But even if this is achievable, why make those socialized to shy away from pressing legal claims more litigious to suit the system when the system could be made less litigious to suit them?

To get a fuller sense of these respective institutional virtues, further questions must be answered. For example, to what extent do they depend on the beliefs and preferences of claimants themselves? Is a claimant's option to bring a civil action valuable even if they would prefer to receive compensation through a scheme? Clearly more must be said to reach an informed judgement on the relative merits of accountability through tort compared with competing institutional virtues. The point I am making here is just that, though we should recognize the accountability value of the tort system, this does not necessarily tip the balance in its favour. That depends on how that particular virtue stacks up against those of the system's competitors.

---

[20] This may be mitigated if the scheme pays out less compensation than would the tort system, as is the case with many actual schemes, but for simplicity we are assuming equal payment.

[21] Cane and Goudkamp, *Atiyah's Accidents* (n 1) ch 8 pt 3.

[22] Anita Bernstein, 'A Feminist Perspective: Private Law as Unjust Enrichment' in Andrew S Gold and others (eds), *The Oxford Handbook of the New Private Law* (Oxford University Press 2021) 195.

C. Causation

One of the most concerning consequences of switching to compensation schemes from the perspective of tort apologists is that victims would not have to identity any specific individual and prove they were the cause of the harm. Some argue that the causation requirement is crucial in linking claimant and defendant. Others argue that the significance of causation is essentially mysterious, and a system focussed on liability for the *ex ante* conduct of defendants is better.[23] We have already rejected the idea that causation is insignificant, so we can hardly avail ourselves of this option. Any defence of the compensation schemes will therefore have to acknowledge rather than dismiss the importance of causation.

i. A solution?
We could adopt a similar strategy to one Victor Tadros uses to derive a justification of criminal punishment from the protective duties owed by wrongdoers. Tadros considers the following case:

> *Double Hit Man 2:* Evelyn hires a hit man to kill Wayne. Fred has also hired a hit man to kill Wayne. Both hit men arrive at the same time. Because of where they are standing, Wayne can only use Fred as a shield against Evelyn's hit man and Evelyn as a shield against Fred's hit man. He manages to do that, resulting in the deaths of Evelyn and Fred.

If Evelyn and Fred are liable to be harmed only for threats they cause, Wayne acts wrongly in this case. But it is not plausible that Wayne must let himself be killed just because Evelyn and Fred are standing in the wrong places. Tadros explains this intuitive verdict on the grounds that, since Evelyn and Fred cannot prevent their own wrongful threats but can prevent each other's, they have a duty to agree to do this. Wayne can then appeal to such a duty to justify harming Evelyn to prevent Wayne's threat and harming Wayne to prevent Evelyn's threat.

There are three differences between *Double Hit Man 2* and the tort context, which might prevent us adopting Tadros' strategy. Two of these differences turn out to be immaterial and the third merits further discussion. The first is that this example is concerned with defensive liability rather than compensatory

[23] See Christopher H Schroder, 'Corrective Justice and Liability for Increasing Risks' (1990) 37 UCLA Law Review 439.

liability. But this difference is irrelevant given that the factors that determine defensive liability are also relevant to compensatory liability.[24] True, there are circumstantial differences, such as the fact that compensation is always divisible whereas defensive harm is not, but if it were possible to compensate Wayne (suppose he survives the attempted hits) Evelyn and Fred would clearly be liable to compensate him, and this judgement would be supported by the same considerations—culpably initiating an unjust threat—as those that justify liability to defensive harm.

The second difference is that the wrongs in *Double Hit Man 2* are criminal whilst the wrongs we are interested in are tortious. One difference between (most) torts and (most) crimes is that the latter involve higher degrees of culpability. This difference is reflected in both the content of the resulting duties and their stringency. Those who commit crimes are (usually) liable to punishment whilst tortfeasors are (usually) only liable to compensate. It is hard to see how this alters the logic of the argument, though. The duty to compensate is still important—sometimes a matter of life and death—and if some injurers are unable to compensate their own victims but can enter an agreement with others to 'swap', then they ought to do this for the same reasons that apply to Evelyn and Fred.

So far, this suggests the following: there is a justified exception to the usual requirement to prove causation when there are multiple wrongdoers, each of whom harms a different victim, but we do not know which injurer harms which victim. Sandy Steel also defends this conclusion by appeal to the idea that it best reflects the wrongdoers' corrective duties, since if they cannot compensate their specific victim, they have a duty to enter an agreement with similarly situated wrongdoers to swap, thus ensuring their duties are fulfilled. The compensation scheme we are envisaging, however, is not restricted to this kind of duty-sharing, since it requires contributions from people who have not caused harm at all. This, then, is the third difference: the duty-sharing argument works only if we assume all parties have corrective duties, but it is controversial whether those who do not cause harm have any such duties.

Even worse, without causation it is difficult to see how any person, wrongful risker or not, can be responsible for any actual damage. Weinrib claims that 'without the causal connection of suffering to the wrongful creation of risk, there is no actor responsible for the suffering and thus no one from whom, as a matter of corrective justice, the sufferer can recover'.[25] Others also reject the

[24] Sandy Steel, 'Defensive and Remedial Liability' in John Oberdiek and Paul B Miller (eds), *Oxford Studies in Private Law Theory* (vol 2, Oxford University Press 2023) 53–78.
[25] Weinrib, *Idea of Private Law* (n 4) 153.

principle that A ought to compensate B for damage if A increased the risk of the damage but did not cause it. Perhaps it is in some sense fair that A should bear costs in proportion to their wrong, but it is not clear why A owes anything *to B in particular* rather than any other victim of harm equally unconnected to A's actions.[26] Thus, the wrong of imposing risk without harm cannot play any role in establishing the wrongdoer's responsibility to compensate for any actual harm.

ii. Two responses

This is an important objection, but it is not decisive. There are two ways we can address the problem. First consider the duties injurers owe their victims. Suppose Ollie wrongfully injures Penny and has three options:

(1) Compensate Penny
(2) Contribute to a scheme that compensates Penny
(3) Do nothing

Perhaps there is some reason to think that (1) is the best option. The state should provide a legal means by which Penny can demand option (1) and a court can enforce it. However, we have already seen that the difference between (1) and (2) is more marginal than we might think, partly because (2) need not result in total loss of accountability for Ollie and partly because the difference between Ollie's insurer compensating Penny and the administrator of a central scheme doing so is not very significant. Nevertheless, let's suppose (1) is preferable to (2). But if (1) is not available, (2) is far better than (3). It is not plausible that, if Ollie cannot directly compensate Penny but can support the scheme, his corrective duties disappear. It is far better for him to support the compensation of Penny indirectly, and indeed the compensation of other victims like her, than to do nothing. (3) would violate *the responsiveness thesis* as it would pay no regard at all to the values Ollie disregarded through wrongdoing. If (1) is not possible, (2) is the next best way of paying regard to those values.

This means that, if it is permissible for the state to replace tort with an at-fault scheme, this triggers a new duty on behalf of wrongdoers, derived from their

---

[26] Arthur Ripstein, *Equality, Responsibility, and the Law* (Cambridge University Press 1999) 72–74; Weinrib, *Idea of Private Law* (n 4) 114–44; Jules Coleman, 'Doing Away with Tort Law' (2007–08) 41 Loyola of Los Angeles Law Review 1149, 1165–66; Peter Cane, *Responsibility in Law and Morality* (Bloomsbury 2002) 136–41; and Sandy Steel, *Proof of Causation in Tort Law* (Cambridge University Press 2015) ch 3 (hereafter Steel, *Proof of Causation*). Steel defends some exceptions to the general rule that the claimant must prove causation, but rejects the principle that A should be liable to compensate B for harm merely on the basis that A imposed a wrongful risk on B.

previous duty, to support this scheme rather than do nothing. Funding for the scheme can then be raised on the basis of this new duty. Of course, the state cannot appeal to this duty as its reason to replace tort with the scheme, as this would be to put the cart before the horse. We will discuss some other reasons for the replacement of tort in the next part, but for now the important point is that the conditional structure of Ollie's duty means that, if the state does set up the scheme, Ollie and others like him have duties to support it.

Can the same argument be made in support of the no-fault scheme? Suppose the four-fold account I defended is correct. If so, there are some cases where Ollie harms Penny non-wrongfully but owes a duty to compensate. Given the three options above, we can again accept that (1) is optimal. But if (1) is not possible, I suggest (2) remains preferable to (3). In this case, *the responsiveness thesis* does not apply because Ollie has not violated any prior duty; he has not wronged Penny and thus disregarded the values that grounded his duty. But there are other grounds, such as outcome responsibility, on which he should still compensate her. If this is not possible through tort law, (2) comes closer to fulfilling his duties than doing nothing, since this is a way of supporting a system that ensures his outcome responsibility is discharged.

The second way to address the challenge is to appeal to duties that arise from wrongful risking rather than harming. Steel says that compensation cannot constitute next-best conformity to a duty not to impose harmless risks.[27] But this does not preclude the possibility that wrongful riskers owe non-compensatory corrective duties. Begin with the observation that imposing pure risks (ie risks that do not materialize into harm) is often wrong. Even if this is false as an interpretive claim about the law, it is true as a normative claim.[28] A person who recklessly speeds through a red light, for instance, narrowly missing someone parked on the other side, acts wrongly, and specifically wrongs the person on whom the risk is imposed. There are different explanations as to why the reckless driver acts wrongly. Two prominent views are that risks are themselves harms[29] and that risks violate a non-material autonomy interest.[30]

---

[27] Steel, *Proof of Causation* (n 26) 111.

[28] In relation to 'damage-based' torts, Ripstein argues that only damage is inconsistent with the plaintiff's right, see Arthur Ripstein, *Private Wrongs* (Harvard University Press 2016) 83. A merely negligent defendant is 'entirely innocent' from a rights-based perspective and has committed no legal wrong. See also Weinrib, *Idea of Private Law* (n 4) 157; Donal Nolan, 'Causation and the Goals of Tort Law' in Andrew Robertson and Tang Hang Wu (eds), *The Goals of Private Law* (Hart 2009) 165–90, 175; and Allan Beever, *Rediscovering the Law of Negligence* (Hart 2009) 446.

[29] Claire Finkelstein, 'Is Risk a Harm?' (2003) 151 University of Pennsylvania Law Review 963; Adriana Placani, 'When the Risk of Harm Harms' (2017) 36 Law and Philosophy 77.

[30] John Oberdiek, *Imposing Risk: A Normative Framework* (Oxford University Press 2017) ch 3 (hereafter Oberdiek, *Imposing Risk*).

I have argued elsewhere that both these views fail as explanations of the wrongness of pure risking,[31] though I will not rehearse those arguments here. I will note that what makes a pure risk wrong is importantly connected with the wrongness of causing the outcome that the risk threatens to bring about. For example, suppose some set of facts {f} ground the wrongness of some non-risk-based act v. Let a person P take a significant risk of v-ing for no good reason. We then have powerful reasons to conclude that P has acted wrongly, without knowing anything more about what is in {f}. For example, if v-ing is wrong because it is contrary to god's will, then it is wrong to risk v-ing because this risks doing something contrary to god's will. If v-ing is wrong because it is harmful, then it is wrong to risk v-ing because this risks doing something harmful, and so on. This suggests that the wrongness of pure risks is intimately related to the wrongness of the things they risk bringing about, whatever they are.

Given these observations, how should wrongdoers respond to their imposition of wrongful risks? Perhaps the least plausible answer to this question is that they should do nothing. True, the wrongdoer has not caused any harm, and the law does not grant remedies in this situation for good reason. But this cannot be accepted as a moral position just because it chimes with the requirement of legally cognizable harm. Consider the previous example in which a person speeds through a red light, risking those in close physical proximity. Certainly an apology is merited, but this seems insubstantial when combined with no further action. When we wrongfully put other people at risk of death or serious injury, I suggest we ought to do more than apologize.

There are objections to this suggestion. One is that corrective duties based on pure risks interfere too greatly with freedom. Wrongful risks are much more common than wrongful harms, and if we were burdened with a corrective duty after every wrongful risk, this would be an intolerable encroachment on our freedom to pursue our goals and projects unimpeded. There are two responses to this. First, when we are talking about wrongful risks, *ex hypothesi* those who owe such duties have *already* behaved as they were not morally free to do. This lessens the concern that their subsequent duties also morally constrain them. Second, for obvious reasons, corrective duties arising from wrongful risks do not involve compensation and are therefore less burdensome. This makes them more likely to be proportional to the seriousness of the wrong. Wrongful risks may be small beans in comparison to wrongful harms, but so too are the secondary duties engendered by wrongful risks in comparison to those engendered by wrongful harms.

---

[31] Adam Slavny and Tom Parr, 'What's Wrong with Risk?' (2019) 8 Thought 76.

At this point we might wonder what a corrective duty arising from wrongful risk would look like. What is there to correct in the absence of compensable harm? Here is one possibility. In light of *the responsiveness thesis* (see Chapter 3), perhaps the most natural way to respond to wrongful risks is to provide equivalent protection for future risks. Suppose that, after risking Penny's death, Ollie can purchase insurance on behalf of Penny, the cost and coverage of which is roughly proportionate to his wrong. The cost is within the stringency threshold and the insurance covers Penny against wrongs similar to the one Ollie committed. Intuitively, Ollie has a duty to do this rather than nothing.

This can be defended on all the leading theories of why pure risks are wrong. On the view sketched above, equivalent protection is a fitting response to the values set back by the wrong, typically physical safety. On John Oberdiek's view, pure risks are wrong because they interfere with a non-material autonomy interest. Risks are like laying traps: they remove or diminish the value of one's options.[32] If this is right, equivalent protection is akin to removing a trap, a fitting response to the laying of one. If we adopt Claire Finkelstein's view that risking is wrong because risks are themselves harms, equivalent protection is an appropriate benefit in light of the harm of risk.

An implication of this is that, if Penny is then harmed by another wrongdoer, she can claim compensation through the insurance policy provided by Ollie, and thus Ollie will indirectly compensate Penny for harm caused by a different wrongdoer, without relying on the idea that he is responsible for this harm in any direct sense.

These duties probably do not merit enforcement through tort law or any relaxation of the causation requirement in negligence. Otherwise, some degree of compensation would be available in every instance of negligence, and this would lead to an overabundance of low value claims and an even greater reduction in efficiency. But these objections do not apply when appealing to these duties to support an at-fault scheme (although they cannot justify a no-fault scheme for the separate reason that permissible riskers generally do not owe corrective duties). This brings us to the question of *how* such duties can justify the at-fault scheme. To answer this, we need to consider the duties owed by the victim of risk rather than the risk imposers.

Victims of risk have duties to extend the protection they are owed to other similarly situated victims. Consider:

---

[32] Oberdiek, *Imposing Risk* (n 30) 86–87.

Gauntlet: Penny must run a gauntlet in which Ollie imposes a reckless risk on her. Penny runs the gauntlet and is not harmed. In compensation, Ollie gives Penny an insurance policy. If she keeps the policy, it will protect her from the risk of being harmed in future gauntlets. Alternatively, she can give it to Qamar, who has not yet run the gauntlet.

To keep things simple, suppose that Penny and Qamar are otherwise equally well off. In this case, I think Penny ought to insure Qamar against the risk of the gauntlet rather than herself. Although Penny has been wronged by Ollie, she is also lucky in the sense that the threatened harm never arose. Given this, she is now in receipt of a benefit without being rendered worse off by the wrong committed against her. She has, in effect, been enriched by the wrong. This means she can benefit Qamar at no cost to herself, and this generates a new duty to assist Qamar. The same argument, of course, also applies to Qamar. If they are luckily not harmed, they have a duty to use any benefit to which they are entitled to insure the next person.

In this way, we can appeal to the general principle that, if a person can significantly benefit another at no cost, they ought to do so. The repeated application of this principle suggests victims of wrongful risks—as opposed to wrongful harm—have duties to insure each other. They can pool the protective resources they are entitled to for the benefit of those who, unluckily, suffer harm. They ought to do this as it substantially benefits these unlucky few and is costless for them.

An objection to this argument is that victims should be entitled to keep any protective resources they are owed for themselves rather than transferring them to others. In the real world, we are subject to iterated or ongoing risk. Protection in the form of insurance is useful for victims, even if they are fortunate enough to escape one instance of wrongful risk without incident. But if this is true then compensation for future wrongs is overdetermined. Victims can be compensated because of the protection they are owed by prior wrongs (that didn't result in harm) as well as the compensation owed by the present injurer. Either way, then, the victim is made better off by the wrong—this follows from the fact that, luckily, they were not injured by the first wrong—and we can engage the principle that they ought to extend protection to others who, unluckily, are harmed by the same wrongs.

Another objection is that most wrongful risks are imposed on groups of people rather than individuals. Negligence on the roads exposes all those in physical proximity to unjustified risks. If all these individuals are owed substantial protection, this might make the duty overly burdensome and exceed the stringency threshold, while if the protection is divided between them, it is relatively useless. All this might fuel doubts about whether pure riskers owe anything to those they wrong. However, the diffuseness of these duties is a strength rather than a weakness in relation to compensation schemes. This fact undergirds the case for victims having a duty to pool any protection they are owed with other victims, since (a) doing so is to their collective advantage and (b) the benefits owed to individual victims of pure risks are too small to be enforceable in any other context.

Those who hold that compensation schemes are inconsistent with corrective justice often emphasize that schemes dismantle the central relationship between injurer and victim embodied by a tort suit. Wright, for example, argues that at-fault schemes are 'inconsistent with the correlative bilateral rights and duties that are a central feature of corrective justice and ignore the logical and normative correlativity of rights and duties *per se*'.[33] The central insight here, which I accept, is that tort duties (and, I would argue, the moral duties that underpin them) are directed. They are owed to particular individuals such that when a person violates this type of duty, they wrong the person to whom the duty is owed, rather than acting wrongly *tout court*. It is tempting to think of the bilateral structure of a tort action as the only natural embodiment of the directedness of these rights and duties. But the claim that alternative arrangements ignore their 'logical and normative correlativity' is an exaggeration. It depends on a host of assumptions: the assumption that pure risks are not wrong, or not directed wrongs, or do not give rise to corrective duties; the assumption that recipients of corrective duties do not themselves owe duties to pool protection; and the assumption that the bilateral structure of the tort action is the only acceptable institutional embodiment of corrective duties. If I have not won over proponents of the strong view that compensation schemes are completely inconsistent with corrective duties, I hope at least to have demonstrated the need for further argument.

IV. Tort Law, At-Fault, or No-Fault

I have argued that three different institutional arrangements—tort law, at-fault, and no-fault—are consistent with our underlying moral duties in the sense that none impose burdens on anyone who does not have a duty to bear them for

---

[33] Richard W Wright, 'Right, Justice, and Tort Law' in David G Owen (ed), *The Philosophical Foundations of Tort Law* (Oxford University Press 1995) 180.

ends they do not have a duty to serve. The tort system is not a required institution. At least in principle, there are multiple permissible institutional arrangements for the governance of a large portion of corrective duties. An implication of this is that the results of relaxing our idealizing assumptions are more important to the overall justification or otherwise of tort than we might initially have thought.

Specifically, we have been utilizing three idealizing assumptions: (1) perfect uptake (that all meritorious claimants receive compensation), (2) zero operational costs, and (3) equivalent deterrence. Obviously, in the real world the three systems we have discussed will vary in terms of uptake, cost, and deterrent effect. The next question, then, is which arrangement is to be preferred once we factor in a variety of non-ideal considerations. One argument in favour of tort is that it reinforces social norms against wrongdoing and has a deterrent effect. An argument against the at-fault scheme is that the operational costs of detecting fault are very high, and thus it lacks one of the benefits of no-fault: that the administrative costs of the latter are much lower.

Philosophers are not best placed to pronounce on the empirical evidence regarding these different institutional arrangements, but we can try to evaluate the normative choice between them based on different suppositions about that evidence. Although the evidence about the deterrent effect of tort is mixed, if it is true that switching to a compensation scheme will significantly increase the accident rate, this counts decisively in favour of tort, all else being equal.[34] It would be different if tort was impermissible from the perspective of ideal theory. Then we would have to ask whether the avoidance of a predicted number of injuries and deaths through deterrence would be enough to overturn this judgement. But since tort is one of a range of permissible options, averting injury and death through deterrence clearly tips the balance in its favour. It is important to note, however, that if this is correct, the deterrent effects of tort are much more crucial to its justification than most tort apologists are willing to accept, not because deterrence is the central aim of tort, or because the pursuit of deterrence should be unconstrained, but because it is necessary to act as a tie breaker.[35]

---

[34] See also Gary T Schwartz, 'Reality in the Economic Analysis of Tort Law: Does Tort Law Really Deter?' 42 UCLA Law Review 377, which argues that the benefits of tort in terms of accident prevention might exceed its costs.

[35] Another argument, which I lack the space to discuss here, is that in some compensation regimes, for example for road accidents, participants are both potential causers of accidents and potential victims, giving them both an incentive to avoid accidents.

The choice between systems is further complicated by (1) and (2). We have assumed all systems operate with perfect uptake, with all parties receiving the benefits to which they are entitled under that system, and with no operational cost. Consider how two realistic suppositions about uptake and operational cost affect the choice. The first is that uptake in tort systems is less than that in compensation schemes,[36] and the second is that the overall administrative cost of tort compared to no-fault is higher.

Suppose, as seems likely, that more people would receive the benefits they are entitled to under the compensation schemes than tort because there are fewer disincentives to claiming. The result is that, under tort, we systematically impose greater risks on potential victims that they will be harmed without being compensated. Risking failing to compensate one's victims when one could do so without greater cost shows the same disregard for them as imposing wrongful risks. It is, in fact, materially similar to failing to insure oneself against future liability. Driving without insurance involves this kind of wrong (or it would do if the Motor Insurance Bureau did not step in to compensate victims of uninsured drivers), and this is part of the justification for making motor insurance mandatory. I am suggesting that, given the empirical assumptions we are working with, the same norm gives us reason to prefer the schemes to the tort system.

Some additional points are worth making about this argument. First, it does not rely on the wrongful risking defence of the at-fault scheme. Suppose wrongful riskers owe nothing to their victims, or if they do the victims have no duty to share this benefit with others. Nevertheless, if victims of wrongful harm are more likely to be compensated under the schemes than under the tort system, they have reason to prefer the schemes even though they would not have such reasons under conditions of perfect uptake. This means the present argument potentially applies to no-fault as well as at-fault schemes. Non-wrongdoers (those who impose neither wrongful risk nor wrongful harm) sometimes incur conditional duties to compensate. If these duties are more likely to be fulfilled under a no-fault scheme than strict liability tort law, duty-bearers have reason to prefer the scheme to avoid violating the same norm that

---

[36] We must be careful here to distinguish between different compensation schemes. The challenges faced by claimants depend on the terms of eligibility defined by the scheme and the procedural requirements for a successful claim. All else equal, it is easier to claim under a no-fault scheme than an at-fault scheme, except perhaps in circumstances where fault can be presumed or inferred. Studies suggesting that difficulties in proving fault are a central reason why people abandon tort claims are cited in Cane and Goudkamp, *Atiyah's Accidents* (n 1) 187.

uninsured wrongdoers violate: risking the possibility that the beneficiaries of their potential duties do not receive those benefits.

How does improved uptake stack up against the value of accountability and the causation requirement? The question is whether those victims who would receive compensation under both the scheme and the tort system can justify tort to those who would receive compensation only under the scheme.

I doubt they can. Suppose Ralph, Stu, Uriel, Viv, and Wren all suffer permanent paralysis as a result of tortious conduct. Under an at-fault or no-fault scheme they would all recover compensation, but under tort law all except Wren would be compensated. Suppose, finally, that they know this in advance and must choose between an at-fault or no-fault scheme and tort. Wren would argue they should opt for an at-fault or no-fault scheme because that way Wren will recover the compensation to which she is entitled. Could Ralph, Stu, Uriel, and Viv reply to Wren that her paralysis is a price worth paying for the sake of their opportunity to hold their injurers to account, and to prove the causal link between specific instances of wrongdoing and their harm? This argument strikes me as weak. The serious permanent injury of some outweighs the interest of others in availing themselves of the accountability process of tort. Wren cannot be expected to forgo compensation for her life-altering injury for the sake of Ralph, Stu, Uriel, and Viv's interest in suing their injurers rather than recovering through a scheme.

It might be objected that this reasoning proves too much. If serious injury is so terrible, doesn't this suggest that compensation for all injury and illness should be given equal priority? Then we might end up, not with a personal injury compensation scheme but a luck egalitarian style universal compensation system. Perhaps we should support such a system, but the argument I am making here has no such implication. We must remember we are assuming that a certain class of victims are owed moral duties of compensation.[37] A broader compensation system that responded only to need, making no distinction between victims of wrongs and victims of other misfortunes, would have to appeal to some other set of duties to justify raising the considerable funds it would require, such as general, positive duties of assistance. Since such duties are more controversial and, in any case, less stringent than the duties of those who have caused harm or imposed wrongful risk, this system is more difficult to justify.

---

[37] See also Martin Stone, 'The Significance of Doing and Suffering' in Gerald J Postema (ed), *Philosophy and the Law of Torts* (Cambridge University Press 2001) 131, 144.

What about the choice between at-fault and no-fault? Assuming uptake is the same, it might seem the present argument does not give us reason to prefer one over the other. However, this may not be the case given plausible assumptions about operational costs. If the operational costs of at-fault are higher than no-fault because of the difficulty of proving fault, this might lead to lower uptake. If this is right, no-fault provides better security for recipients of corrective duties than at-fault. Similarly, no-fault (at least some versions of no-fault) might be justified on the grounds that uptake under at-fault is too low, or improving uptake is too expensive, in the same way some justify strict liability in terms of fault. Not everyone harmed by someone else's fault is in a position to prove it. Relinquishing the fault requirement might be justified if it is better to compensate victims of fault who can't prove it (at the cost of compensating some victims who are harmed without fault) than it is to compensate only victims of fault who can prove it.

Finally, the costs of bringing tort actions may mean their benefits are more likely to accrue to the wealthy than the poor. The schemes, by contrast, may distribute compensation more equitably due to ease of claim. This is where our distributive justice critique becomes particularly relevant. In Chapter 7 we saw that victims of distributive injustice often do not owe corrective duties to beneficiaries of distributive injustice. We also accepted that judges should not generally be empowered to give recognition to this fact in their decision-making. This creates the unfortunate situation whereby the legal practice of corrective justice is systemically unjust and yet the institutions implicit in this injustice have no internal means of addressing it. If compensation schemes improve matters from a distributive justice perspective, and are also supported by our moral corrective duties, this is a powerful reason to favour the schemes.

Conclusion

Let's conclude this chapter, and the book, with some extended reflections on the extent to which our moral account of corrective duties supports some central features of tort law. If previous chapters have not convinced anyone of their conclusions, I hope they have at least demonstrated, despite or perhaps because of their failure, the breadth and complexity of the issues relating to the morality of corrective duties. These issues are thorny enough on their own, and we should be wary of straightforward attempts to read off from them conclusions about enforcement and institutional design.

With this caveat in mind, the view defended in this book neither justifies nor condemns tort law, and therefore provides ammunition neither for the apologist nor the wholesale reformer. On the one hand, it shows how certain features of tort law reflect the morality of corrective duties, which is encouraging for those who think the law is rooted in, rather than separate from, the corrective practices we find in our everyday lives.[38] On the other hand, certain key features of the law cannot be justified with reference to underlying duties, and while they may be justified by appeal to some of the empirical realities of enforcing legal rules in non-ideal circumstances, this is scant comfort for those who view these features as central to a justified, and perhaps even necessary, legal practice.

So what are the similarities between our moral account and tort law? For one thing, the four-fold analysis provides some support for the coexistence of fault and strict liability. Some regard strict liability as an anomaly given that tort is a law of wrongs and strict liability appears to dispense with the notion of wrongdoing altogether.[39] Some fail to see the problem, interpreting strict liability as a form of wrongdoing after all. Jules Coleman, for example, distinguishes between a *wrong* and a wrong*doing*, where the latter does not imply impermissible conduct. Goldberg and Zipursky say that 'standard torts are, in certain common applications, "strict liability wrongs"'.[40]

This move has two disadvantages. First, it creates confusion because the (moral) distinction between permissible and impermissible conduct is crucial for meeting the *undue burden* and *restricted freedom* objections. For many torts, perhaps including negligence via the objective standard of care, some instances of its application involve the violation of enforceable moral duties and others do not. In these latter instances, we need a different argument to overcome the *undue burden* and *restricted freedom* objections. In this respect, instrumentalists have an advantage over other tort apologists, as they at least offer substantive reasons for restricting freedom and imposing burdens when there is no moral wrongdoing present.

The second disadvantage is that forcing permissible and impermissible moral conduct into the same legal rubric seems unnecessary once we recognize that wrongdoing is only one source of corrective obligations among others. Both causation without fault and distributive fairness can ground such duties. It would be misleading, then, to think strict liability can be justified only

---

[38] For this view, see Gardner, *Personal Life* (n 9).
[39] Weinrib has argued that both strict liability and subjective standards of care fail to cohere to corrective justice, see *The Idea of Private Law* (n 4) 177.
[40] Goldberg and Zipursky, *Recognizing Wrongs* (n 16) 192.

by appeal to the kind of 'policy factors'—judicial loss spreading, deterring defensive practices, economic policy, etc—that non-instrumentalists reject or downplay in their theories of private law. The duties generated by considerations of fairness and outcome responsibility are no less important as grounds for compensatory liability than wrongdoing.

Two types of strict liability that may be justified by distributive fairness and conditional permissibility are vicarious liability and the rule in *Rylands v Fletcher*. Vicarious liability engages *The Benefit Principle*. Employers benefit from services provided by their employees, so there is a case that they should share the costs of compensation when those employees harm others in the course of employment. Appeal to this principle does not explain all elements of the law, though, such as vicarious liability for non-profit organizations. But it may be that vicarious liability is subject to other overlapping justifications. If it is based partly on the idea that employees are agents of their employers and so the actions of the former can be attributed to the latter, then this rationale might explain the extension of vicarious liability to charities, while in other cases the two justifications overlap. Alternatively, the case for holding charities vicariously liable might be weaker than the case for holding profit-making organizations liable precisely because this is outside the scope of *The Benefit Principle*.

The rule in *Rylands v Fletcher* has been analysed in terms of conditional permissibility, or licence-based liability,[41] which is well suited to justifying liability for highly risky activity. But *The Benefit Principle* and *The Avoidance Principle* are germane to the rule as well. According to the modern formulation of this rule in *Transco plc v Stockport*, A will be liable for compensation if she brings or keeps on her land an 'exceptionally dangerous or mischievous thing in extraordinary or unusual circumstances',[42] which escapes and causes reasonably foreseeable damage to B's land. Although the damage must be reasonably foreseeable, the escape need not be, which means the rule applies even if A takes whatever precautions can be reasonably expected and thus acts permissibly.[43] *The Avoidance Principle* applies because the party storing the dangerous item generally has knowledge and control over it, which creates an asymmetry between them and those in the surrounding area who might be harmed if it escapes. Avoiding the danger is more difficult and costly for these other parties by virtue of this asymmetry, and so there is a case for the creator of the danger

---

[41] ibid 191.

[42] [2004] 2 AC 1.

[43] For an early version of this argument, see Carleton Kemp Allen, *Legal Duties and Other Essays in Jurisprudence* (Clarendon Press 1931) 193–94.

to internalize the cost in the event of an escape. *The Benefit Principle* also applies when storage of dangerous items is primarily for the benefit of those who store them. Taken together, these principles go some way towards justifying the species of strict liability found in *Rylands v Fletcher*.

Once again, though, appeal to distributive fairness cannot account for all aspects of the rule. For one thing, under the House of Lords' restatement of the rule, recovery is restricted to damage to land, a consequence of situating the rule within the realm of private nuisance and thus a tort against property rather than the person. On *The Benefit Principle* and *The Avoidance Principle*, however, there is no reason why recovery should be so restricted. We can benefit from risks to the person just as we can from risks to land, and we can avoid risks to the person just as we can risks to land. For another thing, the rule in *Rylands v Fletcher* is limited in scope. A more consistent application of *The Benefit Principle* and *The Avoidance Principle* might lead to a more general scheme of strict liability, such as that imposed for ultrahazardous activities in some US states.[44]

Our discussion of outcome responsibility also suggests broader possibilities for strict liability. One worry about the type of outcome responsibility I have defended is that it is too expansive and onerous, far outstripping that found in tort law, where liability is not usually imposed for non-voluntary harm. This discrepancy may be problematic for some who feel that the legal position is more plausible. We must remember, though, I have argued only that there is a *moral* duty for non-responsible injurers to do more for their victims than bystanders, and it is an open question whether this duty is enforceable and in what circumstances. Since imposing legal liability has many costs, there are limits on what moral duties can give rise to liability. The lower the stringency of a person's duty, the less benefit the victim may derive from enforcing it. We should avoid enforcing duties which confer relatively small benefits on others. It is therefore hardly surprising that liability to compensate in tort is not as expansive as the conception of outcome responsibility I have defended. In his original discussion, Honoré makes a similar point, arguing that, whilst outcome responsibility is widespread, it justifies liability to compensate only when a range of other conditions are met.[45]

---

[44] For the view that the current classification of *Rylands v Fletcher* is misguided, see John Murphy, 'The Merits of Rylands v Fletcher' (2004) 24 Oxford Journal of Legal Studies 643 and Donal Nolan, 'The Distinctiveness of Rylands v Fletcher' (2005) 121 Law Quarterly Review 421.

[45] Tony Honoré, *Responsibility and Fault* (Hart 1999).

Nevertheless, it is unsurprising that strict liability regimes have expanded, and negligence has been tightened in response to the increasing availability of liability insurance. Insurance reduces the burden of compensation on the duty-bearer, in many cases bringing it beneath the stringency threshold of their duty. Increasing insurance coverage carries its own problems, of course, but often it succeeds in circumventing the problem that liability would otherwise be too burdensome or simply impossible for one individual. This is one factor that explanations of the relationship between insurance and liability tend to omit. Often the effect of insurance on liability is seen in terms of social policy, or the relevance of insurance is dismissed. But reducing the burden of liability so that it no longer exceeds the stringency threshold of an injurer's duty is one effect of insurance that is neither a form of social policy nor normatively inert—it has a direct impact on how an important feature of interpersonal corrective duties plays out.

We also saw in Chapter 4 that there is no principled basis for the standard of conduct in negligence being capacity and cost insensitive. This conclusion has ambiguous implications for the objective standard of care. On the one hand, the de-individualized standard of the reasonable person suggests that the law embodies a degree of capacity and cost insensitivity. On the other hand, there are exceptions to the objective standard, and much depends on precisely how we define capacity and cost. Beyond this, I conceded that the harshness of the objective standard might be justified on pragmatic grounds, in which case it has a hybrid justification: part principled and part practical.

This raises two problems for tort apologists. First, if the hybrid justification is correct, it means that a defining feature of the tort of negligence is not based on one of the many principled arguments that we considered and rejected, but rather on pragmatic considerations that arise due to the limitations of enforcing legal rules in non-ideal circumstances. This is in tension with the ambition, common to many interpretivists, of conceptualizing tort as a (legitimate and coherent) law of wrongs. A person who violates a capacity and cost insensitive standard but not a capacity and cost sensitive one is not in any meaningful sense a wrongdoer, though they might owe corrective duties on other grounds included in the four-fold analysis.

The second problem is that pragmatic concerns are often contextual, so we should not assume that they justify a rule as general as the objective standard. Pragmatic worries that bite in one area of its application might not bite quite as hard in others. The standard might be relaxed partially, and in a piecemeal fashion, which is already evident in certain areas such as its application to children. Absent a principled justification, then, we should be open to expanding some of the exceptional categories further, such as permitting greater scope for defences based on impairment and incapacity.[46] These changes would not involve the total abandonment of the objective standard but might align it more closely with defendants' moral duties.

Two conclusions reached in the final two chapters present perhaps the greatest obstacle for the justification of tort: that victims of distributive injustice often do not owe corrective duties (or at least duties of full compensation) to beneficiaries of distributive injustice, and that alternative systems for the management of personal injury claims are permissible and perhaps, given certain empirical assumptions, required. As we noted, these conclusions are interrelated because, if the improved uptake of the schemes distributes compensation more equitably, this is a strong reason to prefer them, at least if this does not result in a drastic increase in accident rates.

Both these conclusions challenge the assumption that has structured the debate between reformists and apologists, that tort law and alternatives to the law are supported by irreducibly distinct paradigms. In fact, the morality of corrective duties is far more varied and flexible than this dichotomy suggests. Ultimately, then, our analysis is a double-edged sword from the perspective of tort apology. It reveals the potential to justify tort in a manner that breaks free from the circularity of internalism without falling back on pure instrumentalism, but it also insists on the diversity and complexity of corrective duties and rejects the abiding assumption that the institutional framework of private law is uniquely well-suited to enforce them.

[46] For example, see James Goudkamp's argument that insanity should be a tort defence in *Tort Law Defences* (Hart 2013) ch 8.

Bibliography

Adjin-Tettey E, 'Sexual Wrongdoing: Do the Remedies Reflect the Wrong?' in J Richardson and E Rackley (eds), *Feminist Perspectives on Tort* Law (Routledge 2012)

Alexander L, 'Causation and Corrective Justice: Does Tort Law Make Sense?' (1987) 6 Law and Philosophy 1

Alexander L, Kessler Ferzan K, and Morse S, *Crime and Culpability: A Theory of Criminal Law* (Cambridge University Press 2009)

Anderson ES, 'What is the Point of Equality?' (1999) 109 Ethics 287

Anderson M, 'All-American Rape' (2005) 79 St John's Law Review 625

Avraham R and Kohler-Hausmann I, 'Accident Law for Egalitarians' (2006) 12 Legal Theory 181

Azmat A, 'Tort's Indifference: Conformity, Compliance, and Civil Recourse' (2020) 13 Journal of Tort Law 1

Barcan Marcus R, 'Iterated Deontic Modalities' (1966) 75 Mind 580

Barry C and McTernan E, 'A Puzzle of Enforceability: Why do Moral Duties Differ in their Enforceability?' (2021) 19 Journal of Moral Philosophy 229

Bashshar H and Øverland G, 'The Normative Implications of Benefiting from Injustice' (2014) 31 Journal of Applied Philosophy 349

Bazargan-Forward S, 'Compensation and Proportionality in War' in J David Ohlin, L May, and C Finkelstein (eds), *Weighing Lives in War* (Oxford University Press 2017)

Bedke M, 'Explaining Compensatory Duties' (2010) 16 Legal Theory 91

Beever A, 'The Structure of Aggravated and Exemplary Damages' (2003) 23 Oxford Journal of Legal Studies 87

Beever A, *Rediscovering the Law of Negligence* (Hart 2009)

Benson P, 'The Basis of Corrective Justice and its Relation to Distributive Justice' (1992) 77 Iowa Law Review 515

Birks P, 'The Concept of a Civil Wrong' in DG Owen (ed), *The Philosophical Foundations of Tort Law* (Oxford University Press 1997)

Butt D, 'On Benefiting from Injustice' (2007) 37 Canadian Journal of Philosophy 129

Bernstein A, 'A Feminist Perspective: Private Law as Unjust Enrichment' in Andrew S Gold and others (eds), *The Oxford Handbook of the New Private Law* (Oxford University Press 2021)

Cane P, 'Retribution, Proportionality and Moral Luck' in P Cane and J Stapleton (eds), *The Law of Obligations-Essays in Celebration of John Fleming* (Clarendon Press 1998)

Cane P, 'Responsibility and Fault: A Relational and Functional Approach to Responsibility' in P Cane and J Gardner (eds), *Relating to Responsibility: Essays in Honour of Tony Honoré on his 80th Birthday* (Hart 2001)

Cane P, *Responsibility in Law and Morality* (Bloomsbury 2002)

Cane P and Goudkamp J, *Atiyah's Accidents, Compensation and the Law* (9th edn, Cambridge University Press 2018)

Carleton Kemp A, *Legal Duties and Other Essays in Jurisprudence* (Clarendon Press 1931)

Carter I, '"Ought" Implies "Practical Possibility"' in I Carter and M Ricciardi (eds), *Freedom, Power and Political Morality* (Palgrave 2001)

Casal P and Williams A, 'Equality of Resources and Procreative Justice' in Justine Burley (ed), *Dworkin and his Critics* (Blackwell 2005)

Chang R, 'The Possibility of Parity' (2002) 112 Ethics 659

Chapman B, 'Wrongdoing, Welfare, and Damages: Recovery for Non-Pecuniary Loss in Corrective Justice' in DG Owen (ed), *The Philosophical Foundations of Tort Law* (Oxford University Press 1995)

Christopher B, 'Do Multiple and Repeat Offenders Pose a Problem for Retributive Sentencing Theory?' in J Ryberg and C Tamburrini (eds), *Recidivist Punishment: The Philosophers' View* (Lexington 2011)

Christopher B, 'More to Apologise for: Can a Basis for the Recidivist Premium Be Found within a Communicative Theory of Punishment?' in JV Roberts and A von Hirsch (eds), *Previous Convictions at Sentencing: Theoretical and Applied Perspectives* (Hart 2010)

Coase R, 'The Problem of Social Cost' (1960) 3 Journal of Law and Economics 1

Cohen GA, *Self-Ownership, Freedom, and Equality* (Cambridge University Press 1995)

Cohen GA, 'Where the Action is: On the Site of Distributive Justice' (1997) 26 Philosophy & Public Affairs 3

Coleman J, 'Justice and Reciprocity in Tort Theory' (1974) 14 Western Ontario Law Review 105

Coleman J, 'Moral Theories of Torts: Their Scope and Limits: Part 1' (1982) 1 Law and Philosophy 371

Coleman J, *Risks and Wrongs* (Oxford University Press 1992)

Coleman J, *The Practice of Principle: In Defence of a Pragmatist Approach to Legal Theory* (Oxford University Press 2001)

Coleman J, 'Doing away with Tort Law' (2007–2008) 41 Loyola of Los Angeles Law Review 1149

Coleman J and Kraus J, 'Rethinking the Theory of Legal Rights' (1986) 95 Yale Law Journal 1335

Conaghan J, 'Gendered Harms and the Law of Tort: Remedying (Sexual) Harassment' (1996) 16 Oxford Journal of Legal Studies 407

Dagan H and Dorfman A, 'Justice in Private: Beyond the Rawlsian Framework' (2018) 37 Law and Philosophy 171

Dante A, *Inferno* (Harvard University Press 2013)

Darwall S and Darwall J, 'Civil Recourse as Mutual Accountability' in S Darwall (ed), *Morality, Authority, and Law: Essays in Second-Personal Ethics* (Oxford University Press 2013)

Dickens C, *A Tale of Two Cities* (first published 1858, Oxford University Press 2008)

Dorfman A, 'Reasonable Care: Equality as Objectivity' (2012) 31 Law and Philosophy 369

Dougherty T and Frick J, 'Morality and Institutional Detail in the Law of Torts: Reflections on Goldberg's and Zipursky's *Recognizing Wrongs*' (2022) 41 Law and Philosophy 41

Duff RA, 'Towards a Theory of Criminal Law?' (2010) 84 Aristotelian Society Supp Vol 1, 1

Duff RA, 'Towards a Modest Legal Moralism' (2014) 8 Criminal Law and Philosophy 217–35

Duus-Otterström G, 'Benefiting from Injustice and the Common-Source Problem' (2017) 20 Ethical Theory and Moral Practice 1067

Dworkin R, *Law's Empire* (Harvard University Press 1986)

Dworkin R, *Sovereign Virtue: The Theory and Practice of Equality* (Harvard University Press 2000)

Dworkin R, *Justice for Hedgehogs* (Harvard University Press 2011)

Edwards J and Simester A, 'What's Public About Crime?' (2017) 37 Oxford Journal of Legal Studies 105

Encarnacion E, 'Corrective Justice as Making Amends' (2014) 62 Buffalo Law Review 451

Epstein RA, 'A Theory of Strict Liability' (1973) 2 Journal of Legal Studies 151

Feinberg J, *Rights, Justice, and the Bounds of Liberty* (Princeton University Press 1980)

Feinberg J, *The Moral Limits of the Criminal Law Volume 1: Harm to Others* (Oxford University Press 1987)

Finkelstein C, 'Is Risk a Harm?' (2003) 151 University of Pennsylvania Law Review 963

Fletcher GP, 'Fairness and Utility in Tort Theory' (1972) 85 Harvard Law Review 537

Frankfurt H, 'Equality as a Moral Ideal' (1987) 98 Ethics 21

Frowe H, 'Threats, Bystanders and Obstructors' (2008) 108 Proceedings of the Aristotelian Society 365

Frowe H, 'Risk Imposition and Liability to Defensive Harm' (2022) 16 Criminal Law and Philosophy 511

Gaiman N, *The Sandman* (vol 9, The Kindly Ones, DC Comics 1994–95)

Gardner J, 'The Wrongdoing that Gets Results' (2004) 18 Philosophical Perspectives 53

Gardner J, 'Reasons and Abilities: Some Preliminaries' (2013) 58 American Journal of Jurisprudence 63

Gardner J, 'Some Rule-of-Law Anxieties about Strict Liability in Private Law' in LM Austin and D Klimchuk (eds), *Private Law and the Rule of Law* (Oxford University Press 2014)

Gardner J, 'The Negligence Standard: Political Not Metaphysical' (2017) 80 Modern Law Review 1

Gardner J, *From Personal Life to Private Law* (Oxford University Press 2018)

Gardner J, 'As Inconclusive as Ever' (2019) 19 Jerusalem Review of Legal Studies 204

Gardner J, 'Torts and Other Wrongs' in *Torts and Other Wrongs* (Oxford University Press 2019)

Godden N, 'Tort claims for Rape: More Trials, Fewer Tribulations?' in J Richardson and E Rackley (eds), *Feminist Perspectives on Tort Law* (Routledge 2012)

Gold AS, *The Right of Redress* (Oxford University Press 2020)

Goldberg JCP, 'What are We Reforming?: Tort Theory's Place in Debates over Malpractice Reform' (2006) 59 Vanderbilt Law Review 1075

Goldberg JCP, 'Inexcusable Wrongs' (2015) 103 California Law Review 467

Goldberg JCP, 'Torts' in AS Gold and others (eds), *The Oxford Handbook of the New Private Law* (Oxford University Press 2021)

Goldberg JCP and Zipursky BC, 'Unrealized Torts' (2002) 88 Vanderbilt Law Review 1625

Goldberg JCP and Zipursky BC, 'Tort Law and Moral Luck' (2007) 92 Cornell Law Review 1123

Goldberg JCP and Zipursky BC, 'Tort Law and Responsibility' in J Oberdiek (ed), *Philosophical Foundations of the Law of Torts* (Oxford University Press 2014)

Goldberg JCP and Zipursky BC, *Recognizing Wrongs* (Harvard University Press 2020)

Goldberg JCP and Zipursky BC, 'Replies to Commentators' (2022) 41 Law and Philosophy 127

Goodin R, 'Theories of Compensation' (1989) 9 Oxford Journal of Legal Studies 56

Goodin R, 'Compensation and Redistribution' (1991) 33 Nomos 143

Goudkamp J, *Tort Law Defences* (Hart 2013)

Goudkamp J and Murphy J, 'The Failure of Universal Theories of Tort Law' (2015) 21 Legal Theory 47

Grady MF, 'Res Ipsa Loquitur and Compliance error' (1994) University of Pennsylvania Law Review 142

Harel A, *Why Law Matters* (Oxford University Press 2014)

Harman G, *The Nature of Morality* (Princeton University Press 1977)

Hart HLA, *The Concept of Law* (first published 1961, 3rd edn, Oxford University Press 2012)

Heuer U, 'Reasons and Impossibility' (2010) 147 Philosophical Studies 235

Heyes C, 'Dead to the World: Rape, Unconsciousness, and Social Media' (2016) 41 Signs 361

Honoré T, 'The Dependence of Morality on Law' (1993) 13 Oxford Journal of Legal Studies 1

Honoré T, 'The Morality of Tort Law-Questions and Answers' in DG Owen (ed), *The Philosophical Foundations of Tort Law* (Oxford University Press 1997)

Honoré T, *Responsibility and Fault* (Hart 1999)

Hoskins Z and Duff RA, 'Legal Punishment', *The Stanford Encyclopedia of Philosophy* (Summer 2022 Edition), Edward N Zalta (ed), <https://plato.stanford.edu/archives/sum2022/entries/legal-punishment/>

Howard J, 'Punishment as Moral Fortification' (2017) 36 *Law and Philosophy* 45

Howard-Snyder F, '"Cannot" Implies "Not Ought"' (2006) 130 Philosophical Studies 233

Humberstone IL, 'Two Sorts of "Oughts"' (1971) 32 Analysis 8

Husak DN, 'Guns and Drugs: Case Studies on the Principled Limits of the Criminal Sanction' (2004) 23 Law and Philosophy 437

Ishiguro K, *Never Let Me Go* (Faber and Faber 2006)

James A, 'Contractualism's (Not So) Slippery Slope' (2012) 18 Legal Theory 263

Kagan S, 'Causation and Responsibility' (1988) 25 American Philosophical Quarterly 293

Kamm F, *Creation and Abortion* (Oxford University Press 1992)

Kamm F, *Intricate Ethics: Rights, Responsibilities, and Permissible Harms* (Oxford University Press 2007)

Kaplow L and Shavell S, 'Why the Legal System is Less Efficient than Income Tax in Distributing Income' (1994) 23 Journal of Legal Studies 667

Karhu T, 'Proportionality in the Liability to Compensate' (2022) 41 Law and Philosophy 583

Katz L, 'Exclusion and Exclusivity' (2008) 58 University of Toronto Law Journal 275

Keating G, 'Reasonableness and Rationality in Negligence Theory' (1996) 48 Stanford Law Review 311

Keating G, 'The Idea of Fairness in the Law of Enterprise Liability' (1997) 95 Michigan Law Review 1266

Keating G, 'A Social Contract Conception of the Tort Law of Accidents' in G Postema (ed), *Philosophy and the Law of Torts* (Cambridge University Press 2001)

Keating G, 'Strict Liability Wrongs' in J Oberdiek (ed), *Philosophical Foundations of the Law of Torts* (Oxford University Press 2014) 292

Keeler JW, 'Thinking Through the Unthinkable: Collective Responsibility in Personal Injury Law' (2001) 30 Common Law World Review 349

Keeton RE, 'Conditional Fault in the Law of Torts' (1959) 72 Harvard Law Review 401

Keren-Paz T, 'Private Law Redistribution, Predictability and Liberty' (2005) 50 McGill Law Journal 327

Keren-Paz T, *Torts, Egalitarianism and Distributive Justice* (Routledge 2007)

Kraus JS, 'Transparency and Determinacy in Common Law Adjudication: A Philosophical Defense of Explanatory Economic Analysis' (2007) 93 Virginia Law Review 287

Lamond G, 'What is a Crime?' (2007) 27 Oxford Journal of Legal Studies 609

Lee A, 'Public Wrongs and the Criminal Law' (2015) 9 Criminal Law and Philosophy 155

Lehrer K, 'Cans without Ifs' (1968) 29 Analysis 29

Levy N, 'Expressing Who We are: Moral Responsibility and Awareness of Our Reasons for Action' (2011) 52 Analytic Philosophy 243

Liao SM, 'Intentions and Moral Permissibility: The Case of Acting Permissibly with Bad Intentions' (2012) 31 Law and Philosophy 703

Lippert-Rasmussen K, 'Against Self-Ownership: There Are No Fact-Insensitive Ownership Rights over One's Body' (2008) 36 Philosophy & Public Affairs 86

McMahan J, 'Moral Intuition' in H LaFollette (ed), *The Blackwell Guide to Ethical Theory* (Blackwell 2000)

McMahan J, *The Ethics of Killing: Problems at the Margins of Life* (Oxford University Press 2002)

McMahan J, 'The Just Distribution of Harm Between Combatants and Noncombatants' (2010) 38 Philosophy & Public Affairs 342

McNaughton P and Rawling P, 'On Defending Deontology' (1998) 11 Ratio 37

Miller D, *National Responsibility and Global Justice* (Oxford University Press 2007)

Moran M, *Rethinking the Reasonable Person: An Egalitarian Reconstruction of the Objective Standard* (Oxford University Press 2003)

Murphy J, 'The Merits of Rylands v Fletcher' (2004) 24 Oxford Journal of Legal Studies 643

Murphy J, 'The Heterogeneity of Tort Law' (2019) 39 Oxford Journal of Legal Studies 455

Nelkin D, *Making Sense of Freedom and Responsibility* (Oxford University Press 2011)

Nolan D, 'The Distinctiveness of Rylands v Fletcher' (2005) 121 Law Quarterly Review 421

Nozick R, *Anarchy, State, and Utopia* (Blackwell 1974)

Oberdiek J, 'Lost in Moral Space: On the Infringing/Violating Distinction and its Place in the Theory of Rights' (2004) 32 Law and Philosophy 325

Oberdiek J, *Imposing Risk: A Normative Framework* (Oxford University Press 2017)

Oberdiek J, 'The Wrong in Negligence' (2021) 41 Oxford Journal of Legal Studies 1174

Oberdiek J, 'Wrongs, Remedies, and the Persistence of Reasons: Re-Examining the Continuity Thesis' in H Psarras and S Steel (eds), *Private Law and Practical Reason: Essays on John Gardner's Private Law Theory* (Oxford University Press 2023)

Oliver K, *Hunting Girls: Sexual Violence from The Hunger Games to Campus Rape* (Cambridge University Press 2016)

Oman NB, 'Why There is No Duty to Pay Damages: Powers, Duties, and Private Law' (2011) 39 Florida State University Law Review 137

Øverland G, 'Moral Obstacles: An Alternative to the Doctrine of Double Effect' (2014) 124 Ethics 481

Parfit D, 'Equality and Priority' (1997) 10 Ratio 202

Parfit D, *On What Matters: Volume 1* (Oxford University Press 2011)

Parfit D, 'Can We Avoid the Repugnant Conclusion?' (2016) 82 Theoria 110

Parr T, 'The Moral Taintedness of Benefiting from Injustice' (2016) 19 Ethical Theory and Moral Practice 985

Paul LA and Hall N, *Causation: A Users Guide* (Oxford University Press 2013)

Penner JE, The Idea of Property in *Law* (Oxford University Press 1997)

Penner JE, 'Don't Crash into Mick Jagger while he's Driving his Rolls Royce: Liability in Damages for Economic Loss Consequent upon a Personal Injury' in PB Miller and J Oberdiek (eds), *Civil Wrongs and Justice in Private Law* (Oxford University Press 2020)

Pereboom D, *Free Will, Agency, and Meaning in Life* (Oxford University Press 2014)

Perry SR, 'The Impossibility of a General Strict Liability' (1988) 1 Canadian Journal of Law and Jurisprudence 147

Perry SR, 'Libertarianism, Entitlement, and Responsibility' (1997) 26 Philosophy & Public Affairs 351

Perry SR, 'On the Relationship Between Corrective and Distributive Justice' in J Horder (ed), *Oxford Essays in Jurisprudence* (Oxford University Press 2000)

Perry SR, 'Honoré on Responsibility for Outcomes' in P Cane and J Gardner (eds), *Relating to Responsibility: Essays in Honour of Tony Honoré on his 80th Birthday* (Hart 2001)

Placani A, 'When the Risk of Harm Harms' (2017) 36 Law and Philosophy 77

Prosser W, *Handbook on the Law of Torts* (4th edn, West Publishing Company, 1972)

Radzik L, 'Tort Processes and Relational Repair' in J Oberdiek (ed), *Philosophical Foundations of the Law of Torts* (Oxford University Press 2014) 231

Ramakrishnan KH, 'Treating People as Tools' (2016) 44 Philosophy & Public Affairs 133

Rawls J, *Theory of Justice* (Harvard University Press 2005)

Rawls J, *Political Liberalism* (Cambridge University Press 1993)

Raz J, *The Authority of Law: Essays on Law and Morality* (Oxford University Press 1979)

Raz J, *The Morality of Freedom* (Oxford University Press 1986)

Raz J, *Ethics in the Public Domain: Essays in the Morality of Law and Politics* (Oxford University Press 1995)

Raz J, 'The Problem of Authority: Revisiting the Service Conception' in *Between Authority and Interpretation* (Oxford University Press 2009)

Raz J, *From Normativity to Responsibility* (Oxford University Press 2011)

Ripstein A, *Equality, Responsibility, and the Law* (Cambridge University Press 1999)

Ripstein A, 'Beyond the Harm Principle' (2006) 34 Philosophy & Public Affairs 215

Ripstein A, 'Private Order and Public Justice: Kant and Rawls' (2006) 92 Vanderbilt Law Review 1391

Ripstein A, 'As If It Had Never Happened' (2007) 48 William & Mary Law Review 1957

Ripstein A, *Force and Freedom: Kant's Legal and Political Philosophy* (Harvard University Press 2010)

Ripstein A, *Private Wrongs* (Harvard University Press 2016)

Ripstein A, 'Reply: Relations of Right and Private Wrongs' (2018) 9 Jurisprudence 614

Rosen G, 'Metaphysical Relations in Metaethics' in T McPherson and D Plunkett (eds), *The Routledge Handbook of Metaethics* (Routledge 2017)

Sadursky W, 'Social Justice and Legal Justice' (1984) 3 Law and Philosophy 329

Saprai P, *Contract Law Without Foundations: Toward a Republican Theory of Contract Law* (Oxford University Press 2019)

Scanlon TM, *What We Owe To Each Other* (Harvard University Press 1998)

Scanlon TM, *Moral Dimensions: Permissibility, Meaning, Blame* (Harvard University Press 2010)

Scanlon TM, 'Reply to Zofia Stemplowska' (2013) 10 Journal of Moral Philosophy 508

Scanlon TM, 'Responsibility and the Value of Choice' (2013) 12 Think 9

Scanlon TM, *Being Realistic about Reasons* (Oxford University Press 2014)

Schroder CH, 'Corrective Justice and Liability for Increasing Risks' (1990) 37 UCLA Law Review 439

Scheffler S, 'Distributive Justice, the Basic Structure and the Place of Private Law' (2015) 35 Oxford Journal of Legal Studies 213

Shiffrin S, 'The Moral Neglect of Negligence' in D Sobel, P Vallentyne, and S Wall (eds), *Oxford Studies in Political Philosophy* (vol 3, Oxford University Press 2017)

Singer P, 'Famine, Affluence and Morality' (1972) 1 Philosophy & Public Affairs 229

Slavny A, 'On Being Wronged and Being Wrong' (2017) 16 Politics, Philosophy & Economics 3

Slavny A, 'The Normative Foundations of Defamatory Meaning' (2018) 37 Law and Philosophy 523

Slavny A, 'Benefits, Entitlements and Non-Responsible Threats' (2019) 36 Journal of Applied Philosophy 405

Slavny A and others, 'Directed Reflected Equilibrium: Thought Experiments and How to Use Them' (2020) 18 Journal of Moral Philosophy 1

Slavny A and Parr T, 'Harmless Discrimination' (2015) 21 Legal Theory 100

Slavny A and Parr T, 'What's Wrong with Risk?' (2019) 8 Thought 76

Smith S, *Contract Theory* (Clarendon Press 2004)

Smith S, 'Duties, Liabilities, and Damages' (2011–2012) 125 Harvard Law Review 1727

Smith S, 'A Duty to Make Restitution' (2013) 26 Canadian Journal of Law and Jurisprudence 157

Smith S, *Rights, Wrongs, and Injustices* (Oxford University Press 2019)

Sobel D, 'Backing Away from Libertarian Self-Ownership' (2012) 123 Ethics 32

Steel S, *Proof of Causation in Tort Law* (Cambridge University Press 2015)

Steel S, 'On the Moral Necessity of Tort Law: The Fairness Argument' (2020) 41 Oxford Journal of Legal Studies 192

Steel S, 'Compensation and Continuity' (2020) 26 Legal Theory 250

Steel S, 'Defensive and Remedial Liability' in J Oberdiek and PB Miller (eds), *Oxford Studies in Private Law Theory* (vol 2, Oxford University Press 2023)

Steel S, 'Remedies, Analysed' (2021) 41 Oxford Journal of Legal Studies 539

Steel S and Stevens R, 'The Secondary Legal Duty to Pay Damages' (2020) 136 Law Quarterly Review 283

Stemplowska Z, 'Harmful Choices: Scanlon and Voorhoeve on Substantive Responsibility' (2013) 10 Journal of Moral Philosophy 488

Stevens R, *Torts and Rights* (Oxford University Press 2007)

Stone M, 'The Significance of Doing and Suffering' in GJ Postema (ed), *Philosophy and the Law of Torts* (Cambridge University Press 2001)

Stone M, 'Legal Positivism as an Idea about Morality' (2011) 61 University of Toronto Law Journal 313

Streumer B, 'Reasons and Impossibility' (2007) 136 Philosophical Studies 351

Streumer B, 'Reasons, Impossibility and Efficient Steps: Reply to Heuer' (2010) 151 Philosophical Studies 79

Suikkanen J, 'A Dilemma for Rule-consequentialism' (2008) 36 Philosophia 141

Tadros V, *Criminal Responsibility* (Oxford University Press 2005)

Tadros V, 'Harm, Sovereignty and Prohibition' (2011) 17 Legal Theory 35

Tadros V, 'Independence Without Interests?' (2011) 31 Oxford Journal of Legal Studies 193

Tadros V, *The Ends of Harm: The Moral Foundations of Criminal* Law (Oxford University Press 2011)

Tadros V, 'Orwell's Battle with Brittain: Vicarious Liability for Unjust Aggression' (2014) 42 Philosophy & Public Affairs 42

Tadros V, 'What Might Have Been' in J Oberdiek (ed), *Philosophical Foundations of the Law of Torts* (Oxford University Press 2014)

Tadros V, *Wrongs and Crimes* (Oxford University Press 2016)

Tadros V, 'Secondary Duties' in PB Miller and J Oberdiek (eds), *Civil Wrongs and Justice in Private Law* (Oxford University Press 2020)

Tadros V, 'Two Grounds of Liability' (2021) 178 Philosophical Studies 3503

Tadros V, *To Do, To Die, To Reason Why: Individual Ethics in War* (Oxford University Press 2022)

Tadros V, 'Refuge and Aid' (2023) 31 Journal of Political Philosophy 102

Talbot B, 'The Best Argument for "Ought Implies Can" is a Better Argument Against "Ought Implies Can"' (2016) 3 Ergo 14

Tennyson A, *In Memoriam*, eds S Shatto and M Shaw (Oxford University Press 1982)

Temkin L, *Inequality* (Oxford University Press 1993)

Thomson JJ, *Rights, Restitution, and Risk* (Harvard University Press 1986)

Thomson JJ, 'Self-Defense' (1991) 20 Philosophy & Public Affairs 283

Voorhoeve A, 'Scanlon on Substantive Responsibility' (2008) 16 Journal of Political Philosophy 184

Voyiakis E, *Private Law and The Value of Choice* (Hart 2017)

Vranas PB, 'I Ought, Therefore I Can' (2007) 136 Philosophical Studies 167

Waldron J, 'Moments of Carelessness and Massive Loss' in DG Owen (ed), *The Philosophical Foundations of Tort Law* (Oxford University Press 1995)

Waldron J, 'How the Law Protects Dignity' (2012) 71 Cambridge Law Journal 200

Walen A, 'Transcending the Means Principle' (2014) 33 Law and Philosophy 427

Walen A, *The Mechanics of Claims and Permissible Killing in War* (Oxford University Press 2019)

Wallace RJ, *The Moral Nexus* (Princeton University Press 2019)

Watson G, 'Two Faces of Responsibility' (1996) 24 Philosophical Topics 227

Weinrib E, *The Idea of Private Law* (Oxford University Press 2012)

Weinrib E, *Corrective Justice* (Oxford University Press 2016)

Williams B, 'A Critique of Utilitarianism' in JJC Smart and B Williams, *Utilitarianism: For and Against* (Cambridge University Press 1973)

Williams B, 'Ethical Consistency' in *Problems of the Self: Philosophical Papers 1956–1972* (Cambridge University Press 1973)

Williams B, *Moral Luck* (Cambridge University Press 1981)

Wolff J, 'Fairness, Respect, and the Egalitarian Ethos' (1998) 27 Philosophy & Public Affairs 97

Wood A, 'Humanity as an End in Itself' in D Parfit (ed), On What Matters: *Volume 2* (Oxford University Press 2011)

Wright RW, 'Substantive Corrective Justice' (1992) 77 Iowa Law Review 625

Wright RW, 'Right, Justice, and Tort Law' in DG Owen (ed), *The Philosophical Foundations of Tort Law* (Oxford University Press 1995)

Wright RW, 'The Standards of Care in Negligence Law' in DG Owen (ed), *The Philosophical Foundations of Tort Law* (Oxford University Press 1995)

Zhao M, 'Guilt without Perceived Wrongdoing' (2020) 48 Philosophy & Public Affairs 285

Zimmerman MJ, 'Moral Responsibility and Ignorance' (1997) 107 Ethics 410

Zipursky BC, 'Rights, Wrongs, and Recourse in the Law of Torts' (1998) 51 Vanderbilt Law Review 1

Zipursky BC, 'Pragmatic Conceptualism' (2000) 6 Legal Theory 457

Zipursky BC, 'Civil Recourse, Not Corrective Justice' (2003) 91 Georgetown Law Journal 695

Cases

Bolton v Stone [1951] AC 850

Dunnage v Randall [2016] QB 639

Lagden v O'Connor [2003] UKHL 64; [2004] 1 AC 1067

Latimer v AEC [1953] AC 643

Lawrence v Fen Tigers Ltd [2014] AC 822

Livingstone v Rawyards Coal Co (1880) 5 AC 25

McHale v Watson (1966) 115 CLR 199

Mullin v Richards [1998] 1 WLR 1304

Nettleship v Weston [1971] 2 QB 691
Owens v Liverpool Corp [1939] 1 KB 394
Robinson v Kilvert (1889) 41 Ch D 88
Rylands v Fletcher (1868) LR 3 HL 330
Transco plc v Stockport [2004] 2 AC 1
Vaughan v Menlove (1837) 3 Bing NC 468475; 132 ER 490
Vincent v Lake Erie Transportation Co 109 Minn 456 (1910)
Watt v Hertfordshire County Council [1954] 1 WLR 835 (CA)
Wilsher v Essex Area Health Authority [1988] 1 AC 1074
Woodley v Metropolitan District Railway Co (1877) 2 Ex D 384

Legislation

Compensation Act 2006
Protection from Harassment Act 1997
Equality Act 2010
Social Action, Responsibility and Heroism Act 2015

Online Resources

https://accidentalimpacts.org

Index

For the benefit of digital users, indexed terms that span two pages (e.g., 52–53) may, on occasion, appear on only one of those pages.

Introductory Note
References such as '178–9' indicate (not necessarily continuous) discussion of a topic across a range of pages. Wherever possible in the case of topics with many references, these have either been divided into sub-topics or only the most significant discussions of the topic are listed. Because the entire work is about 'compensation', the use of this term (and certain others which occur constantly throughout the book) as an entry point has been restricted. Information will be found under the corresponding detailed topics.

transitional harm 171–72
transparency 11–12
trespasses, harmless 57, 70

underlying moral duties 21–22, 24, 176,
  178–79, 196–97
undue burden 23, 25, 26–27, 35–36, 58, 59,
  110, 201
  argument 91–93
unequal risk distribution 133, 134
unfairness 25, 26, 84–85, 94, 98
  distributive 149–50, 155
units
  of harm 166
  of wellbeing 166
unity, narrative 52–53, 57
unjust distribution 24–25, 27, 32, 37, 155
unjust holdings 163–67, 169, 170–
  72, 174–75
unjustified risks 35–36, 195–96
unreasonable expectations 170
unwanted benefits 140–42
uptake 7–8, 15, 197, 198, 200
  perfect 180, 197, 198–99
utilitarianism 13–14, 183
utility 154

value pluralism 45, 112
value(s)
  bearers of 48
  expected 131
  loss of 112–13
  non-material 56, 70
  performance 33, 182, 183–84, 185–86
variability objection 97–100
vicarious liability 138–41, 150–51, 202
victims 24–25, 84–85, 125–26, 150–51,
  184–85, 190–91, 195–96, 198–99
  of distributive injustice 156–57, 158–59,
    164, 200, 205
  of fault 200
  individual 70–71, 195–96
  and injurers 123, 130, 137, 144, 150–
    51, 196
  potential 97–98, 185, 198
  of risk 194
  of torts 139–40, 172–73, 187–88
  of wrongdoing 25, 26

voluntary actions 78–79, 101–2
Voorhoeve, Alex 146

Waldron, Jeremy 96, 161, 162–63,
  179–80
weakness of will 94–95, 96–97
wealth 164, 167, 168
Weinrib, Ernest 10–13, 20, 59–60, 63,
  65–67, 120–21, 130, 153, 172–73, 174,
  176–77, 184, 190–91
wellbeing 43–44, 47–49, 51–52, 61–62, 72,
  156, 158–59
  reductions in 49, 63, 120
  units of 166
will, weakness of 94–95, 96–97
Williams, Andrew 146
Williams, Bernard 101–2, 183
Wright, Richard 85–86, 184–85, 196
wrongdoers 23, 45–46, 89–90, 166–67,
  177–78, 181, 185–87
  moral 23, 91
wrongdoing 3–4, 25–26, 69–71, 72–73, 74,
  101, 157–58, 201–2
  centrality 70
  legal 4
  role 42, 64
  severity 69–70
  significance 6, 66, 74
  victims 25, 26
wrongful failures 69, 83, 158–59
wrongful harm 41, 156–57, 159,
  195, 198–99
wrongful injury 59–60, 160
wrongful riskers 190–91, 192, 198–99
wrongful risks 177, 193–94, 195–
  96, 198–99
wrongness 25–26, 55, 92, 193
wrongs
  and duties 28
  legal, see legal wrongs
  moral 20–21, 25–26, 28, 32–36
  negligence 6, 20–21, 35–36, 75–76, 92–
    93, 149–51
  non-relational 68, 69
  relational 68

Zipursky, Benjamin 10–12, 13, 19, 25–26,
  35, 36, 37, 161–63, 201